THE CAVES
OF THE SUN

The Origin of Mythology

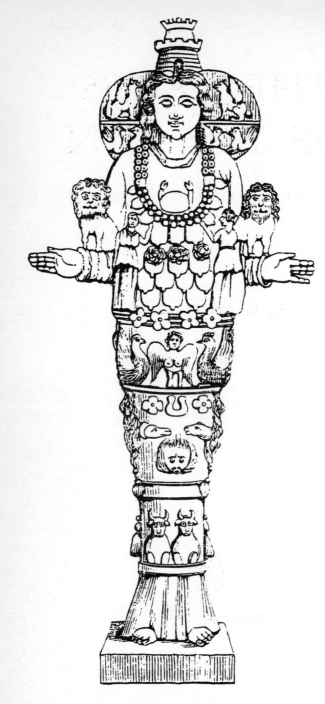

FIG. 1 Artemis of Ephesus

THE CAVES
OF THE SUN

The Origin of Mythology

ADRIAN BAILEY

JONATHAN CAPE
LONDON

To Fiona

First published 1997

1 3 5 7 9 10 8 6 4 2

© Adrian Bailey 1997

Adrian Bailey has asserted his right
under the Copyright, Designs and Patents Act, 1988
to be identified as the author of this work

First published in Great Britain 1997 by Jonathan Cape
Random House, 20 Vauxhall Bridge Road, London SW1V 2SA

Random House Australia (Pty) Limited
20 Alfred Street, Milsons Point, Sydney,
New South Wales 2061, Australia

Random House New Zealand Limited
18 Poland Road, Glenfield,
Auckland 10, New Zealand

Random House South Africa (Pty) Limited
Endulini, 5A Jubilee Road, Parktown 2193, South Africa

Random House UK Limited Reg. No. 954009

A CIP catalogue record for this book
is available from the British Library

ISBN 0–224–03063–9

Phototypeset by Deltatype Limited, Birkenhead, Merseyside
Printed and bound in Great Britain by
Mackays of Chatham PLC

Contents

Illustrations

FIGURES

PLATES

Introduction

Who is the most famous, the most universally known mythological hero? Is it Oedipus, who murdered his father and married his mother? Or is it Achilles of the vulnerable heel? Or Paris, perhaps, who judged the beauty competition and awarded an apple to the winner, Aphrodite. How about Perseus, who beheaded the Gorgon, or Jason who led the Argonauts, or Theseus who slew the Minotaur in the labyrinth?

These are all Greek figures, of course, and Greek myths have become so influential that we are inclined to overlook the contributions of other mythologies – Osiris from Egypt; the Hindu Krishna, and the Scandinavians Thor and Odin and Balder, although the myth of Balder certainly helped to inspire that most weighty piece of scholarly research on myth and folklore, Sir James Frazer's *The Golden Bough*. These characters from the ancient world are so powerfully defined as to suggest that they were drawn from life. There are still those who argue for an historical Robin Hood and King Arthur, but they were most probably the product of the imagination and primitive experiences, and their meaning – for they surely mean something – must be sought in the darkness of prehistory.

Can we throw some light on these remote mysteries, those of a period long before our time of which all that remains are inscrutable myths, and bones and stone ruins? Evidence that might allow access to the past appears at first to be provided by a variety of unrelated things – the cave art of the Ice Age, the isolated ruin of Stonehenge on Salisbury Plain, the Great Sphinx of Gizeh in Egypt, the plumed serpents carved in basalt by the Aztecs in Mexico, the strange bull and vulture shrines in the 6,000-year-old settlement of Çatal Hüyük in Turkey, the 'Rainbow Serpent' (perhaps a snake god) painted on rock surfaces by Australian aborigines. The drawings, the carvings, the monuments of massive, weathered and time-worn stones, whose origins we can barely comprehend, created by long-forgotten people, must surely have been made in response to powerful needs and primitive obligations. While in appearance the Egyptian sphinx has no obvious relationship with the Aztec's plumed serpents, these seemingly disparate things may indeed be closely connected. Were they different ways of expressing the same message?

The people of the ancient world – that is, the very ancient world, many thousands of years before the birth of agriculture – were hunter-gatherers, not short of intelligence but living a primitive way of life in what was certainly an untamed environment. To judge by the wonderful drawings of bison and horses in rock paintings found deep in the limestone caves of France and Spain, they were artistically accomplished. They had discovered that art could imitate life – the lives of the hunters and the animals they pursued – and symbolise things, ideas and concepts that they were otherwise unable to articulate effectively. The plumed serpents that decorate the Aztec temples, the avenues of sphinxes at Karnak in Egypt, these are in effect symbols. There is, of course, no such thing as a snake with feathers nor for that matter a Minotaur – the bull-headed man whom Theseus fought in the Cretan labyrinth (also a symbol). Neither does the sphinx – a lion with a human head, usually the head of a woman – exist in the natural world, yet it has become a universal symbol for all that is mystical and enigmatic. She challenges us, as she challenged Oedipus, to discover her meaning.

As for stone ruins such as Stonehenge and the great circle of Avebury, the silent tombs, the strange geometric patterns carved on the boulders of New Grange in Ireland, are these symbols too? The puzzles of Stonehenge and New Grange, the riddles of the sphinx and the feathered serpents, when traced back in time, may well reveal links and associations that give us the key to the past. Can we go as far back as the Ice Age, and from there even further back to the cults of the Neanderthalers of the Palaeolithic Age, and by interpreting their art and their symbols, unravel their systems of belief? We know that the Neanderthalers, whose brain capacity was larger than that of Homo sapiens who eventually replaced them, not only interred their dead in caves, but practised ritual burial of human and animal skulls and selected bones (in particular, the thigh bones) in stone cists and recesses in cave floors. It is a fact – perhaps one of considerable significance – that Neanderthalers observed a cult of cave bears in which the carefully selected skulls and leg bones of bears were employed for ritual purposes. A ritual, like a symbol, can be a way of expressing the abstract, of conveying a message by way of analogy. It can also, through what has been described as 'sympathetic magic', be thought to encourage a natural event – smashing a water pot in order to induce rain, for example.

Ancient skull and bone burials, or the interment of complete bodies, have been seen as evidence of the first stirrings of spirituality, of a sense of awe and wonder, of a belief in the regeneration of the soul. Perhaps such philosophical concepts did not arise so early in the development of mankind's religious awareness, and the Neanderthalers' burials had a more practical purpose. Could the interment rituals of these hunter-gatherers have been votive, performed in the hope that an offering put in the earth was a form of insurance, promising future benefits from nature? If so, what compelling notion, as such it must have been, led them to place emphasis on the skulls and longbones? Much later, in the Neolithic or New Stone Age, men had graduated to the use of human skulls and leg bones, and those of oxen. The symbolism underlying the reverence for the head and legs must have had profound meaning for it to survive for some 60,000 years in all or most ancient societies.

In the Neolithic town of Çatal Hüyük in Anatolia, the archaeologist Professor James Mellaart found human skulls deposited in the numerous shrines of the settlement, while the bones of skeletons had been interred beneath sleeping areas in the homes, suggesting perhaps a form of ancestor worship. But why the skulls were deliberately separated from the limb bones is just one of the many puzzles left to us by the inhabitants of this ancient site on the Konya plain.

Even more of a challenge is the remarkable and deliberate symbolism featured in the shrines – carved female figures with splayed legs giving birth to horned animals, and clay representations of bulls' heads juxtaposed with modelled human breasts, also in clay, each breast containing a skull of a bird or animal. Here, a vulture's beak protrudes from a red-painted nipple; there, the lower jaw of a boar is likewise enclosed. On the walls of the shrines (Mellaart noticed that these were often the east-facing walls), paintings showed huge red vultures with human legs apparently attacking headless human figures. A female figure (certainly a goddess) is seated on a throne flanked by leopards.

Is it possible to decode such complex symbolism after a gap in time of some 8,000 years? Scholars attempting to explain the mysteries of Çatal Hüyük have proposed that here was the centre of a powerful matriarchy presided over by the figure of a big-breasted, ample-thighed mother goddess with her attendant leopards. That she was also a vulture goddess suggested a predatory, threatening nature to which the men of the town sensibly deferred. To judge by the number of shrines, all the evidence points to a society locked in a bizarre cult with which they were intensely involved.

Ancient societies, then, occupied a world of lost horizons, of virgin forests and springs and rivers, of now long-forgotten beliefs and ceremonies, of cults and sacrifices, of flint axes and broken pots, of red-painted skulls, of gods and goddesses, heroes and monsters, leaving behind a legacy of rock-cut temples, pyramids and ziggurats built of hewn blocks of stone, of scratched images in the depths of caverns, of cairns, dolmens, menhirs, obelisks and labyrinths, barrows, tumuli and cromlechs, all infuriatingly obscure and enigmatic. They also left behind them the symbols and myths and rituals which we still struggle to comprehend.

Could our failure to understand our distant past be due to our method of approach and a strange reluctance to pursue a line of enquiry – well signposted with clues – to its conclusion? More often than not, it seems, we ignore the evidence, preferring instead to accept the most elementary (and sometimes quite plausible) explanation. But where are the most reliable clues to be found? The myths and legends of the Greeks, the Phoenicians and Egyptians, the myths of Mesopotamia, and those of India are among the most accessible sources. Everyone knows that Achilles had a vulnerable heel. It led to his death on the battlefield of Troy, when the Trojan prince Paris shot him in the foot with an arrow, and has since become a metaphor for an inherent weakness. The incident might have passed as a meaningless fragment of myth had we not been told that the Hindu god Krishna suffered a similar fate, that the Egyptian Ra was bitten on the heel by a snake, that the god Osiris was similarly afflicted, and that the Greek smith Hephaestus was made permanently lame, along with a host of other limping heroes, not the least of whom was Oedipus, or 'Swellfoot'. The vulnerable heel is an important clue – one of many – in any enquiry as to the origins of mythology, yet the lameness of Hephaestus was dismissed by the archaeologist and prominent scholar of Greek religion, Martin Nilsson, as being an etiological tale, an occupational hazard, and of 'little importance', and explained by Marie Delcourt as being little more than a token wound of initiation – an explanation that is hard to accept, since the wound was frequently fatal.

The collective opinion of most scholars today is that mythology and ancient religion are so complex, and so diverse, that they defy any single explanation as to their origins. The Greek scholar and mythologist Professor G. S. Kirk said, 'There is no one definition of myth, no Platonic form of a myth against which all actual instances can be measured. Myths differ enormously in their morphology and their social function.' This view is echoed by the historian and classicist Michael Grant, who asserted that 'No single theory, however valuably suggestive, will suffice to explain the whole range of Greek and Roman mythology, or even a major portion of its content.' In other words, there are not one but several meanings to myths, and symbols too may have different meanings for different peoples.

Yet how do we explain the evidence of the swastika, that most famous of symbols, appearing in Mesopotamia as well as in Mississippi? We may guess that it was a symbol in the culture of tribes migrating from the Old World to the New World, but did it mean one thing to the Assyrians and quite another to the American Indians? How do we account for the nineteenth-century Scottish folklorist Andrew Lang finding versions of the Greek myth of the Argonauts as far apart as Scotland and Samoa, Finland and Japan? Were these myths and symbols independently created? It is difficult to comprehend why the Gorgon's head, a popular symbol among the Greeks and Etruscans, should appear in the lore of the Maoris of New Zealand. Cults involving bears began with Neanderthal man and remain as prevalent today in Arctic regions of the world as they have done for thousands of years. Serpents, and especially those with wings or feathers, have been worshipped by the peoples of the Old and New Worlds alike, from Egypt to Mexico, from Africa to Australia.

It is tempting, therefore, to suppose that prehistoric peoples might have drawn their inspiration from a common if extremely ancient source, and that geographical variants, as Andrew Lang surmised, are the result of diffusion and the migration of myths and symbols. Might not this also be true of the monuments, the circles, temples and burial mounds? The construction of stone monuments demanded huge communal effort and dedication, further suggesting that the builders were driven by a compulsion recognised and understood by everyone involved, and the collective response created Stonehenge, just as it created the massive temples of Central America. It may also have prompted the development of cults of human and animal sacrifice, and perhaps inspired the remarkable art deep in the limestone caverns of France and Spain.

At the start of my investigation I was merely guessing, and my first attempt to trace this ancient, common source was unsuccessful. At a certain stage well into the heart of the research I came across an important symbol and feature of ancient religion – again, one of many – that I was unable to explain. The celestial bull, the prime victim of sacrifice, the creature stabbed to death by, among others, the Roman god Mithras at the very height of its potency, was widely featured in the primitive shrines of an earlier age. From the animal's tail sprouted ears of wheat, the wild plant carefully cultivated in the Fertile Crescent, and upon which the Neolithic revolution – the birth of agriculture – had been built. So important was this idea that the Mesopotamian masons placed a stone peg bearing the image of a bull with seven ears of wheat in the foundations of buildings. Yet the Mesopotamian goddess Ishtar begged her father Anu, great god of the sky, to create for her the celestial bull so that she could kill it, as Theseus slew the Minotaur. The bull was the most potent symbol of fertility, and Ishtar was a creation goddess of birth, so why celebrate its death?

Here was a taxing question without, it seemed, a satisfactory answer, apart from the proposition that the bull was a sacrificial offering to the gods and goddesses of fertility. Surely this was not enough. The question – like that of Achilles' heel – was important, and could not conveniently be glossed over. Furthermore, I felt that in the riddle of the celestial bull I might find the answer to some of the other mysteries I had pondered over, an answer that would give voice to those mute messages from prehistory.

The evidence of savage cults and a heritage in stone provokes endless speculation over their purpose and meaning, and so do the enigmatic myths that continue to tease us. All too often the explanations seem inconclusive. Practically every society has its creation myths where a cataclysmic event destroys the old world, from which a new world is born. Some scholars have explained this event as the creation of order from chaos, as occurs when the Babylonian hero Marduk destroys the fearsome goddess Tiamat, or when Zeus destroys the serpent Typhon. Others have suggested that Marduk's victory is really celebrating the destruction of matriarchal societies by stern patriarchies. This does not tell us, however, why the hero decapitated Tiamat and buried her head beneath a mountain. Here is a not unimportant fragment of the legend, for decapitations and the burial of heads seem to have performed a vital function since ancient times and were a persistent theme. The Celts sometimes beheaded women and children prior to interment, and they may have been victims of sacrifice: a head was found in the lining of a well, possibly a foundation deposit put there during construction. In one version of the Marduk-Tiamat myth, Marduk actually decapitates himself – a remarkable achievement!

Were such bizarre features of these legends simply a reflection of the dark side of the prehistoric mind and its impulses, or do they have a message? Only the myths themselves can tell us, their interpretation holding similar rewards to that of the decipherment of scripts. Can there be any doubt that, in the absence of written records, myths and symbols, legends and folklore, passed down from generation to generation, and migrating through diverse cultures and societies while retaining their original meaning, provide us with the most reliable clues to the mysteries of the past?

My researches suggested that little real progress has been made in the study of mythology and religion, symbol and folklore, since *The Golden Bough* was published at the turn of the century. Perhaps recent investigations have been too self-aware and introspective, with too much emphasis on the psyche and the soul, the mystical and the arcane. These facets of modern philosophy and fashionable psychology could be misleading.

Is it not more likely that myths are about man's tenuous relationship with his environment, with the natural world, reflecting his attempts to influence the elements, the sun and the stars, and the animals, rocks, trees, springs and rivers with which he closely identified and was physically involved?

The compulsion to build the monuments of the ancient world may have gone far deeper than a cultural need for impressive architecture in order to express municipal wealth and political power, or even religious conviction. Do they all share a common ancestry and were they inspired less by divine revelation than by apprehension? The Roman writer and poet Petronius said that fear first made the gods. Did prehistoric societies see themselves at the mercy of nature and its forces, or were they aware of a more menacing and sinister threat? Were their efforts to influence nature the true basis of mankind's rituals and beliefs? Could all these beliefs, the gods, the monuments, while seemingly diverse and randomly scattered, have in fact a collective purpose, the meaning of which is at once simple yet profound? These are the questions which this book addresses and seeks to provide rational answers.

CHAPTER 1

Skulls and Stones

Over the past two hundred years the study of mythology has been swayed by changes in fashion, and succeeding schools of interpretation have come and gone. Myths have been explained by reference to totemism, animism, nature worship, phallicism, astronomy, psychology, each theory influencing, rightly or wrongly, the way we read myths and understand them.

Individual myths have been further interpreted in the light of shamanism, fertility rites, mysticism, initiation, the Oedipus complex, and so on. Often, the weight of greatly respected scholarship has lent particular credibility to a point of view or theory to the exclusion of others. Modern scholars are curiously hostile to the 'single theory' or 'single origin' approach to myth, and are generally contemptuous of natural phenomena (such as the sun and moon) as a source of myths, what the Cambridge Professor of Greek and Classics, G. S. Kirk, called 'the wilder excesses of the nature myth school', founded by the German philologist Max Muller in the mid-nineteenth century.

'The obvious truth', says Kirk, 'is that there are such things as nature myths, but that not all or even most myths are of this kind. No one in his right mind has thought so since Andrew Lang finally lost patience eighty years ago and exploded the whole elephantine theory.'[1]

Here, Kirk is referring to Lang's book *Custom and Myth* (1893), in which Lang derides the theories of Muller and others, who attempted to explain myths by the etymological study of the names of gods, goddesses and other participants, relating them to natural phenomena such as the sun, clouds, thunderstorms, the dawn, eclipses, and so on. A myth featuring Zeus is therefore a sky or nature myth because the Greek name Zeus can be traced back to the Sanskrit *dyaus*, 'sky'. As Lang enjoyed pointing out, scholars disagreed as much over the meanings, origins and developments of names, as in their interpretations of myths.

In fact Lang, along with Sir James Frazer, did give support to the theory of natural mythology. Myths, they said, were the expressions of a primitive way of life. Lang and several other contemporary anthropologists decided that the crude and unrefined character of savages lay behind the comparably crude and brutish content of nature myths. The frequent appearance of animals, or of figures part-human, part-animal, was due to the savage's bestial disposition. Frazer, like Petronius, proposed that religion originated in fear, myth arising from the concept of the king who must die, the sacred leader of a savage tribe annually put to death and his successor crowned at the start of the new year, so symbolising the death and rebirth of vegetation.[2] That myths and symbols were created in a harsh world of drought and disease there can be no doubt, and fear of the future could well develop, by way of analogy, the dragons and monsters of legend, while the resilient nature of mankind produces the heroes and heroines to conquer them. Later societies, such as the Greeks, often failed to grasp the significance of the symbols they inherited and merely grafted on their own explanations. Socrates confessed to being baffled, and irritated, by a symbol often stamped on coins, the Chimera, a composite lion-goat-serpent that was said to inhabit the mountains of Asia Minor, across the Aegean Sea.[3] How could the meaning of the myths and symbols be lost? The idea behind the structure of a myth, or of an image presented in symbolic form, shed its original and primitive meaning in the process of time, and was later given a different meaning by the society that adopted it, changing in the same way by which meanings of words – and even of rituals – may change. The Greeks did not understand the underlying symbolism in the limping of Oedipus, the castration of Uranus by Cronus, the beheading of the Gorgon by Perseus. The eighthcentury BC Greek poet and farmer Hesiod, writing the *Theogony* (which describes the origins of the world and the ancestry of the gods), plainly did not understand the myth of Cronus; it was a tale to be recounted, and to seek a deeper meaning was superfluous. The general opinion was that Cronus wielded the sickle to unman his father, Uranus, because the sky-god was in permanent congress with the pregnant earth-mother, Ge. Unless earth and sky were forcibly separated, Cronus and his siblings were obliged to remain in her womb, and could not be born. For the Greeks, the end-product was sufficient unto itself and the inspiration of Greek drama. In other words, you don't need to examine the roots of a tree to appreciate its fruits and its foliage.

How did myths originate, and eventually develop into a finished product? Could it be that natural occurrences (especially life-threatening ones, such as drought) were allegorised and translated into human terms which we call myths? In this way, was man more easily able to relate to the unpredictable and untameable forces of nature, evolving an objective system of performance and response which we call cult and ritual? Certainly the dramatic action, the kernel of the story, is always a form of allegory, subliminally created from a particular circumstance that made a profound impression on mankind. The Greek traveller Pausanius, enjoying metaphor, spoke of myth as 'containing a kernel of deep wisdom under a husk of extragavance'.[4] The prominent mythologist Walter Burkert gives his own definition: 'Myth is a traditional tale with secondary, partial reference to something of collective importance.'[5] Can we look back and 'decode' or identify this something, this circumstance or event, for which Burkert offers no explanation?

Myths employ symbols, or are in themselves symbolic, because in this form they are able to convey an otherwise abstract and perhaps unwieldy concept. For some scholars, this is satisfyingly inconclusive, making the subject a souce of infinite study while conspiring to perpetuate the mystery. The perpetuation of mystery prompted the classics scholar Ken Dowden to say, 'I do not think there is any possibility of an objective account of Greek myth and I think that it would be the poorer if there was.'[6]

This is an understandable attitude, suggesting that objectivity would rob mythology of its magic, and, of course, its value as a perpetual subject of study.

The point was further made by Brian Davidson of English Heritage, who said that 'People like to go to places such as the White Horse of Uffington and Stonehenge because it's a mystery. They don't always thank you for explaining the mystery.' In any case, since we can rarely obtain proof, theories and speculations can be – and are – conveniently ignored, for one man's interpretation may well be another man's poppycock.

We may guess that myths and folktales are not created by the individual mind, yet neither are they the work of a group or a committee. Myths are the collective expressions of a society, or societies, made from regular observations, and synthesised in narrative form over long periods of time. Every single detail carries a meaning, and invariably takes the form of a symbol, but conveyed in such a way as to be downright inscrutable.

Myths are bizarre but, as Plato decided, they have some truth in them. They are also intricately contrived, arising from the day-to-day, pragmatic deliberations of society, more out of concern for the physical rather than for the spiritual welfare of man.

It would certainly not be possible to analyse and understand all of them, since societies are often unable to understand each other's cultural habits and religious ideals – yet often a similarity can be perceived, an identifying feature common to the family of man. Although formidable contributions have been made to our knowledge of the myths of great societies – even of remote tribes – we are still defining the term, as one school of thought treads on the cherished beliefs of another. It is easier to make observations and descriptions than to hazard definitions.

The gods, goddesses and monsters of myth are hiding a purpose which is not readily revealed to us because that which each symbolises, the mask that each wears, has a greater potency in disguise. The more mysterious and unreachable the myth, the more intriguing it becomes, and therefore inherently powerful. Being modified and stylised over centuries of development, the messages of these myths and symbols, their original identities, still retain their mystery. They contain, however, many valuable clues.

A large proportion of mythology thus became a language awaiting translation, and now teases our imagination. The mysteries present a challenge – for many people, the past is more exciting, and more rewarding, than the future. Perhaps this is why, as we approach the millennium, there is a spread of new ideas which seek to overturn established theories and the orthodox views of archaeologists and historians.

Orthodoxy is bred of disciplines which we may see as restrictive, imprisoning freedom of thought and expression. Some authors have sought a purposeful and more rewarding alliance with prehistory, declaring that we have lost, somewhere along the way, a valuable inheritance that might perhaps be reclaimed. They have looked afresh at the bare bones of the past, allowing their interpretations to be influenced by romanticism, by mysticism, by the transcendental and the paranormal. This is encouragingly free of the shackles of fact, and goes some way to satisfy what the biologist Professor Richard Dawkins has called our 'appetite for wonder'. The notion of a pagan mythology, a wealth of esoteric knowledge potentially beneficial to us all, has great appeal. This New Age 'appetite for wonder' conveniently ignores, however, the stern disciplines of science. The mysteries of prehistory are similar to the mysteries of unexplored space – a vast territory where the imagination is free to roam where it will.

Even the traditional seats of learning have weighed in with speculations on influences from interstellar space; in 1995 the Oxford Union came out in favour of the proposition (by 207 votes to 140) that aliens had already visited the Earth. The Crop Circle phenomenon, later found to be a hoax, did nothing to dispel the belief in UFOs or, for that matter, crop circles.

Prehistory has become the inspiration of modern cult movements, linked to a huge interest in science fiction, especially among the young. This was anticipated in the early 1960s with the publication of a popular work based upon the growing interest in astronomy, space travel, UFOs and the like. In *Stonehenge Decoded* the author, Gerald Hawkins, a professional astronomer, sought to show that Stonehenge was designed as a Neolithic 'computer' of the movements of celestial bodies, and he employed a modern Honeywell computer in an attempt to rediscover a lost and meaningful relationship between the stones and the stars.[7]

The results were far from conclusive. Similar ideas had been entertained and discussed in academic circles during the nineteenth century, persisting into our own times. In 1906 the astronomer Sir Norman Lockyer, director of the Solar Physics Observatory, published *Stonehenge and Other British Stone Monuments Astronomically Considered*,[8] in which he connected solar and other celestial associations and alignments with circles and stone rows. It was Lockyer who put the weight of his authority behind the idea of druidic temples presided over by astronomer-priests, at about the same time as Alfred Watkins had a vision of 'ley-lines' criss-crossing the ancient landscape. Both visionaries owed something to Edward Duke, a clergyman and antiquarian living near Stonehenge, who in 1846 proposed that Druid priests had laid out the Wessex monuments in the form of a planetarium or orrery, with Silbury Hill as its axial point.

The temptation to see Stonehenge as a measuring instrument, a clock or a compass, is provided by the layout of the stones which lends itself to geometric earthly alignments and celestial co-ordination. We will learn less, however, from counting the stones (although their number may have some significance), than from trying to understand the preoccupations and motives of prehistoric societies, and we can do that only through the messages in myths and the rituals of cults.

Modern society periodically creates notions about the past inspired by its current preoccupations. The study of prehistory, with few records save the gleanings from archaeological digs, provides a virgin surface upon which we can make our mark. In 1973 the oriental studies specialist and theologian John Allegro published *The Sacred Mushroom and the Cross*,[9] which apparently provoked academics to take to the streets in protest, much as the German scholar Arthur Drews had achieved at the turn of the century with his controversial book *The Christ Myth*.[10] Allegro proposed a theory of phallicism in which rain was analogous to semen ejaculated by a divine penis in the sky. The theory was linked, by way of philology, to a drug culture promoted by the early Christians, the source of which was the hallucinogenic mushroom *Amanita muscaria*, the fly agaric. It was, as an American friend of mine declared, 'a fun book', and timely in view of the influence of the hippy, LSD-inspired movement, and the works of Carlos Castaneda. The poet Robert Graves, perhaps the finest recorder of classical mythology, while not going quite as far as Allegro, certainly took the view that the ancient world nourished a drug culture centred around the *Amanita muscaria*. Graves suggested that LSD, or its Greek equivalent, was the food of the centaurs, and induced the wild excesses of the oriental god Dionysus and his flesh-tearing followers, the maenads.[11]

Allegro's book welded the complex symbolism of a drug culture with religion and phallicism, bringing in another current preoccupation of the times, human sexuality and freedom of sexual expression. While there certainly may have been a cult of sacred mushrooms in the ancient world, there is no firm evidence that it led to a powerful religious movement, and eventually to the spread of Christianity. Yet the bounds of the reasonable can be expanded as far as you care to take them. The science of the anthropologist Gordon Childe has been artfully fused with the fiction of the archaeologist Indiana Jones to a point where it is reasonable to postulate that the ancient Egyptians were preceded, and their monuments constructed, by a super-intelligent society many thousands of years earlier than established archaeological evidence allows. Or that the Maya arrived via Atlantis to settle in

Central America to establish a remarkable quasi-scientific system of prophecy,[12] or that the Giza complex of monuments have their exact counterpart on the planet Mars.

A geologist examining the foundations of the Egyptian Sphinx has suggested that it may have been built as early as 7000 BC (around 2600 BC is the generally accepted date); an engineer and surveyor has claimed that the pyramids of Giza have been planned in the shape of the constellation of Orion – a claim that has good evidence to commend it.[13] The mysterious monuments of antiquity are acquiring a new significance – the pyramids of Mesoamerica and Egypt and the societies that built them might convey a valuable message, ancestral esoteric advice to help solve modern moral dilemmas, and thus they invite investigation and reappraisal.

It is the reason why Stonehenge, as our familiar domestic example, is besieged every year at the summer solstice by thousands of people following their own paths to truth, towards what one New Age pilgrim called his 'spiritual home', for Stonehenge remains an enigma, a cipher, and we can make of it whatever we wish. We project into it, as psychologists say, our individual needs and desires.

When I first saw Stonehenge, as a child, between the wars, the monument's visitors were mainly sheep, and hares raced across the turf. Today, Stonehenge makes a profit. The stones have become the focus in a clash of cultures between those urging a return to the values of an imagined Utopian period of Neolithic life against the uniformed reality of an unsympathetic present.

Like slides hurried through a projector, prehistory gives a fragmentary view of what to us may seem a primitive existence, but is nonetheless remote and magical. Was Stonehenge a temple of the sun? A Stone Age computer? A symbol of the womb of the mother goddess? Was it built by priests skilled in arcane astronomy, or by aliens from outer space? The secrets held by this tumbledown ruin are shared by other monuments of its kind – by the huge stones of Avebury, and the strange hill of Silbury. They are part and parcel of the same mythology, once presided over by long-forgotten gods. A good deal of the mysticism surrounding Stonehenge is certainly due to the romantic inclinations of some scholars, such as Lockyer and Hawkins, and the contributions of the geologist H. H. Thomas, who first suggested that the so-called

FIG. 2 The eighteenth-century view of Stonehenge when its visitors were mainly sheep. From an engraving by Phillip Crocker.

bluestones erected in the centre of the circle had been dragged from Prescelly in Wales to Salisbury plain.

There seems to me to be a central question that has to be faced in any investigation of the origin of myth and symbol: what did their innovators have, without doubt, in common? The imagination and apprehension that created the terrifying mask of the Gorgon must surely have arisen from the same emotive drive that inspired a veneration of death heads, a recurring motif in antiquity which remains prevalent in Mexico, perhaps a hangover of the bloody rituals of the Aztecs. Did the Aztec priests, wielding obsidian knives and stepping through rivers of blood on the temple steps, have a sound reason for their excessive sacrifices, their ferocious gods, their elaborate, savage icons and grimacing, flayed idols? Was an ever-present fear of death the inspiration, in part, of the legends that were handed down from generation to generation, to reach a peak of unparalleled expression in the myths and rituals of the classical world? The life-and-death struggles that feature so prominently in these tales suggest that throughout prehistory mankind was at the mercy of something altogether unpredictable that held life in delicate balance, something that everyone feared and fought to overcome – the fear that Frazer believed to be the origin of religion. Could this fear have triggered the same compulsion that drove men to drag stones weighing several tons over virgin terrain, or to penetrate the darkest recesses of caves in order to paint scenes that were never intended for public viewing? In myth, would it lead the Argonauts to challenge death in their search for the Golden Fleece?

Most modern scholars argue against this reductionist approach, and the consensus of opinion is that there is no single, definitive source, or sources, to the extremely complex pattern of myths. For one thing, it is held to be difficult to make today's interests and beliefs fit those of yesterday, a point made by the archaeologist Peter Ucko, when he wrote that 'the further back into prehistory an investigation leads, the less relevant become later historical analogies.'[14] This may be true in a social and economic sense where people progress and migrate to new areas, but I will argue that they carry their beliefs, concerns and preoccupations with them, like a form of insurance. There is some factual evidence to support the assertion: human skulls covered in red ochre, and dating from the Mesolithic period, about 7000 BC, were found buried in a cave in Bavaria;[15] the same technique was employed in Jericho, and at Çatal Hüyük in Asia Minor, now Turkey, between 6000 and 5000 BC, give or take half a century.[16]

In Jericho, human skulls were discovered arranged in a circle, or in three sets of three.[17] Four thousand years later, on the far outposts of the Western world, the ritual was still being observed: skulls arranged in a circle were uncovered in a barrow near Stonehenge.[18] A skull accompanied by the long bones of the legs were unearthed from a stone circle in Scotland.[19] Also in Scotland, at Loanhead of Daviot, Aberdeenshire, excavators found over fifty fragments of the skulls of children between two and four years old, buried in a stone circle.[20] At Gotha in Germany, there were a hundred inhumation burials with nests of skulls, and six incidences of the wrong skull on a skeleton.[21]

Comparable evidence also appears in myth, religion and folklore, where in Greece the fifty brides of the sons of Aegyptus decapitated their husbands and buried their heads at Argos. Eurystheus, one-time ruler of Greece, was beheaded and his skull buried by a spring, also in Argos. The Biblical Esau's head was interred in a cave, the head of John the Baptist in a crypt;[22] the Mesopotamian hero Marduk beheaded the monster Tiamat and buried her head under a mountain.[23] The Welsh chieftain Caradoc ap Alyn decapitated St Winifride in AD 650, and buried her head in order to create a spring, now St Winifride's Well at

Holywell in North Wales.[24] She was one of several martyred saints whose heads produced miraculous springs.[25] Perseus cut off the Gorgon's head and, after flying three times around the world, carrying the head in a bag and settling old scores by holding it aloft (remember, it turned men to stone), the hero buried it at Argos, or some say by the spring of Lerna.

Any head, it seems, would suffice, from the heads of bulls and horses, down to foxes and weasels and snakes. On several sites in Britain, the skulls and antlers of red deer predominated among the wild animal category of deposits. Hercules cut off the heads of the serpent Hydra, and following Perseus's example, buried them by the spring at Lerna.

The rituals and the myths stretch across the ages, and although the people, places and circumstances were different the purpose remained constant and was universally recognised. Decapitation has a long history in Central America – a find of forty-eight skulls was made at Iximche, an ancient Mayan city, and occupied holes in the plaza floor.[26]

The theme of beheading runs throughout medieval Arthurian legend, and also in Celtic lore. Historical and prehistorical analogies will be found to agree, and the purpose of this cult of the buried head appears to be the same across the span of time and place. Never mind the fact that they were created by cultures as geographically diverse as the Maya in Central America, the Egyptians in the valley of the Nile, the Myceneans in Greece, for their seemingly independent existence is simply the result of diffusion.

The hunting tribes, who travelled through timeless prehistory, took their gods, their symbols, their lore and legends, with them. Is this how the Rainbow Serpent reached Australia, or was it indigenous? Tales may be localised – the well-known Cretan adventure of Theseus in the labyrinth, or Robin Hood in Sherwood Forest – while others such as Cinderella are so widely distributed that they must have followed the migrations of peoples from a common homeland.

The earliest version of *Cinderella* has been traced to China in the ninth century AD but this is very late, indeed it is modern, yet by its very nature the story must be thousands of years old. The great myths of antiquity were forged as language was forged, and probably at the same time.

In Palestine, archaeologists have found dolmens, or 'chamber tombs' (although there is no evidence of their having been sepulchral) similar in design and construction to others in Malta, in Corsica, Brittany, Britain and Ireland. They cannot be the product of independent invention, for they are alike in size, in shape, and in location. There is one by a farm in Devonshire, near a spring. The dolmen builders in Palestine, and those in England, were responding to the same impulse.

The swastika symbol familiar to the American Indians is identical to the swastika first formed in the deserts of northern Mesopotamia. The people of Crete who devised the labyrinth could have compared notes with the designers of Stonehenge. The Bronze Age barrow builders of Etruria would find much in common with their counterparts in North Wales. Over the past century excavation has revealed a wealth of clay models of plump females, the so-called 'Mother Goddesses' or Venus figurines of prehistory, almost universal and found as far apart as Mesopotamia and Mexico.

Some monuments, however, have acquired a unique status. They stand alone in their own strange world, their dark past

FIG. 3 Hesbon, Palestine – a dolmen imitating the entrance to a cave.

FIG. 4 The Greek swastika (above) compared to one from Mississippi, USA, suggests early migration.

defying interpretation. The curious Neolithic chamber tombs of earth and stone called long barrows contained such a rag-bag of bones, all mixed together and partly burnt, that they could hardly have been constructed in deference to and reverence for the dead. A few tumuli, or round barrows of the Bronze Age contained no bones at all – not even a handful of the customary chips of pottery. They were built for reasons other than the sepulchral.

Groups of New Age believers gather in these chamber tombs to conduct mystical communion with the Greek god Pan. Like Dionysus, Pan was an earth and animal spirit, priapic, shaggy-limbed, goat-eyed. The ritual is said to induce a profound spiritual experience, nourishing and encouraging the inner self to be at one with the living earth.

It was perhaps a special relationship with the earth and sky that motivated the building of Stonehenge and Avebury, on the chalk hills of Wessex, and the setting up of the thin skeletal slabs of Callanish, exposed to the Atlantic gales of the Outer Hebrides. These are prime examples of the unexplained, and so is Silbury, the largest man-made hill in Europe, comfortably placed like an inverted teacup in a deep and often waterfilled saucer. Silbury Hill, says Michael Dames, author of *The Silbury Treasure* (1976),[27] was built in the form of the Mother Goddess widely worshipped in prehistoric Europe and Britain. Stonehenge, says Aubrey Burl, Britain's foremost authority on stone circles, was a native monu-ment, and so it is, but is it really unique?[28] The great trilithons, where two massive upright stones support a lintel, have an almost exact parallel in the design of doorways in many of the temples of antiquity, especially those in the entrances of passage graves; in the

Bible lands, the army surveyor Claude Conder, commissioned by the Palestine Exploration Fund in the 1880s, had heard of a stone circle, 'not unlike Stonehenge', above the valley of Wady Waleh, south of Zerka M'ain on the chalk escarpments of the mountains of Moab, though he doesn't mention having visited the place.[29]

While photographing the surface contours of one of the Trilithons at Stonehenge in 1953, Professor Richard Atkinson noticed the engraved shape of what appeared to be a dagger. It was suggested that the shape could be matched with the designs of daggers from Mycenae in Argos, which in turn had their roots in the Mycenaean civilisation of Crete. A possible association between Stonehenge and Crete is interesting. The pattern of the rings of Stonehenge has similarities with the design of the Cretan labyrinth, in which Theseus defeated the bull-headed Minotaur. Was Stonehenge a place of sacrifice like the labyrinth? Did both these ancient mythologies share a common homeland?

Stonehenge, however, is rather late on the scene. In terms of prehistory, Stonehenge is only yesterday. To try and reach an understanding of our pagan past we need to go back as far as possible, to the first cities and first societies of the eastern Mediterranean, to Jericho and Çatal Hüyük, or further still in time, to the cave paintings of Palaeolithic France and Spain, and try to compare the motives of the circle builders to those of the cave artists. Silbury will not yield its secrets by our burrowing into its flanks, nor by measuring its height, or by plotting its 'ley lines', that imaginary grid of alignments connected by some mystic force or influential, spiritual power to other similar monuments. Possible alignments are often cited as evidence of a scientific system established by the megalith builders. The Scottish engineer Alexander Thom spent most of a lifetime plotting with theodolite and tape measure the alignments of stone circles. A few are indisputable – the sun's rays at the winter solstice penetrating the stone chamber at New Grange in Ireland; the rays of the rising sun illuminating the causeway of Stonehenge on the morning of the summer solstice – but these are rather exceptional.

Elsewhere there are no really significant alignments of stone circles, although there appears to have been an agreement between the builders of long barrows, passage graves and burial chambers to align their entrances towards the east and south-east. A Cambridge astronomer and archaeologist, Dr M. A. Hoskin, has measured some 1200 tombs in different parts of Southern Europe and found that 95 per cent face the eastern part of the horizon; tombs facing west are almost unknown. More important than these physical sitings are the motives of the people who built the monuments, of the general and the specific needs of pre-historic man. It seems to me that the only way to understand these motives is through the study of myths and symbols in relation to archaeological evidence, and what we are going to discover is perhaps not what we might expect to find. There was an abundance of choice, in fact: the celestial influences of the stars and space; the legacy of societies with advanced, esoteric knowledge; communion with earth forces; worship of a Great Goddess, shamanism, and so on, and all poised in balance against that single and most persuasive of long-matured theories – fertility, sex and the veneration of the generative organs.

CHAPTER 2

Sex and Symbol

For the past two centuries evidence has been gathered to support the belief that man's spiritual and creative life was expressed through what nineteenth-century anthropologists called 'nature worship', the veneration of stones, springs and rivers, animals and trees, but especially gods and goddesses of fertility, and various manifestations of the human sexual organs.

'One must not be astonished to find in antiquity so many deities favourable to generation and fecundity,' wrote the French historian Jacques-Antoine Dulaure. 'It was the necessity of man that created the powers of the gods. The cult of Venus goes back to the first stages of religion, and evidence demonstrates the indisputable fact that the need for an increase of population was the sole origin of primitive cults.'[1]

The subject was given impetus at the end of the eighteenth century by the antiquary, connoisseur and politician Richard Payne Knight, whose study of Priapus was published to the acclaim of a few and the disgust and disapproval of many. The explorer and orientalist Sir Richard Burton was later to note extensive phallic worship in West Africa, and concluded that man's primal want is for progeny. One Scottish author, James Hannay, a committed anti-papist, intrigued by the wealth of what he saw as suggestive symbolism in religion, spent thirty years in pursuit of this line of enquiry, to his eventual satisfaction: sex was the key to the understanding of the ancient world.[2]

The phallus and vulva as symbols of human fertility and the foundation of nature worship seemed to me a very plausible hypothesis, especially in view of the evidence. Cults involving trees and snakes, upright stones, stalagmites, stones with holes bored through them, obelisks and towers, ithyphallic deities such as Atum-Ra, Osiris, Min, Hermes, Pan, Dionysus and Priapus, the self-mutilating eunuch priests of Cybele, totem poles, the maypole of rustic England, prehistoric rock engravings from Sweden depicting stick-like warriors endowed with erect members of heroic proportions, may all be produced in support of 'the generative organs as symbols of the creative powers of nature'.[3]

Thomas Inman, a Liverpool physician and a keen scholar of sexual symbolism, had decided that fish could represent the uterus, drawing attention to the similarity of a fish's belly to the vulva, and to the Christian symbol of the *vesica pisces*.[4] John Allegro agreed, declaring the red mullet especially symbolic of the womb.[5] The Italian philologist Angelo Gubernatis saw fish as decidedly phallic, while everybody regarded the snake as a prime symbol of the male member.[6] The snake's role as the symbolic phallus needs little encouragement (brushing aside the fact that the mythological serpent is usually female), although some see the serpent as a symbol of the womb and the generative functions,[7] others as the umbilicus.[8] Interpretations that arose from the depths of the unconscious mind fell naturally into the scheme of things. Anything tripartite could be phallic because, as Freud perceived, three is the sum of the parts of the male genitals. The fleur-de-lys, the three-legged symbol of the triskeles, the caduceus or herald's wand carried by the phallic Hermes, the trident in the hand of the phallic Siva.

Many writers and scholars have found no difficulty in perceiving sexual symbolism in myths, even in the works of the established religions. By the turn of the century the way was prepared for Freudian interpretive opportunity. The military surveyor and archaeologist Claude Conder anticipated the psychoanalyst's penchant for word association, suggesting that the biblical 'Fall of Man' was an analogy for the detumescence of the erect penis.[9]

Scholars became fascinated by phallicism, but analogy can be a trap into which it is easy to fall. Following Freud, where umbrellas, walking sticks, ladders, and bananas are accepted as phallic in the analysis of dreams, one might imagine the Eiffel Tower, or the Chrysler Building in Manhattan, or London's Post Office Tower, as being 'phallic', and 'spot the phallic symbol' becomes a game that anyone can play.

The idea of phallic power was carried to its limits by a Freudian disciple, the Hungarian anthropologist Geza Roheim, who had spent much time in the 1920s and 30s analysing the dreams of Australian aborigines: 'The Divine King is the personified penis of the whole community, and it is for this reason that, as has so often been noted, all his insignia and all his ceremonies are phallic. Phallic is his sceptre, phallic is his crown; the insertion of his head into the circlet at his coronation is a symbolic coitus. The oil of his anointing, the water of his lustrations, the cross embroidered on his robe or carried in his hand: all these are symbols of his function, the magical apparatus with which he goes to work. He is the source of all life, by him the people prosper.'[10] But suppose the monarch is a queen – is she phallic, too?

Roheim had no difficulty identifying phallic females, being the author of an essay, 'Aphrodite – or the Woman with a Penis'.[11] He was in fact correct in one respect, since many deities in the ancient world were androgynous. But Freud, Jung and their followers have much to answer for, and in my view they have retarded the progress of the study of myth and symbol by nearly a hundred years. On one hand there is Carl Jung, with his 'archetypes' and mystical revelations of the self, the soul and spirituality; on the other hand there is Sigmund Freud, with his very persuasive style of writing and his seductive theories, urging the psycho-sexual view of man's nature and his motives.

It is tempting to interpret everything in terms of sexual symbolism. After all, fertility means the creation of life from the fecund womb of nature, and the fertile seed of the male, vital to the future of all mankind. If the encouragement of human procreation was indeed the origin of primitive cults, of myth and symbol, then we must expect to find the penis, vagina and uterus as the most basic of archaic models. In *The Wise Wound*, Peter Redgrove and Penelope Shuttle compare the layout of the uterus to the horned heads of sacred bulls (the uterus in antiquity was thought to have 'horns'), while the cervix, identified by the authors as the 'birth cone' was, they claim, a sacred symbol appearing as the Penis of Shiva, cup-marks, Silbury Hill, the tree of life and 'the fruiting of the ovaries,' tumuli, the Celtic cross, even cave art.[12]

For some while, I was certainly persuaded by the idea of a prehistoric society preoccupied with human fecundity, and to follow a route indicated by an American biologist, Clyde Franklin Reed, who declared Stonehenge to be a 'sex machine' in which the fifty-six small pits called the Aubrey holes (marking the perimeter of the circle inside the bank and ditch), represented the 28-day ovarian cycle, the two ovaries providing in total the number of holes in the circle.[13]

Once again Stonehenge is compared to a clock, in this instance a biological clock. A system of counting the holes would indicate which days were propitious for fertilisation since, said Reed, the ovaries do not work in concert, but alternately. The fact that the builders would have been unaware of this staggered ovarian cycle, as even the later Greek physicians such as Galen were ignorant of the structure of the womb, was neither here nor there, but it was an intriguing idea, and 'as good an explanation of the Aubrey holes as most; if it had been published like the others as a short paper in *Nature*, rather than obscurely and privately as a pamphlet, it might have been taken notice of'.[14]

Similar notions had already been proposed in 1958 by Professor A.T. Hatto at the University of London. Hatto identified 'male' and 'female' stones at Stonehenge, especially where the great trilithons suggested the wedge-shaped female genitals enclosed between cyclopean thighs. With the horseshoe-shaped arrangement of stones as a symbolic womb, the potent rays of the midsummer sun penetrated the monument in an act of cosmic fertilisation.[15]

Hatto linked the circle to fertility dances, perhaps to encourage the ripening of crops, and his contribution has much to commend it, in view of the possible male (tall and thin) and female (short and wide) stones in the avenue at Avebury. This can also be seen in the Calderstones circle at Allerton in Liverpool, where a wide 'female' stone is placed opposite a thin, tapering 'male' stone, and in the paired stones along the Avebury avenue. Suggestions have often been made about the 'Heel Stone' at Stonehenge as possibly phallic, and it may be that the so-called and now recumbent 'Slaughter Stone' was its opposite partner. This might indicate 'fertility' in one form or another, and is more acceptable, to my mind, than celestial alignments, even though the Stonehenge entrance points towards the sun rising at dawn at the summer solstice.

Yet sex symbolism, for all its powerful imagery leaves far too many questions unanswered. Is it not more likely that the source of any expression of the genitals in cult and religion comes from the analogy between human fecundity and the seasonal bounty of the natural world? The Mesopotamian goddess Inanna compares her womb to a field, to be tilled by the divine ploughman Dumuzi, and eventually her womb delivers fruit and grain. Although the encouragement of human fertility might be shown by the evidence of the 'Venus figurines' found in quantity from periods of prehistory as early as the Ice Age, these obese little steatopygous (fat thighs and buttocks) modelled figures were not intended to symbolise human reproductiveness.

The anthropologist Peter Ucko suggests that the figurines he found in Crete are either dolls made for children, or dolls used in sympathetic magic as fertility figures in the wish for children.[16] The Venus figurines were designed probably to encourage the

FIG. 5 Female stones
at Stonehenge.
(Crown copyright)

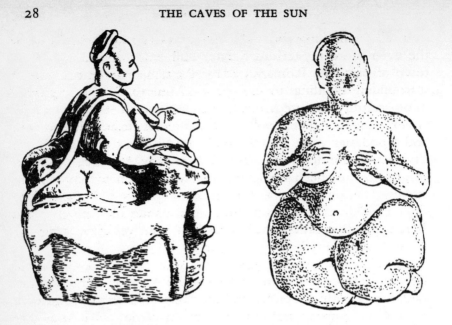

FIG. 6 Venus figurines from Çatal Hüyük, Anatolia.

fertility of the earth, and the cycle of the seasons, not the human birth cycle. At the same time there is a noted relationship between human fertility and husbandry, where ritual sexual intercourse was performed in fields to induce a good harvest, but this aspect of nature worship was never a foundation of pagan cult and religion, nor a source of myth.

Sex symbolism, widely perceived as the manifestation of fertility rites in the ancient world, to encourage the production of food or children, or both, fails to explain the strange and often bizarre features of myth, and the curious monuments of the past. A sexual interpretation (aside from an Oedipal one) does not tell us why Cronus castrated his father. The ancient Greeks thought that the story of Cronus was a creation myth, a dramatic account of the separation of earth and sky. Yet Cronus was not the only one to deprive his father of his manhood. The Hittite god Kumarbi, and the Hindu Indra, performed identical acts of violence on their sires, but in different circumstances; castration in myth, like decapitation, was a theme. A sexual foundation of myth does not tell us why the fifty daughters of Danaus cut off their husbands' heads, why Achilles and Krishna were killed by a wound to the heel, and why Hephaestus was thrown out of heaven by his mother, the goddess Hera.

It tells us nothing about the extraordinary ring at Avebury, or the even more mysterious Silbury Hill; nor why, in my home town of Bath, the Romans dedicated a temple and a complex of surrounding buildings to the goddess Minerva. This is important to our enquiry because Minerva was the Roman equivalent of the Greek goddess Athena, who helped Perseus defeat Medusa, and both goddesses wore the Gorgon's head like a trophy. Bath is a city famous for its hot springs. Is this why Minerva, with her gorgoneion of the hanging tongue, was chosen to represent its interests, because she was a goddess of springs and water? The city's emblem is a Gorgon head, with flames like the sun, and there is precious little sexual symbolism here, yet these things are at the heart of mythology and ancient religion.

Indeed, a great many myths do not seem to be about sex at all. There is nothing sexual in the saga of the Argonauts, the death of Balder, the myth of Perseus and the Gorgon. If Stonehenge with its fifty-six Aubrey holes is a 'Sex Machine' what then are Avebury and the rest of the 900 stone circles in Britain? They could hardly be radically different in purpose, even if they are different in design.

Critics will say that this proves the claim to the diverse meaning of myths and symbols, and that myths were not necessarily related to rituals and monuments. Since so much of prehistory is fossilised evidence and difficult to verify, especially in view of the lack of written information, how could I be sure that my interpretations, and the studies by other authors, were incorrect? Unless, of course, those of us who have made it their business to interpret aspects of prehistory, and with them myth and symbolism, have chosen to ignore or misinterpret vital evidence that has been staring them in the face – like the Gorgon's head – for the past century.

It seemed that sex and fertility had a definite role to play, but that they were really only a manifestation of something else more compelling. Phallicism, though widespread and prominent in many cults and religions, was merely a feature of a much grander design. Is there something quite simple that we fail to recognise? Phallicism, castration, decapitation, lameness, these are all themes because they appear and reappear in the myths of many societies throughout history and prehistory. Another theme that makes a regular appearance is that of numbers. The numbers three, seven and nine are to be found in myth, ritual and monument, right across the Old and New Worlds. More than any other theme, it was this one that encouraged me to seek a single source of myth. Having dealt – for the time being anyway – with sex and fertility, a brief glance at some of the other established theories might guide us in the right direction.

The evidence that shows Stonehenge as being aligned to the midsummer sun, and the legend of the henge as a sun-temple ought not to be be overlooked, but in general the subject of solar mythology has been put firmly away in dusty files in the mythologist's basement since the topic was largely discredited in the late nineteenth century. After all, how could sun-worship explain the drawings of animals in the black depths of the caves, or the bizarre skull and bone cults of the Neanderthalers?

Various societies have shown evidence of sun-worship – the Egyptians, the Aztecs, some American Indian tribes – but solar influences are hard to detect in all the cults and religions of the ancient world unless, again, we persistently fail to recognise them for what they are. The sun's annual rule in those countries bordering the Mediterranean is harsh, with temperatures at the eastern end reaching on average 90 to 100 degrees Fahrenheit in summer, a time when disease is most prevalent.

It is true that Ra was the sun-god of the Egyptians, but he was nowhere near as influential as Isis and Osiris, or Khunumu and Ptah. Zeus, not the sun god Helios, was the great deity of the Greeks, and he was a sky god of storms, as was the Mesopotamian Adad, and the goddess Ninhursag, to whom the sun god Shamash was subordinate. It is a fact that Apollo was a sun god, but he too deferred to Zeus, and the lame Hephaestus was a fire god of sorts, but the Olympians regarded him as a bit of a joke. It appears from these examples that the sun is an unlikely object for veneration; sun worship and solar mythology are considered by many scholars as old hat. What other candidates might be sought as a source of myth? More to the modern taste is shamanism. Shamans are practitioners of mystical rituals, and they are specialist healers but are not founders of cults and religions, although a lot may be learned from the symbolism of their actions and attire. A more suitable candidate is the once and future Mother Goddess. Mother Goddess theories have today a keen following, along with an interest in the Black Virgins of the Catholic faith, and the Green Men carved among the stone foliage in ecclesiatical architecture.

Some feminist scholars, in particular the archaeologist Marija Gimbutas, offer evidence of the ancient and deep-rooted cult of the Mother Goddess possibly pointing to a past age of divine matriarchy.[17] The idea of a benign mother figure as the head of a tribe had gone hand in hand with other nineteenth-century theories, now abandoned, such as totemism and exogamy, and the sacred marriage. Yet the influential goddess in prehistory remains a persistent theme. Ucko tells us that the existence of a Mother Goddess has been discussed since the eighteenth century, but 'the twentieth century's estimation of the prehistoric Mother Goddess has left her character largely undefined'.[18] She was not revered in the form of a single divine being, worshipped by all societies (although some writers have identified her as the Cretan snake goddess), but she is prominent as a celestial, numinous type due to a vital and powerful function which I believe to have been the special preserve of all the goddesses of myth and religion. We make the mistake of supposing that the family structure, presided over by a firm but essentially benign mother figure, contributing to the structure of society, was of paramount importance in ancient times, taking precedence over other, more urgent considerations.

The idea of a matriarchy in a Golden Age was a popular theory among nineteenth-century anthropologists and social scientists such as Engels, Bachofen, McLennan, and others, a theory, like those of solar mythology and totemism, now 'totally discredited and deservedly forgotten'.[19] Totemism describes the tribal worship of an animal or bird chosen as a symbol and guardian spirit, where the totem animal bonded the tribe by kinship, rituals and taboos. The undoubted importance of animal symbols in the long prehistory of myth and cult in primitive societies, as well as in highly developed ones such as Egypt, played a part in promoting this theory. It is prevalent in Scotland today, where my wife's clan, the Macphersons of Newtonmore, are a branch of the clan Chattan of Caithness, the cat people – or perhaps more accurately, the wildcat people.

Totemism does not explain, however, why the young god Horus has a falcon's head, why Apis is a bull, why the Sphinx of Giza has the body of a lion. The Egyptians were not a series of tribes with animal mascots, and it is unlikely that the animal gods were formed from the capricious fancies of Egyptian priests. Could these animals symbolise some other and perhaps more

FIG. 7 The Snake Goddess from Minoan Crete, a version of Ariadne who
helped Theseus to slay the Minotaur. (From Sir Arthur Evans's *The Palace of
Minos at Kinossos.*

powerful influence? Several of the mysteries to be solved can be
by-passed, but others seem to me to represent key issues.

    One of the most prominent, and another feature in the grand
design of mythology and ancient religion, is the riddle of the
Twins. Many and diverse societies throughout the world had, and
still have, myths and folktales and rituals in which twins play a
prominent part. In Greek myths the Divine or Heavenly Twins
Castor and Polydeuces, called the Dioscuri or 'Zeus's Boys',
whose names were given to the constellation, and the zodiacal
sign of Gemini, presented an impenetrable problem, and had been

called by the Oxford classics scholar Lewis Farnell, 'one of the most perplexing features of Greek mythology'.[20]

They were described as the sun and moon, night and day, celestial horsemen, but none of these descriptions fitted the facts. The twins were often hostile to one another; one was weak, the other strong, one rough and hairy, the other smooth and delicate. They were warriors, yet presided over nuptials and childbirth, and give every indication of being male and female, yin and yang, but they are undoubtedly masculine and are of course identical.

One of their duties was to ensure that fertile seed was implanted in the womb of every woman. They were called 'pounders', but also 'witnesses', all of which might suggest that they symbolised the testicles – it was once a custom to place the hand over the genitals while swearing on oath, hence 'testimony' from both the Latin *testis* (witness), and *testis* (testicles); one of the functions of the Dioscuri were avengers against perjury. In the legends a twin often dies, as Cain killed Abel and Romulus slew Remus. A worldwide superstition shows that the mother of twins is regarded as a natural rainmaker, and at their birth it is customary to drench her with water. What could one make of their function in ancient myth?

There are other puzzles too. Why did Perseus behead the Gorgon, and what did she really represent, other than the portrayal of human aggression and 'an expression of the terror the lonely wanderer felt in the beast-haunted night'?[21] Why, then, did the winged horse Pegasus spring from her neck? Why were there so many lame gods and heroes, such as Hephaestus the smith, and Achilles of the vulnerable heel? 'Because', said the Freudians, 'lameness, like blindness, is a symbol of castration. Take the myth of Oedipus, whose name means "Swellfoot", who was lame, and who famously killed his father in order to marry his mother, after which he blinded himself through guilt and remorse. Divine lameness is a manifestation of the Oedipus complex.'

This explanation would seem verified by Achilles, whose mother Thetis caused him to be lame, just as Hephaestus was lamed by his own mother, the goddess Hera, wife of Zeus. Eventually, though, I was persuaded that the Twins were unlikely representations of the testicles, nor were the limping heroes afflicted by the Oedipus Complex – hardly the stuff of primitive myth, but the expansive posturings of modern psychologists.

The answers were more likely to be found through Frazer than through Freud.

Symbolic features such as the Gorgon's head, the winged horse, the Twins, the limping god, must have each had a prototype, an antecedent – they did not just appear out of the blue, unless the Gorgon was an alien. Freud had suggested that the Gorgon's head was a genital symbol, a view shared by the psychoanalyst Ferenczi. Others had said that she was the grim aspect of the Mother Goddess, or the ugly mask of the Death Goddess employed to frighten enemies.

Goddesses were often shown with lions as companions, and certain writers have pointed out the similarity of the Gorgon's head to that of a snarling lion which, when incorporated in a mask, or worn upon a shield, might deter aggressors. But why the mocking grin and hanging tongue? She cannot be explained away by Freudians as an expression of man's fear of female sexuality. One method of tackling a knotty problem is to take a hard look at a detail and try to trace its origins and development. The quirky details in myth, often seen as unimportant, such as the lost sandal of Jason the Argonaut, or the slipper of Cinderella, invariably point the way ahead.

FIG. 8 Athena, Perseus and the Gorgon.

The feature of the hanging tongue had parallels in antiquity. Lion's heads were popular decorative motifs regularly used as waterspouts on fountains, the water gushing over the tongue – they are in fact ubiquitous: there are two outside the British Museum. Was this the prototype? Did the Gorgon's head, like the Twins and their rainmaker mother, have something to do with water? Myth tells us that the winged horse Pegasus, whose name means 'source of water', flew to the eastern slope of Mount Helicon and struck a rock with his hoof to create the ice-cold, crystal-clear Hippocrene spring.

In Egypt, the primeval goddess Tefnut, The Spitter, was a rain deity and had the head of a lioness. There have been suggestions that the Gorgon's head, always perfectly circular, is a symbol either of the moon, or more probably the sun, since the moon usually took the form of a crescent. In this case she is unlikely to have much to do with water, unless, of course, the tongue implied thirst, encouraged by the fierce heat of the arid, Mediterranean summer. Some of the earliest shrines have connections with water – the spring at Jericho, the stone monuments at the headwaters of the Jordan – while springs of healing waters are an essential feature of many myths from the ancient world.

The Gorgon's head, though, is but one of many symbols, and others equally well known do not seem to have much to do with water – the swastika, for example. Yet the swastika not infrequently appears as a decorative motif on archaic pottery, on water-vessels and vases, as did the lion, boar, horse, bull, snake, stag and bear. These animals also decorated the caves of the Ice Age, through which rivers flowed to the subterranean depths of the earth. It may prove to be a route worth following, but for the moment the journey begins nearer to home.

CHAPTER 3

The Lion's Head

We pick up our first clues on the chalkhills of south-west England where Stonehenge was erected, and west to the city of Bath with its thermal springs. It is a fact that the majority of our antiquities – the henges and stone circles, the long barrows and tumuli – were sited on the chalk, and invariably near a source of water: a spring, bourne or river; this watery location is a point to bear in mind, for it is a repeated theme. There are exceptions to the chalk siting – some are on limestone, others in areas of igneous rocks, where outcrops supplied the building material for the monuments.

The chalk terminates rather abruptly in the county of Dorset, where it gives way to limestone and both types of rock are like sponges, soaking up and retaining the rain – they are good acquifers, as the geologists say. The rain percolates downwards to emerge as springs around the chalk escarpment, where the water-bearing chalk meets the strata of impermeable clay, but in the limestone regions of gorges and caves, in Cheddar Gorge and over the heaths and forests of the Mendip hills, the rain seeps through fissures to reach great depths, reappearing as hot springs in the spa city of Bath, the water now sulphurous and incredibly ancient. Geologists, with the advantages of isotope chemistry, claim that the water takes ten thousand years to make this journey.

So the thermal spring that bubbles like green pea soup in the Roman Baths, once presided over by the goddess Minerva who wore the Gorgon-head on her breast, had fallen as rain on the uncovered head of Mesolithic man, for traces of his occupation have been found in the Avon valley. The resident British in Roman times had their own local deity, the goddess Sul – springs are always the special interest of goddesses. The Romans, for their part, had imported their gods and cults – Jupiter of course, Mars and Minerva, but they also introduced the rich oriental deities such as Isis, Mithras, Dionysus, and the odd Syrian figure of

Jupiter Dolichenus, dressed as a Roman soldier, who stands on the back of a bull and waves an axe.

Compared with Isis of the brown Nile, the local water goddess Sul or Sulis was a modest figure, yet she must have carried some weight with the local people, for the Romans acknowledged her influence, and as so often happens when a country is invaded and occupied, native deities are integrated into the religion of the invader. The occupying legions called the place Aquae Sulis, and combined Sul with Minerva. On the pediment of the temple to Sulis-Minerva they placed a stone carving of a Gorgon's head – the mask of Medusa.

Here is a clue that we should grasp and hold on to, although the Bath gorgoneion is curiously different from the classical version with the hanging tongue. For one thing there is no tongue in evidence, and for another it is unmistakably solar, decidedly masculine and with a rather anguished expression which derives, I suggest, from the sculptor's attempt to make the head leonine. In this, he was following the design of the Greek Gorgon's head, or gorgoneion, based upon the features of a snarling lion, for the lion had long symbolised the sun, and in eastern lands was the sun goddess's constant and devoted companion.

FIG. 9 The gorgoneion from Bath, England, and a lion's head
fountain, Phoenicia.

Minerva was identified by the Romans with the Greek goddess Athena, whose dramatic birth from her father's head was a popular subject in Greek art and literature. Her father was Zeus, who had swallowed Athena's mother Metis, just as Zeus's own father,

Cronus, had tried to swallow him. The family showed little in the way of filial piety. When Cronus castrated his father with a sickle, he employed the same type of implement as Perseus, aided by Athena, had used to strike off Medusa's head. Why he did so, and why he employed a sickle, and why Cronus castrated his father, may eventually become clear.

In his youth, Perseus lived on the tiny island of Seriphos in the Cyclades, famously barren but for one significant feature – it had a sulphurous thermal spring. And so, in this small country town of Bath, there are monuments that reach back to the creation myths of the Greeks – due, perhaps, to hot water.

Bath is on the edge of a great complex of antiquities. The heart of this landscape is Salisbury Plain and the Marlborough Downs, the archaeological and geographical region that is still referred to as 'Wessex'. But Wessex no longer exists, except to the readers of Thomas Hardy. Since the time of the Saxons and its heyday as the kingdom of Alfred the Great, it has had no administrative boundaries except to the Wessex Water Board. Neither is this land of valleys and springs and rivers the quietest under the sun, for two motorways cross the region, and the army drives tanks through it, while long convoys of vehicles bump along its winding country lanes.

The 2nd Augusta Legion that marched towards the setting sun under the Roman standards of Claudius, are today replaced by legions of tourists. Here and there, on the clean, open slopes of the downs, ancient shapes have been cut in the turf, to reveal gleaming white figures in the chalk. North of the plain and above the Marlborough Downs near the railway town of Swindon you will find the most famous and most ancient – the Uffington Horse, some five thousand years old. south-west of the plain, almost at the limit of the chalklands, you can visit the ithyphallic Cerne Abbas Giant, whose origins are unknown.

This chalk country was also useful for its huge stones, the sarsens. Long ago, a thick deposit of ocean silt, the residue of primeval seas, covered the Plain and the Marlborough Downs to settle as sedimentary rock, but in time it broke up into huge blocks of almost pure silica. Diamond hard, these monoliths were scattered over the landscape, and provided some of the material for the building of stone circles, and stone avenues, and mysterious mounds of earth, for here in Wessex, along the valleys of the

Kennet and Avon rivers, is the greatest concentration of Stone
Age and Bronze Age monuments in western Europe.

'Greatest' means numerous, and it also means large, and even
famous, for the stone circles of Stonehenge and Avebury have
acquired international renown, though for a visitor it must be hard
to understand why, at least so far as Stonehenge is concerned, for
the monument is a ruin, dwarfed by the Plain on which it stands,
by the expanse of sky above, and by its companion monument
some twenty miles to the north – the huge Avebury circle and the
mound of Silbury, the biggest man-made hill in Europe. The
persistent idea that Stonehenge is a temple erected to the sun, that
the axis of the monument is aligned to the summer solstice, and a
claim from antiquity that it was dedicated to the sun-god Apollo,
or his Celtic equivalent, might be seen to have a similar source in
the folk legends of Silbury Hill.

According to John Aubrey, antiquary, traveller and diarist, who
discovered Avebury in the seventeenth century, Silbury was the
tomb of a king buried upright on his horse – King Sil. Could this
name be related in any sense to the goddess Sul, so that perhaps
Sil, like Sul, are masculine and feminine words meaning 'sun', or
perhaps 'water'? The horse was a potent solar symbol in prehistory, while the legends of magic horses, with riders, imprisoned in hills and mountains were known throughout Europe.

Taking into account the usual folktales of buried treasure, is it
coincidence that the story of King Sil was later embroidered so
that horse and rider were said to be of pure gold, or that Sil was
buried in a golden coffin? A further fragment of folk memory
maintains that the hill was raised 'while a posset of milk was
seething'.[1] Would this be about the time it takes for the sun to rise
in the morning? The sun-god Apollo 'burst through his swaddling
clothes' and grew to maturity with astonishing quickness.

Echoes of pagan animal sacrifice sounded in the eighteenth-
century, when rustic celebrations witnessed bull-baiting, followed
by the slaughter of the bull, and roasting the carcass on top of the
hill. There are further clues to be found in the structures of
Silbury, Avebury and Stonehenge, as there are in the hot springs
of Bath and Medusa's head, but first they have to be recognised
for what they are, and we will have to go a long way away, in
time and in place, to discover their true meaning.

In that far distant age that we call prehistory, in an environment
and a landscape still affected by retreating glaciers a mile thick, a

landscape now difficult to imagine, European man left behind
sufficient evidence to enable archaeologists to piece together his
way of life, his occupations and preoccupations, dwellings, habitat,
and to identify some of the foods for which he foraged and
hunted. We know from excavated sites that in one area they were
fond of pork (in Neolithic Wessex, England), in another they
consumed huge quantities of snails and pistachio nuts (Mesolithic central Turkey), in another area they ate a lot of reindeer
meat (Upper Palaeolithic France) and used arrows with sharp
flint heads, expertly and beautifully fashioned. Studies of ancient
human bones show that, in general, people suffered from osteo-
arthritis, tuberculosis and toothache. Of the Neolithic population
of the Orkney Islands, studied by the archaeologist John Hedges,
most people died before the age of thirty. Life expectancy on
arriving at fifteen years of age was a further thirteen years for men
and nine for women. Many others would have died during
childbirth. The life expectancy of Neanderthalers was about
eighteen years, of Neolithic hunters between nineteen and
twenty-five. According to the Belgian archaeologist Dr Paul
Janssens, death was decidedly premature, although his claim that
most people died around fourteen years of age makes one wonder
how the human race survived. Infant mortality was high, as it
always has been in parts of the world. An Iron Age burial site
revealed 225 skeletons of which fifty per cent were young
children, while the remains of 29 adult burials from a Mesolithic
site (about 8000 BC) suggest that they died between twenty and
thirty years of age.

The periods or divisions of time, from the Old Stone Age or
Palaeolithic, through the Middle or Mesolithic to the Neolithic,
the New Stone Age, during which agriculture began, also saw the
establishment of Homo sapiens over the less progressive Neanderthal man of the Mousterian culture, or Middle Palaeolithic. Some
arrowheads were found embedded in human bones, and it is clear
that in addition to slaughtering animals, they slaughtered each
other. Perhaps they — or rather, we — always have done so; or
perhaps the desire to kill is a product of a higher intelligence, and
is now part of the human condition.

The stones, bones and snail shells are a few of the firm clues that
allow us to construct a picture of man's early lifestyle, but of his
mental and spiritual life the picture is less clear. The evidence is
tantalising, for it is insufficient to be conclusive, and the further

back in time one goes, the more scanty the evidence becomes, so that, from 40,000 BC, all we are left with are enigmatic scratchings on stone and bone. There have been a few isolated finds where, for example, a Neanderthal man was buried with the jawbone of a boar, another where the corpse was covered with flowers. These isolated examples have persuaded some writers to the view that Neanderthalers of 60,000 years ago had indeed developed a concept of life after death, a view with not much substance to support it, except that the bodies in some burials were tightly flexed in a foetal position, suggesting a 'return to the womb' for rebirth. Yet an equal number of skeletons were found not flexed but extended.

The flexed bodies were also tightly bound, leading to the theory that this was to prevent the dead from returning to haunt the living. But the flexed and bound bodies could point to their being victims of sacrifice; the trussing must have taken place quite soon after death or rigor mortis would have made flexing difficult. The trussing suggests, perhaps, that the victims were buried alive, while flexing might indicate the foetal position as simulating new life, and therefore a form of dedication to the earth in winter, encouraging the birth of nature. In France a multiple burial was discovered in which an adult male and female were found tightly flexed, the woman bound with thongs, and accompanied by four children in an extended, supine position.[2]

Of greater significance is the jawbone of a boar. For thousands of years boars have been a feature of cult practices: tusks and jawbones placed in graves, clay effigies found in pits, and boar images in art and dress (the crest on a warrior's helmet) seem to have had a deep, symbolic meaning. Medusa has boar's tusks. Adonis was killed by a boar, and so was Osiris, and it was a huge boar that ripped open the thigh of the great hero of Homer's Odyssey. Perhaps the most bizarre example is the jawbone contained within a clay model of a human female breast, decorating the wall of a shrine in the Anatolian village of Çatal Hüyük, and dating from about 6000 BC.[3] This was not witchcraft, but a form of talisman in the service of the goddess whose breasts were represented.

One regular phenomenon, though, was widespread and fairly well documented. A sixth of Palaeolithic (Old Stone Age) burials across Europe to Russia, from as far south as Malta and up to Finland in the north, were strewn with red ochre or iron oxide,

the naturally occurring earth pigment related to the rust that
appears on iron. Inhumations were by no means abundant, and
the vast majority of people were probably not buried at all. (Until
quite recently certain African tribes, notably the Masai, exposed
their dead to the vultures and jackals.) Nevertheless a significant
proportion – located as far afield as Australia, Africa, North
America and China – were covered with red ochre, or were laid
on top of a scattering of pigment. The floors of Mousterian
dwellings have been found to be streaked with it, a practice which
persisted for many thousands of years, through to the Neolithic
Near East. In support of the rebirth theory, it has been suggested
that red ochre is a representation of blood, but it does not
necessarily follow that rebirth is symbolised.

What is so special about the mineral pigment known as red
ochre? It is the only earth colour found in quantity, apart from
black manganese dioxide, and during prehistory it was mined and
transported. Ranging from yellow, through brown and brick-red
to the colour and appearance of dried blood, the redness of ochre
can be intensified by heating. Thus the red colour of the soil in
Mediterranean countries and the Near East, in the tropical and
desert regions of Africa, is due to the high proportion of iron
present, the rapidity of evaporation, and the fact that these soils are
rich in organic matter which oxidises the iron. This is apparent in
the remarkable variety of red soils across the Portuguese Algarve.

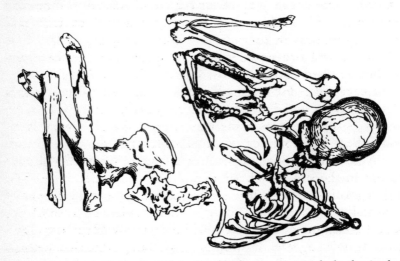

FIG. 10 Neanderthal cave burial in Israel. The remains include the jawbone
of a boar.

Iron is present in every known type of rock, especially in red sandstone and limestone areas, and the ochre is found in quantity where acid-bearing water has percolated through rock, where running streams have oxidised the iron like rust, and leached it to form crystalline deposits following evaporation. Iron-rich terra-cotta earth and ferruginous clay formed the fabric of early pottery, and remains one of the most malleable of pottery materials.

This fact gives us a clue to the sanctity of red ochre. It was believed by prehistoric and early historic societies that the first man was formed of clay, a fact well-supported by myth. The Egyptian potter-god Khnumu formed man from the mud of the Nile. In Mesopotamia, the mother goddess Ninhursag of the Zagros mountains was the 'Lady Potter' who helped shape mankind, aided by the god Ea, called Nudimmud – 'God of the Shaping' – who provided the water to soften the red clay.[4] Adam, the first man, derives his name from the Hebrew אָדָם which means 'man' and 'red', and also has the sense of 'to make or produce', and is perhaps related to *admah*, 'red earth', since Adam was made from the dust (Genesis 2:7), or the red earth by the spring called Ain-el-Judeideh.

The discovery of deposits of pure oxide, resembling dried blood, and the presence of oxide in the earth and impregnated in rocks, especially in caves, engendered the belief that man was created from earth and stone, 'the rock that begat thee'. Perhaps this is why red ochre was venerated in prehistoric times, and widely employed. Prometheus fashioned Pandora of clay, and stole fire from heaven to give his figure the spark of life. The Greek smith and fire god Hephaestus made men of clay, who were then clothed and given the spark of life by Athena.

The quality of redness may also refer to the sun. Tribes such as the Crow, Creek and Hopi Indians of North America, each tribe separated by distances of a thousand miles, share a Promethean legend where the founder of mankind makes the first human beings from the residual clay of the Deluge. When the figures dried out in the sun they became endowed with life, as the new spring vegetation appears in response to the quickening power of the sun following the rains. This is so close to the myths of Osiris, Ptah and Khnumu, to the myths of Prometheus, Hephaestus and Athena, that it suggests a common underlying idea that perhaps originated in the Middle East. The redness of blood, of clay, of the sun, fused together in the mind of prehistoric man to suggest that here was the stuff of life itself, a substance vital to the cycle of nature. It was painted on the walls of caves, on the Venus figurines to encourage vitality, on artefacts, the floors of dwellings, anywhere in fact where it might do some good, where it might promote the continuation of life. In a cave at Great Ofnet, Bavaria, occupants had dug two holes in the limestone floor, and interred thirty-three human skulls, all facing west, and covered them with a pile of ochre. A fragment of mythology from Greece tells of how two brothers slew a third, cut off his head, wrapped it in a crimson cloak – as once they might have used ochre – and buried it at the foot of Mount Olympus.[5]

Iron oxide in its pure mineral form, collected from surface deposits, from river terraces and the depths of caves, was believed to possess great healing properties, as shown in the Greek myth of Telephus, the infant son of Heracles and Auge. Telephus was exposed and left on a hillside to die, a fate not uncommon among the divine children of mythology, in particular Oedipus whom Telephus in some respects resembles.

Suckled by a hind, and found by shepherds, he became king of Mysia. Involved in an incident where he was wounded in the leg by Achilles, and the wound refused to heal, Telephus sought the advice of an oracle, who said that a cure could only be achieved by Achilles himself, for the wounder should be the healer. Achilles, scraping some rust from his spear, applied it to the wound, and cured the limping hero.[6]

In myth such details as rust to cure a wound are never accidental, and we may suspect that in this case it is a central clue. Nor is it accidental that rust is iron oxide, a substance valued in prehistoric ritual, as the Greeks would perhaps have known. The need for people to understand and attempt to influence their environment by certain acts of repetitive behaviour that we call ritual have certainly contributed something to the formation of myths. Rust was included in a list of treatments in *Natural History* by the Roman writer Pliny, and in the myth of Telephus it is instrumental in one of the great sagas of the classical world, for Telephus was the guide who led the Greeks to Troy.

Red-haired Achilles was a healer. The 'wounder' and the 'healer' may both be aspects of the sun. He heals Patroclus on the battlefield, and gives his name to a plant, *Achillea*, the yarrow or milfoil, used throughout the world for its medicinal properties, and applied as a haemostatic agent to coagulate blood.

The connection between the sun and healing has long been recognised, but imperfectly understood, though the meaning is simple. It comes from the sun's apparent ability to recover from the 'death' of winter, and to promote life in the spring, and because the declining sun of autumn coincided with the arrival of rain, for water was both a healer and promoter of fertility.

This could be the purpose behind the clutch of Bavarian skulls, mentioned above, covered in red ochre and buried in a cave, and all facing west, where the sun declines, and which is the direction of the arriving rains. The Akkadians thought that the sun sank through a hollow in 'the mountain of the world', to travel by night through the dark abode of death, and to escape at dawn by the eastern gate.[7]

Where a reasonable claim might be made for ritual behaviour of a religious nature, and evidence found of a cult, such as where stacks of cave-bear skulls have been discovered in cists set into the cave floor, we can perhaps start to look for the foundation of a myth. A Neanderthal cave-bear sanctuary in Switzerland (Drachenloch) dating from around 40,000 BC had a bear skull surrounded by a small stone circle, and skulls carefully arranged with long bones, suggesting some form of bear worship.[8] It also suggests that here was a precedent to those skulls and long bones found in chamber tombs, mentioned briefly in the first chapter. Perhaps bears were seen as worthy adversaries in the hunt, for they were a source of food and clothing, but plenty of other equally worthy contenders were met with in the course of hunting – including mammoths, wolves and lions.

The period in question, when the bear cults flourished in France, Switzerland and Germany, was called the Mousterian (from a cave site at Le Moustier, Dordogne) and was associated with Neanderthal man; also during the Riss-Würm interglacial, when conditions were still decidedly cold. Why was the cave bear an object of reverence? One of the more recent statements on the subject was made by an American mythologist, the late Joseph Campbell, who took a Jungian approach in which interpretation is clouded by references to mysticism and things transcendental. Perhaps I am being unfair. Campbell supposes that in the cave-bear cults we are witnessing the first stirrings of religious feelings, the awakening of religious awe and spirituality. Campbell quotes the French ethnologist and expert on cave art, André Leroi-Gourhan, who declines to make any interpretations, other than remarking that 'Certain facts sufficiently well authenticated suffice to show that practices not related to techniques of material life existed before the period of Homo sapiens; we may call them religious, because they testify to interest beyond those of vegetative life.' Yet none of this helps us to understand why cave bears were the object of mankind's earliest known rites. What is special or particularly unusual about the habits or appearances of bears? We know that they are noted for a certain aspect of their annual life cycle – they hibernate, and seem to be able to exist without nourishment through the winter.

Could the bear, emerging from hibernation, resemble the return of spring and the powerful influence of the sun, forming a symbiotic relationship, so that the cult was essentially solar? Is this perhaps why the Drachenloch skull and bones were surrounded by a stone circle, to represent the disc of the sun, a distant forerunner of the stone circles of Britain?

The value of animals as subjects for symbolism, or theriomorphism – a deity in animal form – may have arisen from the seasonal behaviour of certain species. Bears were seen to reappear with the spring sunlight. The rutting stags, the *Cervidae*, with their newly formed antlers, were noticeably active at the decline of the sun in mid-autumn, which coincided with the arrival of the fertilising rains, followed by the birth of nature in the spring. In Brittany, archaeologists found an ochre burial within a setting of antlers.[9] A further clue to the possible solar nature of the bear might be found the cults of Artemis Brauronia, 'Artemis the Bear', sister of the sun god Apollo. At her festival in mid-April, girls wearing saffron-coloured robes, perhaps in imitation of the sun, danced in her honour.

The reverence paid to the bear by Neanderthalers is the earliest evidence of cults yet discovered. The hunters may have been impressed by the observation that bears do not seem to need nourishment during their period of dormancy; bears do not actually hibernate, where the body temperature is dramatically lowered, but retire into a dormant state through the winter. The belief that bears find nourishment by sucking their paws is an ancient one, and is perhaps behind the fables of gods, such as Zeus, who was born in a cave and nourished on honey. The infant Telephus was nursed by a mother bear.

If bear cults were indeed solar, it would partly explain why cults still persist in circumpolar regions of long winters – from

Lapland along the Arctic Circle through Siberia, and including Japan and Labrador – and why the circumpolar constellation Ursa Major is 'The Great Bear'. Bear cults could have a simple explanation. The cave bear was revered because, like the sun, bears entered the earth at the onset of winter, as the sun was thought to do; in the Sacred Books of the East, the Persian sun god is buried in the cave of gold in the west, only to rise in triumph in the spring. Moreover, caves especially were held in awe by prehistoric peoples, because here was where the sun's winter magic was performed, and the earth was quickened for the return of spring.

Perhaps the most remarkable thing about these bear cults is that they reveal the practice of solar worhip to have existed among Neanderthalers, attesting to its great antiquity, and what is more, the symbolism was considerably developed. This may be inferred by the discovery in the Drachenloch caves of a bear skull with the long bones thrust through its eye sockets, a sort of 'skull and crossbones' image. Did the skull represent, in some way or another, the sun? The long bones had a particular significance right through prehistory, and the combination was still in existence in Britain in Stonehenge times. If the Neanderthalers were maintaining a solar skull cult, it is likely that solar cults had been established perhaps for thousands of years.

Much later, during the Upper Palaeolithic, the period between 25,000 BC and 15,000 BC, men penetrated the limestone caves of southern France to model bear images from clay, and to drape them with real bears' pelts, presumably to endow them with life. This act reappears in the Greek creation myths, where the smith Hephaestus models men and women from clay, while Athena clothes them and breathes life into them. The cave artists produced work of delicate geometric patterns carved in bone; modelled figurines mainly of ample-thighed females – the 'goddess' or 'Venus' figurines – and the astonishing animal figures painted and engraved on the walls of limestone caves, often in their darkest recesses.

They are astonishing because of their remote location, and also because the artists have managed to convey the impression of movement and agility. We know how they did it. The artists crawled on their bellies through cramped passageways in the rock, facing difficulties that only cavers and potholers will recognise, pushing before them their wooden poles and animal-fat lamps, their lumps of red ochre and manganese black pigment, on slivers of limestone or on barnacle shells, to reach the vaulted ceilings of the cathedral-like caves ahead. What we would like to know is why they did it – and this poses one of the great questions in the study of prehistory. Is it possible to discover, on these walls and along the subterranean galleries gouged by the racing waters, the origin of at least some of the mythological legends, of ancient symbols and primitive religions, and trace a continuous thread – like Ariadne's – through the labyrinth to the upper world?

These myths and symbols almost certainly look back into the darkness of prehistory, into the darkness of the caves where artists scratched images of bears and painted red-ochre bison, deer, and horses by the poor light of flickering candles. Why, though, did they make the drawings on the same stretch of wall, time and time again, creating a sort of palimpsest, leaving other areas untouched?

In reference to the mysteries of cave paintings the archaeologist Anne Sieveking spoke of a 'language for which we have no vocabulary'.[10] A closer examination of the hidden languages of myth and symbol and of art might pave the way towards a greater knowledge of prehistory. The art galleries of the cave dwellers may prove to be the best place to begin an understanding of myth and symbol, and to trace our journey forward in time, to our goal on the hills of Wessex.

CHAPTER 4

The Breasts of Venus

Could the caves of the Ice Age and the wonderful drawings of the Palaeolithic hunters yield clues to the mysteries of mythology and the animal gods? The painted caves of France and Spain were a nineteenth-century discovery, and a phenomenon that at first provoked disbelief, much acrimony and mud-slinging in academic circles. The idea that the murals could be really ancient was met with ridicule; the drawings were considered too well executed to be the work of primitive cave-dwellers. Their discovery went directly against the orthodox views of the time in which there was no such thing as prehistory. The stern upholders of faith had declared that the creation of the world was fixed at 4004 BC, although this view was soon to be profoundly shaken by Darwinism. It took more than a quarter of a century from their discovery in 1876 until formal academic acceptance in 1902 before the paintings were recognised as the work of Palaeolithic or Stone Age artists covering a period from 25,000 BC to 10,000 BC, the bulk of the work dating from a flourishing period around 17,000 BC.

The history of these discoveries and the art of the Ice Age is thoroughly discussed by Bahn and Vertut;[1] Ucko and Rosenfeld;[2] and by Coles and Higgs[3] who wrote: 'our understanding of its significance is extremely vague and insecure. It has been studied endlessly since its recognition in 1895 as the earliest mural art in the world, but today its meaning to late glacial man remains beyond our comprehension.'

The caves were not decorated as a pleasing, aesthetic exercise, 'art for art's sake', this much is clear, nor were they painted in order to enhance living conditions, since only undecorated caves served as dwellings, and certainly not the deeper recesses where many of the compositions are to be found. The most enduring theory about why the pictures were executed has been that of 'sympathetic magic', first proposed by Saloman Reinach in 1903, when he postulated that the artist/hunter drew his prey on the wall, then ritually killed it by stabbing at the image, or by including arrows and spears in the drawing. Bahn saw this as a sort of 'voodoo', like sticking pins into a wax doll to ensure a satisfactory kill during the next hunt. But the weapons are by no means clearly defined, and of 2500 to 3000 animals depicted, fewer than ten per cent (one source claims five per cent) were depicted as 'wounded' in any way, with missiles in or near them. Indeed one missile is known to have been engraved before the animal was drawn.[4]

The sympathetic magic hypothesis should not be dismissed too lightly, however, for if the drawings were not solely decorative, then they may have been made in order to induce some form of influential force to act on behalf of the artist or his or her group. A painted image can have the numinous power to arouse emotional responses in the viewer or worshipper: I have seen Hindu devotees near Jaipur pressing food into the mouth of an image of the goddess Kali painted on a temple wall. The concept of mural art as representing a living deity – animal or human – is as powerful today among some societies as it must have been in prehistory. The theory of hunting magic would have more going for it were the subjects game animals, but on the majority of sites animals killed for food hardly figure at all; where, for example, reindeer bones – animals of decided economic importance – were abundant on a site, the reindeer does not appear as a subject of wall paintings. Conversely, animals that feature in art are often absent from the local fauna. 'It is known from actual animal bones that throughout much of the Magdalenian period at least, the reindeer was staple food in western Europe but it is extremely rare in Palaeolithic parietal art.' This discrepancy also applies to the saiga antelope, hunted for food, yet no drawings are known.[5]

If the cave art of the hunter-artists did not feature hunting, their main occupation, what was its purpose? Fertility magic (animal and human), totemism and shamanism, initiation of adolescents – each has been proposed as an explanation. But cave art is only a part of a variety of art forms. The earliest known examples are of human or lion-headed figures carved in mammoth ivory some 40,000 years ago. The so-called 'Venus' figurines with their exaggerated forms, emphasising breasts, abdomen and thighs, often at the expense of heads, limbs and extremities, date from the Ice Age, and have been found in the locality of caves. A typical example is the obese Venus of Willendorf, Austria, carved in limestone and coloured with red ochre.

Why are these tiny figurines, many only a few inches high, so gross in their shape, so impersonal, so essentially female but never really feminine? Bahn suggests that the proportions of the figurines merely represent women whose bodies are worn by age and childbearing,[6] an interpretation that doesn't explain, however, the lack of features that could add charm, personality and the essential element of sexual attractiveness, a vital part of motherhood.

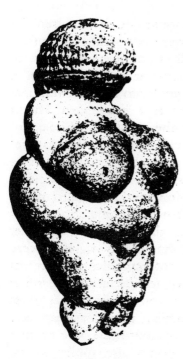

The Willendorf Venus comes from the Gravettian culture. The names are taken mostly from the cave areas of southern France where the tools were discovered and evaluated as belonging to a distinct time and place – the Gravettian from La Gravette, the Magdalenian from La Madeleine on the Dordogne. The cultures are further recognised by those periods in the Upper Palaeolithic in which scientific dating techniques (radiocarbon analysis) show them to have been active – the Gravettian from 22,000–18,000 BC; the Magdalenian from 15,000–8000 BC.

The Gravettian Venuses set a style that was to persist for over 16,000 years. At Tepe Sarab in the Zagros mountains of Mesopotamia, archaeologists found many clay figurines, ample of breast and thigh, minus heads, hands and feet, and dating from c. 6000 BC. Clark and Piggott noted that 'The most outstanding products of Gravettian art were beyond doubt figurines of animals and women'.[7] A peculiarity of the carved or modelled figurines is that they were mostly of women (examples of male figurines are rare), and in many instances only those parts of the body associated with fecundity were emphasised. Several, including the Willendorf figure, and the famous Venus of Laussel holding a bison horn, were painted with red ochre.

FIG. 11 Venus figurine from Willendorf, Austria – four inches high.

Why is the masculine principle absent? Could it be because the role of the fertilising agent was represented by animals? A parallel situation (although of a much later date), is to be found at the site of Çatal Hüyük in Turkey, circa 6000 BC, where the cult of a Mother Goddess, prominent on shrine walls, is associated with bulls, boars, leopards and vultures. Here, the bull would appear to fill the masculine role since there is scant evidence of a male deity or consort in the shrines. The famous figurine of a very over-weight Mother Goddess in labour, seems to show her giving birth to a calf. It was found in a grain store, suggesting 'sympathetic magic' to enhance future crops, and perhaps bread making.[8]

A comparable symbolism was observed on the other side of the world near Mexico City. Archaeologists excavating the prehistoric site at Tlatlico found 'an extraordinary number of figurines, all of them female, naked and adorned with jewellery'. They were also painted, mostly yellow, some white, black or purple. Laurette Séjourné says in her book on Mesoamerican religion, *Burning Water*, that everything about these figurines suggests they repre-sent the tender ears of maize.[9]

Bahn points out that figurines in Europe were never found in any kind of privileged position – a shrine for instance – except where they were buried in pits in the floors of dwellings. A figure dating from 23,000 years ago had been buried upright in soil mixed with red ochre, and facing the hearth.[10] The Venus figurines were never intended as votive deposits to promote the fecundity of mankind, but instead to invoke continual blessings of nature, of fire and water, sun and rain. They do not represent the Mother Goddess in any conventional sense, for they were created as symbols of future productivity, and this is why most of them were depersonalised.

The sculptors of these stone and clay figures had no intention of idealising the female character, only coalescing into a symbolic entity those parts of her body representing nourishment and the fecundity of nature. This had nothing to do with the 'flagrant male takeover' of the Mother Goddess and her womb as the emblem of fertility and containment as some feminists have claimed, but was an essential part of pagan religions everywhere. It was thus more appropriate to convey the quickening powers of the generative solar heat, the rains – powers which are essentially abstract – through the exaggerated human form, with the enlarged breasts, abdomen and thighs suggesting bounteous providence.

The march of the seasons, linked to the fertile cycles of nature, and the behaviour of the cosmos – these were an enduring mystery to those for whom the earth was flat and surrounded by water, whereas the human reproductive process was regularly observed, participated in, more or less understood, and not restricted to seasons.

While there are few male figurines, comparable male symbols abound in the form of phalli. If expressing the idea of female fecundity by abbreviation (dispensing with heads and extremities) was purely functional, so it was to represent male potency through the phallus alone. It would appear to deny anthropic influences, making the phallus an abstract symbol of nature's fertility, perhaps to throw emphasis on the fertilising properties of the natural elements. In Neolithic Europe, carved phalli in limestone, sandstone, rock, wood and bone, and especially in areas of chalk were, as one author puts it, 'almost ubiquitous', and more often than not buried in pits.[11] Was this a form of 'sympathetic magic', the burying of chalk phalli a way of encouraging the fertility of the earth?

This system of the physical minimalising of figurines, male and female, may have had little to do with the increase of the population but everything to do with the rhythm of the seasons, the arrival of the rains, the return of the sun, the birth of animals and plants. A fair proportion of female figurines have an undeniable 'phallic' appearance which has much to do with the androgynous character of ancient cult deities and, it seems to me, relates to the belief that the sun itself was androgynous.

FIG. 12 Phallic female figurine.

The symbolism of the figurines of prehistory was expressed by societies far more concerned with the propitiation of natural forces, rather than the worship of the human male and female body, elevated to divine status. Huge stone phalli, the so-called 'boundary stones', or kudurru of Mesopotamia, were decorated with snakes and scorpions, symbols of rain, and dedicated to deities such as the Babylonian Marduk, god of fertilising rains and of the sun. Because animals were in close harmony with these natural rhythms they were perhaps thought to influence them, as the cave bear influenced the sun and vice-versa, as the stars were thought to influence weather patterns. When much later the

Zodiac was devised, astronomers drew upon animals to represent eight of the twelve signs, several of which had served as symbols for centuries.

When in Mesopotamia the much-needed rains arrived in the late autumn, a symbol was created both to evoke and to celebrate this season. The rising constellation in October looked like a scorpion, and so Scorpius eventually took its place in the Zodiac. October and November were the season of ploughing, and Scorpius became a female sign, representing the earth that received the seed, and was thought to grasp the phallus of the centaur-archer Saggitarius, who also represented the time of seed-sowing, hence its appearance on the phallic stones mentioned above.

The cycle of vegetation began with the first winter rains and lasted until the harvest in May. From late June through to September, everything was burnt up. This period of fecundity was represented by bizarre and composite animal-figures, by scorpion-bodied archers with the legs of an eagle, by horned lions with scorpion tails, a griffin with the forelegs of a lion, the rear legs of an eagle, and wings. The symbolism was entirely seasonal, and recognised by all societies. The seed-sowing propensities of goats and rams in the tupping time of autumn led the Greeks to

FIG. 13 Composite animal figure from Assyria.

develop the satyrs and centaurs who follow the god of wine and frenzy, Dionysus.

Because autumn is the peak period for the sexual attentiveness of ungulates, coinciding with the time when the newly fermenting wine is drunk from goatskin flasks, the satyrs and centaurs were known for their fondness for the grape, and their Bacchanalian revels. Saggitarius, the centaur-archer, with the body and legs of a horse, or a goat, the torso of a man with a bow looses the arrows (sagitta) of the sun, and like the solar Apollo could 'shoot from afar'.

Returning to the caves of the Palaeolithic, we can now start exploring with the notion that the animals in the caves might have something to do with seasonal cycles, and with the reproduction of nature. The caves have been so thoroughly documented over the past century of study that it is necessary to mention only some of the more prominent animals.

Horses and bison predominate, and occupy the centre of all surfaces used and may be repeated many times in the same cave.[12] The equine/bovid group is always present and dominates the groupings both numerically and topographically. There are also ibex, deer, aurochs (wild cattle), mammoths, bears and lions, fish and birds – mainly water-birds.

The various locations of certain species has led to a theory, proposed by the French anthropologists Annette Laming-Emperaire, and André Leroi-Gourhan, that the caves were divided into areas or symbolic constructions where certain species predominate. Horses and bison in the main, central areas, felines in the further recesses, bears and rhinos at the entrances. The theory was further developed into a dual system where certain animals represent the male, others the female – bison were female, horses male; ibex male, mammoth female.[13] A few caves contained abstract signs which seem impossible to interpret, although some investigators have seen them as sexual, while in two of the caves were found figures of bison modelled in clay, and the model of a headless bear with a real bear's skull at its feet.

One of the problems with the French interpretations is that they present a decidedly complex 'structural' approach to cave art, drawings and engravings 'full of conceptual ideas – they were the means by which the artists expressed some more metaphysical concept.'[14] In seeking a solution to the mysteries of cave painting over the past century, explanations and theories have tended to become more and more abstract and conceptual, as each of the simpler and more straightforward theories were in turn weighed and subsequently discarded.

To be fair, Leroi-Gourhan's theories, as he was at pains to explain, were at best tentative. 'We may imagine that the caves were shrines in which highly elaborate rituals took place, but all we have is wall decorations'.[15] Were these artists attempting to convey abstract, philosophical and religious ideas? If so, to whom were they meant to appeal? Many of the drawings are so remote, and hidden in places where access was difficult and at times dangerous, that only the artists themselves may have known where to find them.

The suggestion has been made that an introduction to these labyrinthine passages, so forbidding and difficult of access, in a total silence broken only perhaps by the drip and trickle of water, in a velvet blackness of a deep and claustrophobic intensity, even to the least susceptible was a form of initiation. The initiate would crawl into one of the vast caverns, lit by the dancing flame of a lamp, to be greeted by shadowy forms of huge animals seemingly moving on the cave walls and ceilings. How could this fail to impress the cowering neophyte?

While nomadic hunting societies are perceived as being 'nearer to nature' than the later, progressive, sedentary farming societies, we are inclined to be swayed by the idea that they were also more closely connected to the imagined spiritual forces of the earth, that perhaps they sought communion with animals in the sanctuaries of the caves. While it is quite possible, indeed likely, that the caves were seen as 'wombs of the earth', and as places of increase, I am none the less inclined to think that cave art was above all practical and corporeal in its aims and execution.

The hunting societies may certainly have been superstitious and riddled with all kinds of taboos, but they were also likely to have been down-to-earth pragmatists, like the Neanderthalers, seeking to enrich their material rather than spiritual lives. Sympathetic hunting magic is certainly a pragmatic approach to the enduring problems of spearing game animals, and would have been a welcome and acceptable theory had the facts squared with the evidence.

It would seem that the artists were making their drawings on behalf of the tribe, and were charged with the task of crawling through subterranean tunnels to perform a ritual whereby certain

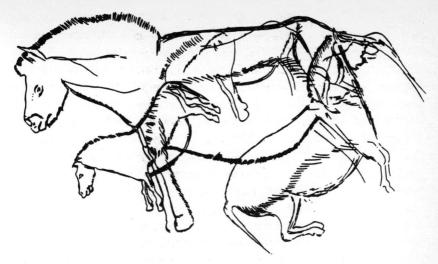

FIG. 14 Engraved horses from the Ice Age in the Cave of Les Trois Frères, copied by the Abbé Henri Brevil.

animals were repetitiously drawn at a significant time during each year, and this may point to why the drawings were made repeatedly on the same rockface. In other words, it was the act of representation itself, more than the final visual result, which was important to the Palaeolithic artists.[16] Support for this view is lent by the fact that it is not uncommon to find animal paintings unfinished, or indicated only by part of an animal instead of the whole. No attempt was made to portray animals to scale, in relation to each other, or even the right way up, and no indication of a setting or landscape. In the cave at Teyjat in the Dordogne, Magdalenian artists engraved a cervid (probably a reindeer) upside down over the image of a horse the right way up, over the tilted rendering of a cave bear, a rendering unlikely to impress an initiate.

This superimposing of images has created a tortuous mass of interwoven lines, the result of thousands of engraved or painted animals, without apparent regard to the condition of the surfaces. 'It is a real characteristic of the art that the artists chose to execute their works irrespective of the rock curvature, cracks and fissures, nodules, stalagmatic formations etc.'[17] Superimposing also appears in portable art, engraved on slivers of stone, and is thus not confined to cave art, but complements it.

In attempting to explain the purpose of cave art, the basis for a reasonable hypothesis raises three important questions that need to be answered. First, why are drawings superimposed in such a way that the images are lost in the confused mass of lines? Second, why did the artists seem to delight in rendering their drawings in almost inacessible places in the caves? Some paintings were carried out so high on the cave walls or the roof that they must have needed some form of scaffolding, or perhaps a brush on a long pole. Others were placed in extreme corners where the roof is only a few metres from the floor, so that the artist was obliged to crouch low on the ground.

Finally, why is the horse the most frequently drawn animal? The regularity with which the horse is depicted is equalled only by the bison, followed by aurochs and ibex. The largest piece of three-dimensional Palaeolithic sculpture ever found was that of a horse. Some rare engravings on open-air rock surfaces in southern Europe also depict wild, shaggy-maned horses.

To deal with the first question, it would seem that the act of making a mark on a certain piece of stone, or wall, was thought to be influential, a creative act with consequences. It is an ancient idea, and is found in the Greek word *deltos*, 'a writing tablet' or any flexible surface prepared for an inscription, a virgin surface waiting for a mark to be made; a womb ready to be fertilised. It is cognate with *delphus*, 'womb', derived from the Sanskrit *jartuh*, 'vulva', a word related to *delta*, the fourth letter in the Greek alphabet.

The Cretan craftsman Daedalus, father of Icarus, gets his name ultimately from *delta*. Daedalus made the labyrinth (a form of cave) and also a wooden cow for the sun goddess Pasiphae, a labyrinthine dancing ground, and the thread for the fair sun-goddess Ariadne to guide Theseus out of the maze. Daedalus was an artist, a supernatural inventor and carpenter who made statues and brought them to life. It is possible that in Palaeolithic times the rendering of an image on a suitable surface was a sacred act, a 'hieroglyph' or sacred sign, and one of sympathetic magic, capable of inducing a favourable response, especially when buried in the earth, or hidden in a cave.

Many such engravings, mainly of animals, were scratched with flint on animal bones and dusted with the obligatory red ochre. There may be a thread linking the art of the Palaeolithic with these mythological creators of life from the classical world. The

Greek god Hephaestus the goldsmith, he who split open Zeus's head to liberate Athena, was a divine crafstman whose forge was in an underwater grotto, a Promethean figure skilled in magical creations. Athena herself was a creator, who made horses from clay and breathed life into them. The smith gods worked deep in the womb of the earth because they were busy fashioning nature from the two prime elements of fire and water.

Human gestation, and the gestation of the earth's crops under the influence of the spring sun were, and are, closely identified, as we have seen with the fertility figurines. Remember that many of these were moulded in clay, and hardened by the sun, and so the Stone Age sculptors who modelled their Pandoras and buried them in the earth, were encouraging the emergence of life. In a Pyrenean cave at Bedeilhac, a Magdalenian artist modelled a relief bison, and close by an undeniable vulva drawn, perhaps with a finger, in wet clay. It is one of the very few such images in the whole of cave art, and was either a rare example of crude grafitti sketched in a moment of boyish enthusiasm, or a potent 'fertility symbol'.

Was fertility the aim of the Palaeolithic sculptors who moulded a group of bison from the clay floor of the Tuc d'Audoubert cavern in the Pyrenees? Speculations about the purpose of these clay animals have included the predictable sexual interpretations, claiming that the bison are mating, although more sober investigators, such as Peter Ucko, have pointed out that the figures are separated from each other by nearly a metre. The bison are by no means isolated examples of three-dimensional and relief figures, while many have probably been destroyed.

The cave of Montespan in Haute Garonne contained a clay model of a bear, minus the head, fashioned by Magdelenian artists some 15,000 years ago, over which a bear hide was draped to which the real head was once attached. A bear cub skull found between the front paws may be the remaining evidence.[18] The 'wounded' bear in one of the most famous of caves, the Trois Frères in Ariège, is covered with circles, and appears to be vomiting. Interpreters have claimed that it represents a bear pelted with stones, and vomiting blood, and is thus a victim of 'hunting magic'. A careful count of the circles shows that there are 189 of them, and not all are confined to the body. There are also several apparent 'spears', some of which miss their mark. What else could the circles represent? The number 189 could be significant, if we credit the Palaeolithic artists with numeracy and primitive astronomy. It adds up to the number of days, or 'suns' from the summer solstice to the winter solstice – give or take a day or two – although this may be a coincidence and a fanciful interpretation. The vomiting 'blood', and the 'spears' too, are just as likely to be water, the rainfall that arrived at the time of the winter solstice; the imagery has later parallels in Mesopotamian engravings, where winged lions vomit rain. There is another, smaller bear in the same location, also expelling 'rain', and decorated with three circles. Three, like seven, is a number of ancient significance.

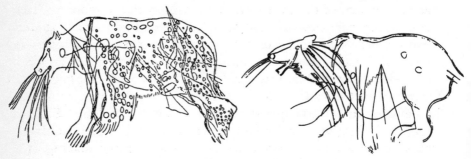

FIG. 15 Bears in Les Trois Frères caves, vomiting water.

Once the bear cult had became established by the earlier Neanderthalers its original symbolism would have persisted unchanged over thousands of years. Thus in spite of the misgivings of some writers stressing that customs and beliefs undergo many changes in the course of time, the solar symbolism of the bear remains in Greek myth. Hecuba, mother of the Phrygian prince Paris who judged the famous beauty contest, dreamed just before his birth that she brought forth a firebrand that also spewed writhing snakes, and burned Troy to the ground. The great epic of the Trojan War is almost certainly a solar myth. At the advice of an oracle, Paris was exposed on a hillside, like Telephus and Oedipus, and left to die. He was found nursed and suckled by a she-bear.

Paris was a solar hero, an identity that will later become clear, and his exposure represents the wintry birth of the sun, the 'infant' suckled by the solar animal that emerges from hibernation at the appropriate time. I suggest that this is the idea behind the myths of all heroes suckled by animals, as Romulus and Remus were suckled by a wolf, Zeus in his cave (the sun always winters, and is born in a cave) by the goat Amalthea (whose kids would be born in the early spring), and the doves that continued to nourish him with honey. Telephus, ursine, who survived a wound through the agency of Achilles, with rust from his spear, was an aspect of the sun, healed by virtue of solar power.

Access to the bear of Montespan – as it is to the bison of the Tuc d'Audoubert, located a mile and a half into the cave complex – is gained by crawling along extremely narrow passages, in some places barely wide enough to squeeze through, although we cannot be sure that this was the original route pioneered by the artists. Several of the limestone caves have water in them, and the conditions were probably the same in Palaeolithic times. 'Montespan's art can be reached only by wading upstream, with water up to one's waist and, at one point, having to duck right under when the ceiling comes down to water level; yet on very rare occasions, as in 1986, the cave is dry.'[19]

Wet or dry, many of the parietal sites are forbidding. Perhaps long ago they were forbidden, sanctuaries to be visited only by those explorer-artists versed in the ritual of image-making. Yet according to archaeologists, children were permitted deep into the caves, for their footprints have been found in the mud floors. Neophytes? Initiates? Probably not – the value of having children in the caves may well have been due to their ability to negotiate narrow passages in advance of the adults and return to base for fresh supplies and materials, when the lamps and pigments needed replenishing.

The key question is perhaps the one concerning the species of animals depicted on the walls, ceilings, nooks and crannies of the caves. If we can discover why the horse was so favoured, followed closely by the bison, we might learn in what particular way horses were viewed – that is, what they represented symbolically to the people of the Palaeolithic. If, as I suggest, the symbolism surrounding the cave bear was solar, did the horse have a similar meaning? And did this also apply to the bison?

The nearest living relative or equivalent to the ancient herds of European horses is said to be Przewalski's wild horse of East Europe and Asia, although strictly speaking this horse is native to the Gobi, and so conditioned to a desert climate and not to life in the Ice Age. Either way, the Stone Age horse is unlikely to have provided much to the economy. There is tenuous evidence that horses were bridled, but as far as we can tell, they were not domesticated and ridden until about 2000 BC.[20] Horse flesh doesn't appear to have been a staple in the hunter's diet – a privilege reserved mainly for reindeer.

Horses were admired for other qualities, and the only means we have of telling what these qualities might have been is to seek later analogies through lore and language. The Indo-Europeans, who domesticated the horse, used the word *acvas* to describe swiftness, and *acva* for 'horse', deciding that the two had much in common. Herd animals were fast and vigorous, like a running stream, bison powerful and aggressive. Before the domestication of the horse, the prehistoric hunting tribes were obliged to chase their quarry on foot, and so swiftness and long-distance running were no doubt greatly admired qualities.

Caucasian wild horses are reputedly very fast movers – and so for that matter are bison, the second most regularly painted animal in cave art. Both species travel in herds, bison thundering along at speeds of up to 25 miles per hour; horses are even quicker. The other most frequently depicted animals, wild cattle (aurochs) and ibex, also run in herds, and deer have been clocked at speeds of more than 30 miles per hour.

Perhaps the hunters first noticed the next attribution – the similarity of horse to water. The Greeks myths featured horses that could strike water with their hooves. The famous horse Pegasus, born of the Gorgon Medusa, created the spring at Hippocrene with his hoof. Poseidon, god of the sea and of fresh water springs, was also 'Lord of the Horse'.

Words were found to link the two ideas. Compare the Latin *equus*, 'horse' with *aqua*, 'water', both derived from the Sanskrit *akra*, 'water', and *asva*, 'horse', from the root AK, 'to go', 'to hasten'. The word *asva* is further related to *ava*, meaning 'flow down', giving the word *avarsti*, 'rainfall', and the idea of horse and water is found in the description of the swift-flowing Indus, a river that is 'rich in horses'.[21]

One of the most indefatigable and inspired researchers into Palaeolithic art, Alexander Marshak, drew attention to the signs and symbols used for water or, as Marshak puts it, 'iconographic acts of participation in which water symbolism or a water mythology played a part'. Marshak avoids calling a spade a spade, identifying water as represented unequivocally by the zigzag or meander. He suggests only that the meander is broadly generic, representing rain, a river or a stream, and possibly 'the continuous flow of other processes, seasonal, biological, ceremonial and ritual'.[22]

Marshak does draw attention, though, to the fact that meanders are strongly represented with images of the horse. It seems to have been a persistent connection, for 12,000 years ago someone in what is now Wales scratched a zigzag pattern on a horse mandible (in the British Museum) and left it in a cave (Kendrick's Cave, Llandudno).

The areas in which the painted caves are located, in Franco-Cantabria, the Massif Central, Pyrenees and Cantabrian mountains, are mostly limestone and well supplied with springs. It has been noted that the principal sites are often located near springs, or clustered around rivers, anywhere that supports a supply of running water. Erosion by water, the impressive 'cathedrals' of caverns with stalagmites and stalactites, hidden galleries and deeply carved recesses containing water, caves with rivers running through them – all contributed to a powerful water mythology.

The caves in Franco-Cantabria, like those in the west of England, were probably formed during the Pleistocene in late glacial times, when icy and slightly acid meltwater ate through limestone like mice through cheese. The French caves, however, were subject to long intervals of dryness unlike the caves in more temperate places, and this may explain the absence of comparable cave art in Britain.

At Maz d'Azil in the Pyrenees, people collected little pebbles from the river, and decorated them with designs, mainly in red ochre. These have been interpreted by archaeologist Aubrey Burl as 'ancestor stones ... involving the manipulation of these pebbles, the evoking of great spirits, muttered incantations to awaken the sleeping dead who might give protection to these small, isolated communities'.[23]

The various geometric designs appear to be random, with no deliberate symbolism as far as one can tell (although one pebble bore an engraving of a horse) unless they were collected simply because they expressed the value of water. In fact, if the ochre can be accepted as symbolising life and the sun, the river pebbles symbolising water, the combined effect with each stone may have created a powerful talisman, a suggestion supported by the number of pebbles so far recovered – almost 2000 of them.

The horse could have symbolised the power of running water, and, if so, we have to decide why it should be celebrated on cave walls; water seems not to have been in short supply, and the rivers where many sites are located do not dry up in the heat of summer. Water may have contributed towards the imagery in cave paintings, but there was another strongly influential contribution, a source well known in antiquity, and this was the sun. The combination of sun and horse was a motif on coins struck during the Iron Age, a combination with a long history. A French proverb asks, 'What is swifter than a horse, crosses water, yet never gets its feet wet?' The answer is 'the sun'.

Coins of classical Greece featured the sun-chariot of Helios and Apollo, the quadriga drawn by four horses. It was a popular theme in Vedic India, with the sun god Surya's chariot drawn by seven mares, sometimes by a mare with seven heads. Seven, like three, is a mysterious number that was of considerable importance in antiquity.

The word mare derives ultimately from the Sanskrit root MR which, along with a host of related words, gives the meaning of 'shining'. Indra, the god of sun and rain, battle and storms, rides the 'shining white' steed named Uccaihcrava; the twin horsemen, the Acvins, were the sons of the mare Saranyu by Vivasvat, the sun. 'The sun is at the same time a hero and a horse. He is *acra*, "the swift one".'[24] The Rig Veda refers to the horse as 'the winged one darting from heaven'. In examples from folklore, magic steeds are stabled in caves. Three horses are kept in a cave in a glass mountain. These wonder steeds help a hero to win and rescue a captive maiden of gold. The maiden alludes to the sun in winter, captive in a cave, 'rescued' by the solar hero.

The Japanese sun goddess Amaterasu retired to her cave after the autumn festival of first fruits, plunging the world into winter darkness. The legend of a wonderful Arabian horse hidden in an almost inaccessible cavern may reach back to the caves of the Palaeolithic; on finding and mounting it, the hero is able to rescue the sun-maiden from the grip of winter, bounding across the spring sky towards summer.[25]

Is this what the cave artists were attempting to do, contributing towards the revitalising of the sun with the aid of vigorous, swift animals, repeatedly engraved each winter in almost inaccessible limestone chambers? The idea of the sun, either captive or deliberately wintering in a cave, will lead us to the legend of the Deluge, the primal Creation myth that was perhaps first narrated in the light of flickering animal-fat lamps in the caves of the Ice Age.

CHAPTER 5

Caves of the Sorcerer

The creation legends show that refugees from the flood waters of the Deluge escaped by boat or canoe, climbed trees, sought safety on a mountain top, or hid in caves. The cave refuge is especially marked on the American continent where it features in many Indian myths, but it also turns up in Persia and Japan. The existence of myths with shared features in widely dispersed locations are an inheritance of ancient tribal movements, but with many local variations to suit the environment. It is natural that in Eskimo myths the survivors escape by kayak or canoe, or climb mountains, although this could be seen as a distant echo of the Bible legend of the ark coming to rest on Mount Ararat. Like Noah, the Algonquin hero of the flood sends out three messengers, a detail that is unlikely to have been created independently, and thus has Old World origins.

Flood myths could reasonably be interpreted as being about survival, followed by birth or rebirth in the form of reappearing survivors. One persistent feature describes how survivors find refuge in caves, so suggesting that such myths are of great antiquity and arose among cave-dwellers of the Palaeolithic. The cave theme is found especially among the American Indians, and in Mesoamerican cultures, where the Aztec Creation myth tells how the first members of the race emerged from Chicomoztoc, the Cavern of the Seven Chambers, following a flood caused by the 'water sun'.[1]

Presumably, tribes with cave or mountain refuges in their legends were no great distance from mountain ranges, or had originally come from a mountain area. Are these Deluge legends of caves and mountain refuges evidence of a sort of residual folk memory, like accumulated silt and detritus, left behind by that river of life that spread from a common homeland? I do not mean that they recall an actual primeval event, of course, but that the cave or the mountain was a perhaps symbolic feature of the original myth.

The myth itself is found worldwide. 'Quantitavely speaking,' says the American folklorist Alan Dundes in a recent collection of essays, 'the flood myth must surely be the most studied narrative ever. No other myth or folktale or legend has been subjected to anything like the intensive scrutiny that has been lavished on the story of a cataclysmic deluge.'[2] The fact that the myth deals with the creation of mankind, and contains details shared and recognised in the mythology of societies as far apart as Iraq and Mexico, clearly has a fundamental meaning unless, of course, the myth actually does record an historical event.

One of the reasons for the intensive study of the Deluge was that nineteenth-century developments in science, geology and the study of comparative religion challenged orthodox belief in the Bible (as did the discovery of cave art) since the story of Noah is one of the foundations of the Old Testament. Archaeologists claimed (and are still claiming) to have found physical evidence of cataclysmic floods in the Middle East, or the remains of an ark, or boat-shaped object, on Mount Ararat in Turkey, currently being excavated. Whatever they discover is unlikely to be the ark of the Flood, for the ark is pure legend. In the late 1920s the archaeologist Leonard Woolley found definite evidence of a great flood in the levels at Ur, although his findings – a stratum of silt carried by the Euphrates and indicating an inundation of floodwaters some twenty-five feet deep – was later disputed by one of Woolley's own team.[3]

Cataclysmic though the flood may have been, such inundations are by no means unusual. In Bangladesh where the Ganges, Meghna and Brahmaputra rivers form a great delta, flowing into the Bay of Bengal, disastrous flooding is frequent. In America, devastation occurred in 1993 when the Mississippi flooded vast areas of the Midwest, while in China millions were made homeless by the flooding of the Yangtze in 1995, but local incidents do not worldwide myths make, no matter how severe they may have been.

Geographically, Ararat was an unlikely landfall for the ark, one authority – the *Encyclopaedia Biblica* – claiming that the location was 'in the highest degree improbable', preferring the mountain of Nisir in the Babylonian version, and Elburz in the Hebrew.[4] The story of the Deluge in the familiar version of Genesis was borrowed wholesale from the Mesopotamians. The Babylonian ark was built in seven days, and loaded with 'the living seed of every kind' in groups of seven (though Noah guides them in 'two by two'). Readers will perhaps be more familiar with Noah than with his Sumerian version Ziasudra, or the Babylonian Utnapish-tim, but the Deluge myth is much the same and varies only in detail. Named *The Preserver of Life*, the ark set sail over the waters in the year of the Great Serpent.

Originally, the myth would have seen the refugees on a mountain top, or in a cave, and indeed the ark does come to rest on a mountain. The details of the ark's construction and voyage are important to the story, however, for they express a deliberate symbolism. It was a curious box, measuring 190 feet each way, mounted on a basin-like coracle sealed with bitumen. The interior had seven storeys and nine divisions, and a hole in the top to admit light. The ark sailed for seven days across an ocean on which there were seven islands. After a further seven days, the vessel came to rest on dry land on the seventeenth day of the seventh month. Note the weighty use of number symbolism, for it has a profound meaning. Before reaching land, Noah had sent out three birds, a dove, a swallow and a raven. Presumably the dove represented spring, the swallow summer, and the raven winter, while the three collectively represented the annual passage of the sun.

Many people have seen in the ark a symbol of the womb, particularly in view of the popular and modern idealistic concept of rebirth, for the ark does indeed suggest this; the progress and development of orthodox religion sought to add to the story of the Deluge a moral message about the wickedness of man, his destruction by the flood, followed by man's physical and spiritual rebirth.

Some interpreters, notably Dundes, following the analogy of human birth, have declared the floodwaters to represent the discharge of amniotic fluid.[5] This is not a bad idea, since childbirth is a human experience that might explain the universality of the myth. In several Vedic tales from India, the flood comes from a spilled water pot (*kumbha*), which in some versions is golden and contains the seed of the Creator; in Sanskrit the word *kumbha* stands for both 'pot' and 'womb'. This golden pot could be interpreted as combining the generative contributions of the sexes. It represents the feminine, incubating influence of the sun, while the seed of the Creator is rain, which overflows the pot and fertilises the earth. Once again, the symbolism might be seen in reference to natural rather than to human events.

The concept lies behind the birth of Erichthonius, who was born of the semen of the smith Hephaestus, god of fire, prematurely ejaculated on to the thigh of Athena. The virgin goddess, with a delicate shudder, wiped away the offending seed with a hank of ram's wool, and dropped it to the ground, where it promptly fertilised the earth mother Gaia.

In due course, Gaia gave birth to the half-human, half-serpent offspring who, by my reckoning, represents the infant sun. The sun-child is born of three parents, whereupon Athena placed him in a chest and gave him to the care of the three daughters of the Athenian king Erechtheus. Forbidden to open the chest, the girls however did so, and in fright at the contents, leaped off the Acropolis and were killed. Their demise represents the fall of the sun towards winter, and Erichthonius the birth of the new sun from the earth. Here, the chest doubles for a cave. That it does so is partly supported by the similar actions of Aphrodite, who put the solar wunderkind Adonis in a chest (actually in a *larnax*, or coffin) and sent him to the nether regions.

Because Deluge myths are so widely diffused, some authorities suggest that they were independently created, though I think it more likely that they migrated with the spread of peoples from an original source. An impressive number of North American Indian and Mesoamerican cultures recognise a creation myth where people take refuge in caves. The archetypal foundation of New World myths contains the residue of extremely ancient ideas formed in the Old World.

The myths of creation are a product of the earliest 'origins' thoughts of mankind, and probably date back a million, not thousands, of years. Because myths and symbols take such an enormous time to devlop, we must assume that primitive man was in fact far from primitive in thought. Some symbols could only have come about with the development of cultural advances – the swastika, for example, most decidedly migrated from central Europe to central America: such a unique and curious motif could never have been created independently by two widely separate cultures.

In many of these stories the flood is preceded by a conflagration, while in some tribal myths it is followed by a conflagration. This might suggest a dramatised account of the passage of the seasons, where the fierce summer heat is followed by torrential rainstorms, followed in due course by summer heat. The myth of the great Flood thus describes an annual event observed by many societies in temperate as well as tropical zones. Yet the Deluge is found in Eskimo tribes well above the Arctic Circle, where the flood was caused by the sea, and is well-established in Canada among, for instance, the Cree and Tlingit Indians; among the Algonquins a lake overflows.

Add to this the number symbolism that recurs in the various Creation stories: the Cavern of the Seven Chambers, refuge from the Deluge caused by the 'water sun' of winter that accompanied (or was thought to cause) the rains, the winter that had metaphorically destroyed life on earth; the three messengers sent out to find land; the three brothers in the Coem Indian myth who sought a cave refuge; the ark with its seven storeys and nine divisions, and with a 'window in the roof to let the light in'.

Actually the window is not to let the light in – but to let it out. The hole in the roof is a not uncommon theme in folklore where the hero, or heroine, or magic horse, all solar, escape from a cave by making a hole in ceiling, as the sun escapes from the confines of the earth following its winter 'imprisonment'.

The ark of life is the barque of the sun, Noah is a solar hero, and the voyage is the reappearance of the sun following its journey after the winter rains; the ship of the sun is a motif found in the myths and rituals of many societies, and cult vessels were carved on the rocks in Scandinavia by Bronze Age artists, who clearly were sun-worshippers.[6] The sun travels by ship during the time of the rains, and the north European fire-festivals of winter, when ships are burned, or buried in the earth, encourages the coming of the rains, and prepares for the rebirth of the sun and the fertile spring. Such vessels were buried alongside the pyramids of Giza, for the sun-god Ra travelled by boat.

All water-borne vessels – whether boats, the reed basket of Moses, the coffin of Osiris, the chest that transported Perseus to Seriphos, or the Argo that carried Jason and his crew to Colchis – all these could be viewed as symbolic carriers of the winter sun, transporting the solar hero. 'Solar hero' means he who has the power to affect and control nature, he who is responsible for the favourable outcome of events, because he is acting on behalf of mankind. Perseus and Heracles and Mithras are solar heroes. Nata, the Aztec Noah, was commanded by the god Tezcatlipoca,

'Smoking Mirror', the sun in winter, to build a ship to save himself from the Deluge. The winter refuge of the sun is an ancient and solar concept that I am certain lies behind the Neanderthaler's cave-bear cults; it is perhaps no coincidence that Tezcatlipoca has the head of a bear, and brilliant yellow eyes.[7] Those first races of men that emerged from the caves – as the Aztecs emerged from the Seven Chambers – worshipped the sun, as did the Mixtec Indians, who took refuge from the Flood in the Nine Caverns.

The idea of the winter sun living in a cave will perhaps explain the New Year's rite of Hunting the Wren that thrived in predominantly Celtic areas until the late nineteenth century. It was popular among children in Ireland, the Isle of Man, and Wales, and in Brittany and other areas of France, and is observed on 26th December, or on St Stephen's Day.

Celebrants were supposed to catch a wren – not easy since wrens are extremely active, skulking and subarboreal – put it in a decorated 'Wren House' (there's one in the Welsh Folk Museum, at St Fagans near Cardiff) to be paraded around the village. The Tyr Dryw, 'wren house', not much bigger than a shoe box, was made roughly in wood and decorated with red and white ribbons. The European rust-coloured wren is of the species *Troglodytidae*, 'cave dwellers', so called from the wren's spherical nest with an entrance hole. This, and the wren's appearance during the winter months (like the robin), may have given the bird solar associations.

The children, bearing the Wren House, sang 'The Cutty Wren', a song about killing the victim and preparing it for the pot, and needing a huge vessel, and cooking utensils that get bigger and bigger as the song progresses – as the sun grows from birth to maturity? Is this why the rite is conducted by children? There can be little doubt that it is a fertility celebration, for the bird that enters its 'cave' dwelling might be a symbol of the sun that penetrates the earth in winter to bring about the birth of spring.

There is perhaps a simple explanation for the Deluge myth. The fire that comes to earth and precedes the flood is the declining sun of late summer, heralding the autumn and winter – the 'water sun' as the Aztecs called it. Fire is followed by thunderstorms and heavy rains, a feature of hot climates, and these are followed in turn by the disappearance of nature as winter arrives. The survivors of the flood may collectively be a symbol of the sun that takes refuge in caves, or on a mountain top. The return of the sun, and the re-emergence of life was the foundation of many Creation myths worldwide. Fear that the declining sun might be extinguished by torrential rains, along with the destruction of mankind, or that it might cease to move at all, was of great concern.

To the Indian tribes of Mesoamerica, in particular the Aztecs, the danger menacing the sun was inertia.[8] There was good reason to fear the sun's immobility, for were the sun to halt the march of the seasons, the rains would fail to arrive and the maize crops would wither and die. Inertia threatened Osiris, who was called 'the Great Listless One'. He was urged to 'lie on his side', to enable the waters of the Nile to gush from his thigh.[9] In Aztec thought, the sun must regularly be propitiated and fed with human blood, the symbol of fire. In other cultures the Deluge was thought to be the result of man's failure to assist the dying sun. Later religious developments perceived it as a punishment for mankind's indifference and failure to worship and defer to God.

The sun's decline, however, did lead to the apparent death of nature, a seasonal change that would have been the more dramatic, and of some concern, in the colder climate of the northern hemisphere, and particularly so during the Ice Age. That the sun wintered underground is the idea behind the descent of Ishtar; the sharing of the sun-god Adonis between Persephone, in the underworld for a six-month lease, and Aphrodite, in the upper world for the same period. It refers to the concern of the goddesses of spring waters to hasten the sun's winter decline, and to encourage the arrival of the rains which would surely follow.

In Greek myth, new life was forged underground by the smith-god Hephaestus. The sacred trees of many cultures were nourished by underground rivers, and sacred trees stand beside sacred springs. In the Highlands of Scotland, at the 'Clootie (cloth) Well' (see plate 1) near Munlochy on the Black Isle, the trees around the holy spring are today and every day hung with thousands of rags, for each donation of cloth represents new life, continuing good health and relief from illness.

In the Deluge myths, where the sun took refuge, the caves were the source of new life because they combined the elements of sun and water. But they also represented the womb of the earth in which the sun resided, like the 'Cutty Wren', the rufous bird of winter in its cave-like nest. This is why new life emerged from the caves in the Creation myths, for the Aztec Cavern of the Seven Chambers is the womb of the earth.

The imaginary caves of the Deluge shared the same underlying symbolism and purpose as the actual caves occupied by Palaeolithic artists, which was to reawaken nature. Cave art must have been carried out during intervals of dryness, perhaps one long arid period spanning several centuries. The Middle Magdalenian of 15,000 BC may have witnessed cold conditions with little rainfall, conditions which fostered the art, because some drawings are actually underneath a glassy transparent skin of hard calcite, formed gradually by the later effects of moisture spreading down the cave wall.[10]

When we consider the fact that reindeer were a prominent feature of the fauna during the Ice Age, we can assume long winters and short summers that brought only temporary relief from the hard grip of winter; the warmth of the returning sun and the melting of ice to release water being a longed-for event. Climate may therefore have had a direct influence, for the wonderful surge of creativity that led to the development of animal drawings seems to have died out with the end of the Pleistocene (roughly 8000 BC) and the melting of the glaciers, with correspondingly warmer conditions, and the fairly rapid decline of herds of reindeer, a prime source of food for the hunter–artists. This period succeeding the Ice Age permitted the 'Neolithic Revolution', the beginning of agriculture.

So the drawings almost certainly had a practical purpose, since prehistoric societies must have been a practical and realistic people in order to survive the harsh climate, and the (presumably) primitive conditions in which they lived. The purpose of their art was to induce the sun to warm the ice-bound earth and renew life. The animals drawn on the cave walls and ceilings were not generally the hunter's quarry but mainly horses and bison, animals that move swiftly in herds, rapid, vigorous and virile, like a tumbling torrent. Their companions were sometimes bears, often stags and deer, occasionally fish (identified mostly as salmon) and such water birds as geese and ducks, more usually found in portable form engraved on bone, ivory and stone.

This last group all have something in common: they have distinct seasonal habits. The bears, as we have seen, are dormant through the winter. Stags harden their antlers in winter, and shed them in spring. It has been noted that the drawings of red deer and reindeer often include features which indicate the rutting season in late autumn,[11] while bison and wild horses mate in late summer.

Salmon migrate upriver to spawn in late autumn, returning to the sea in spring. Engravings of male salmon have notably included evidence of the kype or hook on the lower jaw,[12] which only develops at the spawning period. An engraved baton from the Pyrenees has antlered stags with leaping salmon, a design in which 'the total composition is clearly seasonal'.[13] Geese and many types of waterbird migrate south in winter and return in spring.

In Greece, the migratory movements of cranes (*Grus grus*) to the south in autumn, returning in the spring, led to the bird's direct indentification with the sun. There are examples of vases decorated with cranes and horses stamped with swastikas. A relief from Roman Gaul shows a bull bearing three cranes perched on its back.

The fourth most regularly drawn animal, the ibex, later became sacred to the Babylonian Ea, god of fresh waters and rivers, much as the horse was sacred to Poseidon, also god of rivers and the sea. The ibex or antelope, combined with a fish, was Ea's special sign, and eventually took its place in the zodiac as Capricorn. Both Ea and Poseidon were part of a triad, and solar, but water was the element that they so powerfully represented.

Ea appears on cylinder seals with streams of water in which fish swim, flowing from his shoulders, or from a vase which he holds.[14] This is why their sacred animals were the antelope and the horse and the bull, because they moved swiftly in herds, seeming to imitate the fast-running waters of springs and rivers in spate. Yet ultimately these animals – the horse, the bull, the ram and the antelope – represent the sun, for it was the sun that was perceived to hasten the arrival of rain.

It could be argued that the cave artists were drawing their subjects in their autumn or winter phases since the work was probably executed during that period of the year. Some of the caves can only be entered in the autumn: access to the Tuc d'Audoubert cave in Ariège is through tunnels which are usually running with water in winter and spring.

The drawings were not made from life, although portable reference may have been employed, the artist using a sketch made previously on stone or bone. They were 'symbolic illustrations' of the season of autumn, and were probably made during that time and repeated seasonally. Their purpose was to encourage new life, and especially to encourage rain and spring water, and the generative powers of the sun.

The most famous drawing in the entire corpus of cave art is the 'Sorcerer' of the Trois Frères cave, a part-human, antlered figure that seems to be executing some kind of dance. Such representa-

tions are rare, and much has been made of this Sorcerer, owing to
supposed shamanistic origins. This prancing male figure on human
legs, apparently hung with human genitals and wearing the antlers
of a rutting stag, symbolises a vital period in the year which
welcomes the autumn and winter rains. The Sorcerer is the sun,
the rutting stag who delivers his seed in autumn, penetrating the

FIG. 16 Palaeolithic
cave art from Les
Trois Frères, copied
by Henri Abbé
Breuil.

caves as the sun was thought to do in the period heralding winter, when the drawings were made. If the physical condition of the drawings seems to indicate a period of dryness during which cave art flourished, it is possible that the artists were hoping to generate new life, and especially water, by the 'sympathetic magic' of their drawings. The deeper they went, the more influential and effective their efforts became.

More than any other aspect of nature, except for running water, animals were the stuff of life, especially the horse which prehistoric man seems so greatly to have admired: one of the earliest examples of known sculpture is of a horse in mammoth ivory from the Aurignacian cultures of 30,000 BC. It showed evidence of long handling and perhaps ritual usage.[15]

FIG. 17 The Sorcerer, drawn by Abbé Henri Breuil.

The purpose of the animal drawings was a seasonal votive performance intended to re-awaken nature. As mentioned in the previous chapter, a significant number of animals portrayed appear either to be giving voice, expelling breath, or vomiting blood. The opinions of scholars are divided between the two latter possibilities, and as usual the weight of emphasis is shared among bison, horses, cervids and bears.

Some of the drawings show that the animals appear to be struck by missiles, thus it follows that blood is a reasonable hypothesis. Yet the blood does not spurt from the wounds, but from the mouth and nostrils.[16] It is possible, though, that the spears are indeed the weapons of the hunters, and that the killing of an animal was intended as a form of sacrifice. The animals drawn on the walls of the caves each represent solar activity, and they are expelling not blood but water, as the winged lions of Assyria spewed rainwater, and as the Greek river god Acheloos spewed river water when challenged by Heracles. (See Figure 38, p.211.)

The water and solar animals, the horse and bison, were

portrayed by the Magdalenian artists in the darkest, and most inaccessible places. Where water and alluvial mud was present they used it to form figures. This is why we find several clay bison grouped together, or engravings and fingertip sketches in the mud. It has been noted that horse images were strategically placed where the caves descend to dark and mysterious pools of water.[17]

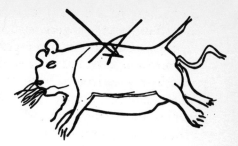

FIG. 18 Animal spewing water, perhaps a bear, from Lascaux.

The swift and shining white horse is also a messenger of the sun whose appearance in the autumn caused the springs to flow. The archaeologist Dr Miranda Green, one of the few writers who appreciate the importance of the sun in ancient religions, notes that 'The sun and the horse were tenacious companions',[18] because the horse was the prime symbol of the 'water–sun' that touched down on the earth with the rains, and entered the earth through the caves. The idea of the sun's winter journey in the earth was probably already ancient by the time it was expressed by Neanderthal man during the last interglacial era. The winged horse Pegasus, progeny of Medusa, created a rainstorm with his hoof, which then gave rise to the Hippocrene spring. In the Hindu Rig-Veda the horses of Agni, god of fire, struck water from their hooves.[19]

By venturing into the caves with lamp and pigment, man was insuring for the future. As a symbol of sun and water, the horse generated life, and this is shown much later on Celtic Iron Age decorations in which horses have vegetation sprouting from their mouths.[20] It seems to me fairly certain that the widespread portrayal of symbolic animals in ancient cults and religions was because of their response to seasonal changes, and in particular the performance of the sun. Yet the evolution of symbols from a fundamental idea took an enormous span of time, and it is unlikely that such well-founded concepts would change their meaning in the passage of the centuries; if the horse represented the sun, water and life to the Greeks and the Celts, it is likely that it did so to the Magdalenian artists, though the period during which cave art flourished was a mere fragment of prehistory. The artists came and went, leaving their efforts to posterity. A practice or ritual which might seem strange to us was probably perfectly normal for them. They were helping to create life, having gathered the fruits of autumn, putting the germ into the womb of the earth, represented by those animals which were the very essence of fertility.

When man's struggle with the environment became transformed into myths, animal symbolism was essential to the structure of the story, and animals were chosen to nurse and suckle many of mythology's great gods and solar heroes, as Telephus was suckled by a she-bear, and Zeus by the goat Amalthea in a cave on Mount Ida.

The great mythologies of Europe and the Near East, and eventually the myths of all nations, grew from a need expressed in the caves of the Palaeolithic, and which had itself been inherited from a much earlier period in the prehistory of mankind, when it was recognised that water was the first essential to survival.

The great agent that appeared to bring the blessing of water, and breathed life into the hard, cold earth at the start of the year was, of course, the sun. Its warmth brought about the seasonal miracle of spring, and it also gave inspiration to something equally miraculous – the flowering of human creativity and its expression in myth and symbol and art. The developing creativity of man gradually drew upon nature to establish what we might call the 'mechanics of myth', in which human action symbolised the dramatic and untameable forces of the elements that so harshly determined life and death.

CHAPTER 6

Numbers Code

No one – certainly not the Mediterranean people in classical times – could have been surprised by the theatrical savagery of the cast of performers in their myths. The acts of castration and swallowing and beheading are the allegorical mechanics of myth, to which we can add the rather more subtle theme of lameness. Hephaestus was lamed when he fell from heaven – or rather, he didn't fall, he was pushed by his mother Hera. Hephaestus is one among many mythological figures who limp or who, like Achilles, have vulnerable heels. Although this is the stuff of drama, which the Greeks introduced to the world, the persistent themes – decapitation, lameness – have a definite purpose.

The details are often so contrived that we are inclined to gloss over them as being merely fanciful. Zeus engages in battle with the fearsome monster Typhon, who robs him of his sinews. One might be forgiven for thinking that this is what Robert Graves would call a 'silly Olympian fable' of no consequence, but would not Zeus's stolen sinews have the same disabling effect as, say, Achilles' vulnerable heel, or Hephaestus's limp? The story acquires greater significance when we learn that Hermes found the sinews and returned them to Zeus; Typhon had hidden them under a bear's pelt in a cave, and Typhon was the offspring of Hera who crippled Hephaestus. It seems then, that Hera benefits from the deformity of her husband and children, perhaps in the same way that Athena benefits from Medusa's demise and this is why she wears – like Minerva – the Gorgon's head on her breast.

All the evidence so far gathered from the ancient world, the myths and folktales, the cults and rituals, the signs and symbols, the mysteries and monuments could be interrelated to form a network, finally giving us a whole remarkable pattern. A useful analogy in our computer age would be to say that we could gain access to this network of information if we had the right code, if we could, say, punch in the correct numbers or the right formula to get into the system. Number symbolism is particularly useful because, like the theme of lameness, it might provide clues that lead to the origins, the identity of myth, especially the traditionally potent numbers three, seven and nine. The influence of arithmetical thought in the structure of myth and ritual is presumably of great antiquity. It cannot have emerged spontaneously and fully fledged in the myths and religions of early societies. The Babylonians venerated the number seven, their tree of life having seven branches each bearing seven leaves, their pyramids or ziggurats constructed in seven steps, glazed with bricks of seven colours. 'So we may multiply the 7's of Babylonian cosmogony and religion,' wrote the American mathematican Vincent Hopper (1938), 'and add to them their uncounted descendants in other lands and later times, for few other numbers were to be so universally venerated'.[1] Perhaps from them the Greeks inherited the symbolic value of seven. Apollo was a seven months child who grew in three days, and Cronus was the seventh of the Titans. In their creation myth, Cronus castrates his father Uranus and the drops of blood engender three Furies and three nymphs. Hector is dragged by Achilles three times around the walls of Troy, and Perseus flies three times around the world, later to sire seven children. The Persian (and later the Roman) god Mithras was closely associated with the number seven, as was Agni, the Hindu god of fire. The Hurrian god Kumarbi, grasping his father by the feet, bit off and swallowed the parental privates, and at once became pregnant with three gods.

The employment of numbers is a regular feature of folktales. The numbers lend weight and a certain authority to the story, and any myth, parable, rite, or incantation containing the deliberate repetition of three, seven or nine might be found to share a common, if distant, ancestry. No myth or folktale is complete without some reference to a 'mystic' number. The regular use of the number seven runs throughout mythology and ancient religious texts, especially the Bible, reaching a point of absurdity in Revelation where it appears fifty-nine times. According to the early Christian writer, theologian and philosopher St Augustine, seven is composed of the first odd and even numbers, becoming the symbol of all numbers – therefore seven means perfect completeness. 'Augustine,' says Vincent Hopper, 'gave the final stamp of approval to number symbolism.'[2] He saw in number the image of the absolute. 'There is a relation of numbers which cannot possibly be impaired or altered, nor can any nature by any violence prevent the number which comes after one from being the double on one.' Rituals are solemnised by numbers, when certain functions have to be repeated. For example, pilgrims to Mecca walk around the Ka'aba, the Holy of Holies, seven times, representing, they say, the seven attributes of God.

A popular theory is that seven comes from the lunar cycle of twenty-eight days, and represents the four quarters of the month. Thus 'seven' is a basic unit of time. Early societies recognised the difficulties in reconciling the lunations with the solar year. The moon's monthly cycle of 29½ days is incompatible with the solar year of 365 days, and the first calendars calculated 12 lunations with a 13th month intercalated from time to time. It was easier to fix the year as having 360 days with each month of thirty days, as the Greeks chose to do, while the Babylonians used alternate 29- and 30-day periods.

Another suggestion for the sanctity of seven is that it stands for the seven planets (Sun, Moon, Mercury, Venus, Mars, Jupiter and Saturn) or the stars in Ursa Major, The Great Bear, or the Pleiades group of stars in the constellation Taurus, the 'Seven Stars' familiar in Britain as an inn sign. Yet it requires a keen eye to see more than six stars in the group. The identification of seven planets was probably the work of Babylonian priest-astronomers, to whom seven had long been a sacred number. The naming of the seven days of the week after each planet was a later development, 'a notion,' Hopper observes, 'that seems not to have gained general currency until the first century BC at Alexandria.'[3]

The number seven, though, had a special significance long before the Babylonians, Egyptians and Greeks had scanned the night sky and developed the science of astronomy, the cult of astrology, and the zodiac. The seven planets, for example, were late arrivals on the astronomy charts. 'We do not know,' wrote Hutton Webster in Rest Days, 'when all five planets were set off against the fixed stars, or when they were first connected with the sun and moon to form a group of seven planetary luminaries.'[4]

The Italian astronomer Giovanni Schiaparelli (father of Elsa, the couturier) said that both achievements required centuries of close observations and did not belong to primitive astronomy. 'Hence we may safely conclude,' Webster continues, 'that the symbolism of seven, reaching into remote Babylonian antiquity, long preceded the recognition of the seven planets.' The problem was but briefly acknowledged by the scholar A. B. Cook, who in 1925 wrote, 'On the whole it must be admitted that as yet no single or simple explanation of the sanctity attaching to the number seven has been reached.'[5]

The ancient world set great store by a structured numbers system, a code recognised from India to Central America, from Iberia to Siberia, in myth, cult, ritual and religion, each of which was influenced from time to time by astronomy and astrology. They perceived a mystique attached to certain numbers, and saw in mathematics a logical process and a powerful agent in symbolism.

The Maya civilisation, for example, evolved a chronology decidedly provocative in its complexity. Authors Adrian Gilbert and Maurice Cottrell, in *The Mayan Prophecies*, explain how 'The Mayan number system has been investigated by many scholars to date and has mystified them all'.[6] It has so far defeated every attempt to decode it, but we can crack the Maya's code, and I will show that the choice of certain numbers evolved from a simple idea, a formula, shared by all ancient societies.

Our persistent use of such favourite numbers as three, seven and nine, may be regarded as mere superstition, but it is a decidedly powerful compulsion, in use for at least 30,000 years. And so number symbolism is lastingly influential, having become an established part of our culture and behaviour. There are nearly forty English-language movies with the number seven in the title – and fifty with the number three, and doubtless many more in other languages.

We use certain numbers to emphasise action and as verification – when drowning we are said to go down 'for the third time', and medicines are the more effective if we take them three times daily. Other numbers that have established themselves in worldwide cultures are four, five, twelve and thirteen. Four and five are especially important to American Indian tribes, to the Chinese, to the Buddhists and Hindus, who also recognise seven and three.

The medieval city of London had seven gates (as did the Greek city of Thebes), though this may be due more to convenience rather than to deliberate symbolism. Angkor has five gates, the roads leading to them are bordered by a row of 108 stone statues, 54 each side of the avenue, the total number being 540, which will be seen to have a decided significance.

The ziggurat pyramids of Babylon were constructed of seven

layers and decorated with glazed tiles of seven hues because the designers were undoubtedly observing a religious or superstitious precedent, just as most polytheistic religions observe a structured hierarchy, at the top of which is a triad of gods, or gods and a goddess. Even monotheism acknowledges the power of three, so that the Christian religion refers to Father, Son and Holy Ghost. When Jesus was crucified, he was flanked by the two thieves as part of a triad attended by three Marys (John 19:25), and was fixed to the cross with three nails.

There is a remarkable catalogue of things in triple form that persist in everyday life, most of which we take for granted. Our passion, or perhaps our need, for abbreviation has created DNA, SOS, BBC, USA, CIA, FBI, UFO, MGM, LWT, ICI, DDT, PTO, and so on – you could probably find hundreds more examples to add to the list. We enjoy a three-course meal with a knife, fork and spoon, washed down with red, white or rosé wine. Winners in an athletic contest come first, second or third, may win a gold, silver or bronze medal, and are further rewarded with 'three cheers'. These things may be seen as mere convention, a matter of tradition and no more. Perhaps, but tripartition is certainly a part of the very fabric of universal cultures. Why then does the number three run so persistently through our lore, our language and our customs?

The first and one of the few serious investigations of trichotomy was made by the German philologist Hans Usener in 1903,[7] while the most recent is by Alan Dundes, the American anthropologist and folklorist.[8] Dundes enlivens his study with such examples as the versatile sandwich, consisting as it does of two slices of bread and a filling. Sometimes the filling has three ingredients, as in the popular BLT sandwich – bacon, lettuce and tomato.

Later on, Dundes points to the fundamental structure of language in terms of threes: first, second and third person; three distinctive forms of any one pronoun: he, his, him. The third person nominative singular is divided into he, she and it, corresponding to the genders masculine, feminine and neuter. And of time: past, present and future; hour, minute and second; yesterday, today and tomorrow. Society is three-tiered, forming itself into an upper, middle and lower class. Our national flag, the Union Jack, is made up of three crosses – St George's, St Andrew's and St Patrick's. Many national flags are based on three divisions of three colours, the eponymous French tricolore being the prime example.

As indicated earlier, suggestions for the origin of trichotomy have included the idea that its foundations might be sexual. In Eastern symbolism, three was the number of the masculine principle embodied in Siva, the Hindu god of fertility, who has three heads, three eyes, and carries a trident. His attribute is the phallus or lingam which, with the testicles, is of course a threesome. Freud pounced on this 'phallic' theory, adding the triskeles, the clover-leaf and the fleur-de-lys as examples of the symbolised male organ.

The theory holds good until you discover plentiful evidence of female threesomes – in Scandinavia the Three Norns who daily watered the three roots of the sacred ash tree Yggdrasil. In Greece the Three Fates, Three Sirens, Three Hesperides, Three Furies, Three Graces, Three Gorgons (Medusa and her sisters), while the statue of the goddess Hecate had a triangular base supporting three heads pointing in different directions. It generally stood at a place where three roads met – as did herms, the crude ithyphallic statues of the messenger-god Hermes. Interpreters quick to spot sexual symbolism might see a road junction as representing the inguinal triangle, the vulva or yoni, while those with a psychoanalytical approach could find rich Oedipal overtones, for the crossroads was where Oedipus killed his father Laius.

In common with most symbols, the significance of the number three is a result of long, slow development. Again, it is a product of synthesis, a process that takes a thought, an observation, and 'matures' it over centuries, over millennia. It is the outcome of a collective effort, of contributions by generation after generation. The number three, as a masculine procreative symbol, seems only to appear in some examples of sacred and folk art, but the almost universal use of the number in everyday life suggests that it has developed from language and from social order. It establishes the positive, comparative and superlative degrees, so the number three has the power of the infinite. Yet its origins may have come from an observed and regular phenomenon.

There is one possible source, the repetitive performance of which can be traced by evidence in art and language, and this was the daily and annual passage of the sun. The moon also has its phases, and quite complex cycles, similarly the planet Venus, appearing as the morning and evening star. But for millions of years man has looked principally to the sun as the most powerful influence on his life and his natural surroundings. The sun's routine penetrated the subliminal layers of the mind long before it was consciously registered.

Dawn, noon and sunset is an unfailing pattern, repeated in the annual phases of the solstices, with the 'birth' of the sun in spring, to its zenith with the summer solstice, the 'sacred marriage' of the solar representative with the goddess of earth and water, and the descent to 'death' in the dark days of winter. In the Rig-Veda this is analogous to the three strides of Vishnu. Others have long ago pointed to the solar recognition of the number three. The remarkable persistence of this number in myth and ritual, along with the numbers seven and nine, might suggest that it has a foundation more concrete than abstract, one that powerfully influenced the lives of primitive societies. The cycle of spring, summer and winter had a more urgent effect on the thoughts of Stone Age people than the science of numbers, and it is from the Palaeolithic that number symbolism evolved.

The sun was ultimately reassuring and predictable through the unfailing regularity of its threefold pattern, therefore 'three' is the number of power and determinism. Shakespeare's Earl of March, in *Henry VI*, declares that 'I will bear Upon my target three fair-shining suns.' It is reassuring because it always survives winter and is thus 'Sol Invictus', for there was considerable concern that the sun might one day slow down and darkness would fall permanently over the land.

And so where one is chance, two is coincidence, three is certainty. Because of this completeness, this reliability and reassurance, three is the number of authority, not because it represents the phallic power of the dominant male, dominant group or society, but because it accentuates the positive and eliminates the negative. Next time you listen to a politician give a speech, notice how frequently he or she repeats a phrase three times. Once to establish the message, twice for conviction, and three times for authority. 'A single occurrence,' writes Hopper, 'is of no significance. A repetition is noticeable, but might easily be the result of coincidence. A third occurrence of the same nature gives the event the impress of law.'

The symbolism of this powerful number has its origins in the solar phases, and has become established as an intrinsic part of our culture. The national flags of most European nations, even though they are the representative emblems of powerful, patriarchal societies, are not phallic but are often divided in three parts in recognition of the sun, for flags have a strong tendency to trichotomy. This is why they are based on three divisions, with some notable exceptions such as the national flag of Japan with its straightforward motif of the rising sun. The solar origin of flags led to the ritual observance of raising the standard at dawn, and lowering it at sunset.

Supporters of the psycho-sexual approach to myths may argue that the rise and fall of the sun, like the raising and lowering of flags, can nonetheless be construed as phallic, imitating erection and detumescence. This is a fair comment. There are clear associations between the sun and the image of phallic power and procreation. They appear in Bronze Age rock carvings in Scandinavia and in the Camonica valley in the Italian Alps. Ithyphallic sun-men brandishing weapons, or copulating with female figures, or with animals, suggest the quickening, fertile properties of solar heat.

The images convey a dynamic concept, to equate fertility and strength with the sun. The rock-engravings, some of them superimposed on others on the same piece of stone, were probably carved at an appropriate time of the year, namely winter and spring, to celebrate and encourage solar power. This is why so

FIG. 19 Phallic sun-men. Bronze Age rock engravings in Sweden. (From Gelling and Davidson's *Chariot of the Sun*.)

many of them are related to phallic humans, and images of antlered stags. These curious figures, with their sun-disc bodies and idealised phalluses, waving their spears and axes and displaying their copulatory prowess, were anthropomorphised images of the sun, and the intention was probably to speed the sun's return and encourage its fertile influences on nature. Many of the male figures, as well as being extravagantly endowed, wave their battle axes for, like a Norse warrior, the sun was invincible.

The representations of rams, bulls, boars and stags are overt symbols of masculinity, and because they are virile they are solar, and because they are solar they are virile. The autumn stag, proud with his newly hardened and now mature antlers, was simply an animal version of the human male, and was dominant in the rutting period that begins with the autumn equinox (antlers are cast around the time of the spring equinox), when the sun was waning in strength, and thus supplemented solar energy.

As I have stressed in previous chapters, this graphic sex symbolism was intended to put across the idea of fertility per se, not to encourage the procreation of humans, but of the powers of nature – sex symbolism by analogy. Human sexuality was a useful frame of reference to which the processes of nature could be compared. In this sense the figures are comparable to the Venus figurines and phalli of the Palaeolithic, and it is why Siva with his trident is phallic, not because he represents sex and procreation, but because he is a solar deity embodying the sun's fertile influences.

Where does that other regulator of primitive timekeeping, the moon, fit into this cosmic symbolism? The number three in recognition of the phases of the moon appears, for example, in a magical incantation to the moon goddess, Selene, who is described as a three-headed, three-named, three-formed goddess of the three ways, something she shares with Hecate. Although the Greeks consistently regarded the moon as feminine, it was masculine in some cultures. The feminine moon 'held and purified the seed of the celestial bull', and links with the lunations and the menses were of course widely recognised. The moon was the symbol of the winter goddess, and sometimes her consort, and the life-giving waters that sprang from the ground.

The power invested in the number three was so influential that it formed the structure of early religious belief, in polytheism, or perhaps 'polythreeism' would be more appropriate, with its

leading triad of deities, even the word 'tribe' may be derived from
the Latin *tribus*, thence from *tres*, 'three'. In classical Greece, the
throne of Zeus, and the home of the gods and goddesses, was on
Mount Olympus, and I have no doubt that this particular
mountain commended itself to the Greeks for its three peaks,
celebrated as 'the three peaks of Heaven'.

The Olympian creation myths include the birth of three giants
– Briareus, Gyges and Cottus, and the three Cyclops – Brontes,
Steropes and Arges. When Cronus castrated his father Uranus, the
blood fertilised the earth and gave birth to the three Erinyes, or
Furies, who may be compared to the three Fates – Clotho,
Lachesis and Atropos. The three leading gods of the Greek
pantheon, Zeus, Poseidon and Hades, may be compared to those
of the Vedas, namely Brahma, Vishnu and Siva. This Hindu triad
is described in the Vedas, of which there were originally three, the
fourth Atharva Veda being a later addition; the triad is related to
the sun as the sun is described as *Treyitenu*, 'three-bodied'. In the
Vedas Trita, the third of three brothers, is cast into a well. The
Vedic god of fire, Agni, has three heads, and three legs. So have
examples of terracotta rams with three legs, and bulls with three
horns from the early Neolithic.

FIG. 20 Bull-headed
human figures with three
horns fighting monster snakes.
From Burkert (1976). Accademia Nazionali del Lincei.

The number nine was also respected as a powerfully symbolic
number, not because it represented the months of human
gestation, but because it is three multiplied by three. Thus nine

was revered in Egypt, in Babylonia and India, among the Greeks, and the societies in Central America.

There is a decided refinement of numerical thinking in mythology. The name of the goddess Hecate, according to Graves, means 'one hundred', because it is three times thirty-three and a third.[10] The view that she represents the moon's phases is incorrect – Hecate is the sun goddess in winter, and so lives in a cave. Hecate had several triple attributes and associations with fire. She speeds along, a torch held high in each hand; she is related to the sun-god Apollo, and bore the epithet 'Phosphorus' which could refer, as some believe, to the moon. She, too, had three heads, and one of them bears a modius, or grain measure, hardly a lunar reference.

She presides over the time of the year when the sun descends to the land of the dead, the time of rains. Fish were sacrificed to her, perhaps in the month of January – and not just any fish. They had to be gurnards, of the family *triglidae*, so called because the gurnard has three fingerlike feelers under its mouth. The Greeks must have searched for some time to find a fish with the power of three.

The gloomy nature of the winter sun is why Hecate is associated with ghosts and the dead. As we saw above, she also presides over crossroads, typically at places where three rather than four roads, or three rivers meet, because the sun is a wanderer, a traveller, and the junction seems to be where wandering, and life, comes to an end.

Due to the tenacious connection of the number three with solar power, the crossroads represents the place where the sun enters the earth, and is therefore associated with winter and the underworld. Here is the parting of the ways, traditionally where criminals were hanged, and suicides buried. This would explain why Hermes, in the form of stone herms with a prominent phallus, was sited at crossroads. Hermes was the phallic solar messenger entering the earth and acting as a guide to souls descending to Hades.

The Vedic god Siva, in his avatar aspect of the sun in winter, was in the habit of wandering around graveyards at night, a pastime he shares with the Aztec sun god Tezcatlipoca, 'Smoking Mirror', who carried his head in his hands, and wore a grey veil. Like Hecate, Siva has three heads, three eyes, and he carries a trident. The fact that Oedipus killed his father Laius at a crossroads has nothing to do with incest, or guilt, or castration as a talion punishment, for the myth of Oedipus is solar.

It is difficult to decide whether some types of myth grew out of the dynamic effects that phases, time factors, and numbers had on communities, or whether numbers were subconsciously added because they were a recognised and approved convention. In the Deluge myth, when the rains cease, Noah sends out a dove three times. In the Passion of Christ, the cock crows three times, Peter's denial is threefold. Jesus died in the ninth hour, and rose again on the third day.

This appears to lay foundations for the identity of Jesus as a sun-god, a claim that was famously proposed by Arthur Drews in *The Christ Myth* (1910) and contested ever since. Has this clear emphasis on tripartition occurred 'because that's how it has always been done', or is it fundamental to the meaning of the myth?

I believe the latter to be the case, that numbers are a key issue, because the pervasive, almost numinous power of numbers is recognisably solar, and that such myths were spontaneous creations of this power, expressed through human thought and language. The sun brought light, warmth, healing, fertility, but was also recognised for a benefit even more vital, valuable and life-enhancing, and with which it was intimately associated, and without which life would cease.

CHAPTER 7

Gods of Fire

Will the number seven be found to have the same solar origins as three and nine? In the same way that three has become a part of our culture and language, the number seven seems to have pervaded every religion and every society, and examples can be found in abundance. In Northern India, a girl's puberty rites required the propitiation of the 'Goddess of Sex' – probably Lakshmi, a golden goddess usually depicted sitting on a lotus – with seven lamps, seven golden pots, and seven banana trees.[1] The rite was observed for seven days. Should we infer from this that the number is in some way 'sexual'?

Remaining in India we find that Agni has seven arms in addition to his three heads and three legs, seven tongues of fire (each one a goddess), seven abodes and seven sources. Seven sacrificers worship him in seven ways. Seven books of the Yajur Veda of the Brahmans are assigned to Agni, and he is the seventh of seven brothers.[2] Indian symbolism is nothing if not thorough.

We are told that Agni sometimes steals the semen of Siva, and like the Egyptian Set and the Hurrian god Kumarbi, swallows the semen of the gods, in particular that of Prajapati, whose name means 'progeny', and who of course was the seventh of seven brothers. Does Agni represent the sun, since he is a fire-god? This idea receives some support when we discover that the number seven is sacred to Apollo and Mithras, both sun gods, yet neither Agni, Apollo nor Mithras seems to represent the sun itself.

The Hindus already had a sun god (in fact they had three – Surya, Savitri, and Vivasvat) while Mithras, whose name is derived from a Persian word *mihr*, 'sun', is shown on a sculptured relief shaking hands with the sun-god Sol, whose head is crowned with seven rays. These figures, then, were intermediaries able to influence the course of the sun and the vital elements through the seasons of the year. This suggestion is perhaps helped by another meaning to Mithras' name, that of 'contract'.[3]

'Seven' refers to a period of time. Plutarch, the Greek philosopher (and priest at Delphi) referred to this period in his work on religion, Isis and Osiris, when the golden cow of Isis, covered by a black cloth, was perambulated seven times around the shrine of Osiris, as pilgrims walk seven times around the Ka'aba in Mecca. 'The circuit is called "The Seeking for Osiris" for in winter the Goddess longs for the water of the Sun. And she goes around seven times because he completes his passing from the winter to the summer solstice in the seventh month.'[4] This will present some difficulty to those who would rightly argue that there are only six months between the solstices. Plutarch must have been referring to a lunar count of the months, where the new moon denotes the first day of the month during which the solstice occurs; although there are six months between the winter and the summer solstice, the latter would take place either before or after the seventh moon. In the Jewish pre-exilic period it was natural years that regulated the chronology, the change of the year fell in the seventh month of Tishri (October) and the months which followed the moon were allowed to take their own way, without concerning themselves much about the solar year. Most ancient societies reckoned time by the lunar phases. 'So far as we know, the Babylonian calender was at all periods truly lunar, that is to say, the "month" began with the evening when the new crescent was for the first time again visible shortly after sunset. Consequently the Babylonian "day" also begins in the evening and the "first" of a month is the day of the first visibility. In that this was the beginning of a month is made dependent upon a natural phenomenon which is amenable to direct observation'.[5]

The number seven was also made to fit usefully other periods of the year, from the start of autumn in October to seven months later in April and the harvest, and the start of summer; from the summer solstice in June to the winter solstice in December. In the zodiac, this was covered by the signs from Cancer to Capricorn, the equinoxes from Aries to Libra.

The sun rises at a different point along the horizon each day, and travels north-east to its furthest position at the summer solstice around the 21st June, when it appears to stand still for a few days before returning south-east. It finally reaches its southernmost position at the winter solstice about the 21st December, where it appears to rest for a day or two before heading back north again. This annual passage of the sun, and the sun's ultimate resting points, north and south, marking the solstices, would have been observed over countless ages.

The period from the winter solstice to the summer solstice in June sees the birth of new life, the blossoming of nature, crops sprouting green and growing to maturity. It sees the offspring of domestic animals, the harvest, and has come to symbolise human as well as crop fertility. It was also noticed that 'seven' was the period of rains, the seven months from October to May in the Near East, and from October to April-May in Europe. In Palestine and the Lebanon the rains can begin in September, falling at intervals until April, or even as late as May.[6]

The number seven was therefore directly equated with periods of gestation, with the fertility of the earth and the progeny of the animal world. It was also indirectly related to human fertility, for the uterus was believed to be constructed of seven cells. This alone reveals the priority that the cycle of nature had over the cycle of human reproduction; wherever it occurs, the number nine as a symbolic number never refers to the nine-month period of human gestation, but to the solar power of three times three.

The reproductive system was imperfectly understood by the Greeks, and there had been a reluctance among physicians to perform dissections on human subjects. Galen, lecturing on anatomy to Roman students, preferred to use pigs and sheep. Although Greek physicians practised surgical intervention, such as

FIG. 21 Fifteenth- and sixteenth-century drawings representing the human uterus. It was once believed the womb was horned, with seven cells. The labyrinth, with its seven winding passages, is probably related to this idea.

foetal excision (the removal of a dead foetus from the womb), neither Aristotle nor any of his contemporaries dissected adult human subjects post mortem.[7] The Dark Ages of science, which persisted almost from the time of Aristotle until the Renaissance, meant that the idea of a 'seven-cell womb' held sway among physicians until well into the sixteenth century of our era. An anatomical drawing from the thirteenth century shows the seven cells, three on the right side, in which male embryos developed, three on the left in which females developed, and the seventh in the middle for hermaphrodites.

In the following two hundred years, anatomical dissection had developed to the extent that enabled the Italian physician Berengario to declare 'It is a sheer lie to say that the uterus has seven compartments.'[8] The uterus was also thought to have 'horns' although it is unique among mammals for not having horns — only animal uteri are bicornate. This idea inspired Redgrove and Shuttle, the authors of *The Wise Wound*, to declare that 'The womb is two-horned with its Fallopian tubes. It is the emblem of fertility and containment, and the sacred bucranium or ox-head decorating Greek and Roman temples was a womb emblem.'[9]

'Seven' represented the feminine influence of solar power in the earth, and this is why the Babylonian month of Elul in September was called 'The descent of Ishtar', for this was when the goddess was believed to enter the underworld, passing through seven gates, each gate representing a month, comparable with the seven cells of the womb. The goddess would make the earth ready to receive the fertilising rains which were shortly due — she herself was the earth ready to be tilled by the plough, a sexual analogy. She would also warm the earth with the fires of gestation. Ishtar returned in April at the start of the barley harvest, and the time of her sacred marriage to the god Tammuz. Her seven months in the underworld are comparable to the fertility cycle in Scandinavian mythology, where winter is prolonged for eight or nine months. 'The number 9 thus became the northern counterpart of the southern number 7,' notes Vincent Hopper, 'being particularly connected with fertility, religion and magic. The Celtic need-fire was kindled by 81 men (8 + 1 = 9), 9 men at a time being employed.'[10]

If I have interpreted correctly the meaning of seven, the

number symbolises the months of the solstices, or more likely the seasonal months of rains (coinciding with the weakening sun), ploughing and sowing, leading to the springtime and the harvest. 'Seven' is thus the gestatory period of nature. The sun has delivered the fertilising rains (perceived as a sort of celestial semen), and has entered the earth as subterranean fire to quicken nature's womb. This led to the idea of the sun being androgynous, capable of performing the roles of both sexes. This is why many sun and fire gods are closely associated with the number seven. It appears in Hindu myth when the fire god Agni swallows the semen of Prajapati. The fertilising and the later gestatory activities of the sun are indicated by the effeminate reputations, or direct evidence, of solar gods and heroes. It is why Agni's 'seven tongues of fire' are all goddesses,[11] and why Hephaestus's golden assistants are women, why the solar heroes Achilles and Heracles dress in women's attire. Now we can see why a girl's puberty rites required seven lamps, seven banana trees (not because bananas are phallic, but because they are yellow, like the sun) and seven gold pots.

The septenary influence in the ancient world is perhaps the reason for the Pleiades being thought of as seven in number, in preference to the visible six, because their period of visibility corresponds to the period of gestation of the crops of barley or wheat; they rise to herald the harvest during the period between the solstices, they set seven months later at the time of the rains. Like Agni's goddesses, the seven stars of the group are all female, the most important being Taygete who lay with Zeus, and gave her name to a mountain whose melting snows water the fertile plain of Sparta.

Because seven was known to be powerfully significant, and that numbers invested myths with a special vitality, they took their place in the structure of religions. The gospel writers used the number seven indiscriminately, to lend weight of authority. Numbers are often a vital part of the structure of myths, and a good example of the way in which this symbolism works is found in the well-known myth from Homer's Odyssey in which the wandering solar hero Odysseus, with twelve companions and a goat-skin filled with red wine (a clue that points to late September) is trapped in the cave of the giant cannibal Polyphemus. Both Odysseus and his adversary are both aspects of the sun – Polyphemus with his one glaring eye, the giant of folklore who holds the sun captive, and the solar hero – Odysseus, 'The Angry One' (like Achilles) because fire rages, and is unpredictable – with red hair and rather short legs, and a scarred thigh. Polyphemus, blocking the cave's exit with a huge stone, terrorises the band of adventurers, killing and devouring them two by two. When the giant has eaten six of Odysseus's crew, with seven now remaining including the hero, they devise an escape plan. Odysseus gets Polyphemus drunk with the wine, and armed with a pointed olive-wood stake, heated in the fire and 'glowing terribly', plunges it into the giant's single eye, spinning it about like a fire-drill.

Pushing the blocking stone aside, Polyphemus staggers out of the cave and so allows the men to escape. Odysseus, the wily trickster, his mind wonderfully concentrated through fear that the giant may yet prevent his escape, gathers nineteen (a solar number – 3+7+9) rams and lashes eighteen together in groups of three, and to each ram in the centre Odysseus ties one of his companions, under the animal's belly. The hero chooses the nineteenth and most powerful ram for himself, and clinging to its underside is carried among the flock as they head for the pasture. In this manner the seven voyagers collectively symbolise the liberated sun, and head for freedom, out of the dark cave of winter and into the spring where, after seven months in the cave, the ram takes his place in the night sky as Aries. The myth has parallels with the return of Ishtar, back through the seven gates from the underworld.

Myths usefully draw upon elements from folktales, and the tale type where a giant, or despot, holds captive a hero or heroine and sets them impossible tasks, is a common theme that is always solar. It refers to the sun that must be set free at the end of winter, else disaster will befall mankind. This tale from the *Odyssey* uses the solar numbers three, thirteen (Odysseus and his twelve companions, the lunar months in the solar year) and seven, the extinguishing of the sun's eye by fire, and the ram – the animal closely associated with the sun in many cultures; Jason's ram with the golden fleece is a symbol of the sun.

Where myths set the scene for the action which follows, we need to look extra carefully at the detail, because it is always trying to tell us something. Apollo was born on an uncharted islet, later identified as Delos in the Cyclades. In myth, Delos was said to be a floating island or, when Apollo's mother Leto was in labour (which took nine days and was assisted by wolves), Poseidon covered the island with the sea, and the moment Apollo was born, Delos was clad in a dazzling mantle of gold, a fitting tribute to a sun god. Thus Apollo was born under water.[12]

Some might argue that this represented the amniotic fluid of birth, but what it really means is that Apollo was closely associated with both fire and water, symbolising the birth of the sun after or during the rains of winter. Hegel thought Apollo 'the most Greek of all gods, in art the ideal type of young, but not immature manly beauty'. In fact he is too perfect, representations of Apollo revealing a figure of almost feminine proportions and grace, his delicate, beardless head adorned with golden curls.

Apollo is the perpetual *kouros*, enduring youth, yet the gods of Olympia rise to their feet when he enters the house of Zeus. Even so, Apollo is, like Agni, or Mithras, or Attis, androgynous. By the same token, Apollo's sister Artemis follows the male calling of the hunter. Apollo wears his tunic, the chiton, flowing to his ankles like a woman's, his features are delicate as he thoughtfully plucks his lyre.

His habitual companions were young maidens, the Muses, whose number varies from three to nine. Apollo, powerfully invested with the number seven, and endowed with feminine characteristics,[13] included among his many activities those of healing, of prophecy, of law and philosophy. He was called Phoebus the brilliant, and *hekebolos* – 'he who shoots from afar', a reference to shafts of sunlight loosed from the god's mighty bow that only he and the flame-headed, scarred warrior Odysseus could bend. The lyre of Apollo is a further vital clue to his function – the duty of all sun gods and heroes to create water, as Poseidon created the springs at Lerna, and Heracles the river Scamander by striking a spring in the earth.

The attribute of music often refers to water, from the sound made by water flowing and splashing over rocks in mountain streams, and the drumming of the rains, and the winds that herald the rain sighing through the reeds. Orpheus, Apollo's son, inherited this musical talent and gift for playing divine music on the lyre, and met a watery death. He was torn to pieces by Thracian women, his head and lyre thrown into the river Hebrus. The head of Orpheus, singing and prophesying like the singing head of the Celtic god Bran, was carried out to sea as far as the island of Lesbos.

The sanctuaries of Apollo were located in the countryside and their exact position determined by the presence of a spring. The temple of Apollo at Delphi, containing the sacred navel-stone, the omphalos, was built by two springs, which is perhaps why the site was originally chosen, just as watery places were selected for other oracular temples of Apollo – those at Didyma, Claros and Ptoion, at Ismenion, Tegyra, Thourion and Hysiai. At Ptoion by a cave and spring, male prophets gave consultations as late as the third century AD. At Claros the temple was built directly over a spring from which the priest drank before giving his responses.[14]

There is however another path to follow in respect of Apollo's solar character, and it leads to Delphi where he presided over the oracle at the earth's navel, just as Agni was worshipped at the Hindu version of the omphalos. The Babylonian sun god Shamash was also a diviner and seer, and the association between diviners and the sun points to a simple explanation, but one with many ramifications. Because the sun was the all-seeing eye, the sun's anthropomorphic representative had the gift of foresight; the association between the sun as the all-seeing eye, of wisdom and divination, has long been recognised.

The possession of knowledge, of wisdom (including sexual knowledge), was especially the province of women: Metis, who counsels Zeus from within the god's belly; Athena, whose pet owl is the byword for wisdom, are prime examples. The famous Greek seer Tiresias spent seven years of his life as a woman; it was Eve who took a bite out of the apple from the tree of knowledge, while the Pythia who utters the responses at the oracle of Delphi is a woman priest.

There are I think several reasons for this, apart from the recognition of female intuitive skills. One is due to the above-mentioned solar gestatory influences. The other is the recognition that knowledge nourishes the mind, for it is the supreme function of women as nourishers of mankind, and this is why all goddesses are the creators of springs and rivers.

Apollo and his sister Artemis, both famed as hunters, shared one persistent and marked attribute – the bow and arrow. Artemis roams the wild forests, apparently loosing her arrows at anything that moves. There are other shared features, too. The interest in birth, and in water. When Artemis was a child, she tore a tuft of hair from the chest of the giant Bronte, which made him thunder and produce rain.

Artemis of the shrine at Carian Didyma had a sanctuary close to five springs, and her priestesses were called *hydrophoros* (water-carriers, an office of considerable prestige). Like Hera, she was identified with Eileithyia, the goddess who assisted women in labour, just as Apollo increased the progeny of the womb. He presided over Delphi, a word associated with *delphos*, 'womb', and his creature was the dolphin, the 'uterine beast of the sea'.

The arrows of the sun's rays strike the earth and they produce water, particularly in winter; the 'water miracle' in the cult of Mithras occurs when Mithras strikes a rock with an arrow and a spring bursts forth. This is part of the sequence of events in the death of Robin Hood, a sun hero and archer like Apollo who, when dying, shoots an arrow to mark his burial place.

Apollo and Artemis are therefore prime fertility deities. With their bows and arrows they are the agents of sacrifice, afflicting cruelties with a savage indifference, like the bloodthirsty goddesses of the East. Apollo kills the female Python with his arrows, replacing her with the priestess Pythia, and through her agency delivers his oracles. Artemis turns the innocent Actaeon into a stag, to be devoured by his own hounds, and shoots down the goddess Callisto. She also 'accidentally' shot the hunter Orion, or sent a scorpion to sting his heel. Orion dies in the sea, Python and Actaeon by springs, Robin Hood by the Nun Brook.

This is ritual slaughter, the action of the goddess of earth and springs, in league with the sun god, who sends her lions, panthers or wolves, or her griffins to kill the victim, whose blood and seed will generate her fecundity. Is this why Apollo accidentally kills the young god Hyacinthus? The story is a straightforward nature myth, to emphasise the growing power of the sun's heat. Hyacinthus was a beautiful youth loved by Apollo, who accidentally slew him with a stray discus which struck his head. The wild hyacinth, like the bluebell *Endymion nonscriptus*, is an early spring plant with an all too brief lifespan, and the tale is a simple analogy of the wilting and death of the plant as the sun increases in strength – hence the discus. By the same means Acrisius, the grandfather of Perseus, met his death.

The myths confirm the identity and nature of Apollo and of his sister Artemis, who may well have been created from an original androgynous figure (or perhaps were twins) responsible for the death of the sacrificial victim, the death of Orion, of Actaeon who dies as a stag in the autumn before the rains arrive to nourish the earth. The victim's blood invigorates the waters, and to ensure the life-supporting supply of water, from the sky and from the earth, a price must be paid, a sacrifice offered. This condition is played out in the story of Danaus and his daughters, who massacre and decapitate their husbands in a night of the long knives.

CHAPTER 8

The Nuptial Murders

The story of the daughters of Danaus who beheaded their husbands on their wedding night will reveal a message hidden in numbers, especially the number seven. Essentially, the principal players in the drama are the rival twins Danaus and Aegyptus. Danaus had fifty daughters, Aegyptus fifty sons. One of the foundation myths of the Greeks, the legend of the Danaids is set in Argos in the Peloponnese, where the people had been suffering a prolonged drought. Argos was the land of the sea god Poseidon and centre of the worship of Hera, who in addition to her duties as the wife of Zeus, was a goddess of spring waters.

Zeus fell in love with Io, a priestess of Hera, and daughter of the river god Inarchus. Any extra-marital targets of Zeus's affections – and they were legion – found themselves trapped in parlous circumstances, and suffered Hera's wrath. Zeus, more for his own protection that that of the vulnerable priestess, turned Io into a cow to hide her from Hera. This was a simple yet cunning move, since Zeus was well able to transform himself into a bull to achieve his desire.

The great goddess, however, was not deceived. Enraged by yet another example of her husband's infidelity, Hera sent a vicious, stinging gadfly to attack Io, who fled across the world (that is, the known Greek world), eventually to find refuge in Egypt where she was relieved of her torment by the hand of Zeus, who returned her to her human shape, or rather, part-human shape – a mural at Pompeii shows Io, still bovine with horns sprouting from her forehead, being presented to Isis, who holds a snake, and reclines against a background of reeds, a crocodile at her feet.

'The hand of Zeus' has been recognised by some scholars as a euphemism for sexual union, and the result is Io's offspring, the bull-child Epaphus. The child's name means 'touch of the hand', for the god's hand is the instrument of fecundity. The Vedic sun-god Surya or Savitri had a golden hand, and Hobal at Mecca an arm of gold, the Persian Zoroaster had hands of gold and silver. According to Claud Conder, the Victorian explorer and student of Near Easten religion, 'The gold or silver hand is a well-known emblem of the sun, the great workman of heaven'.[1]

The action of the myth now shifts back to Argos from whence Io had fled, where the god Poseidon had petulantly dried up the rivers and springs, because certain rites of worship due to him had not been observed. A substantial number of myths begin with a drought; it was an essential part of the myth of the Danaides that the plot and characters deliberately shifted between arid Argos and the Nile delta.

Epaphus, the Egyptian-born offspring of Zeus and Io, becomes the progenitor of the Danaides. The tauriform child is an ancient and ancestral figure; Pasiphae, the wife of King Minos of Crete delivers the bull-headed Minotaur; earlier still, the obese goddess of Çatal Hüyük gives birth to a bull. The myth of the Danaides is the beginning of a dynasty featuring the rivalry between the twins Danaus and Aegyptus, both tauric and descendants of Epaphus. The story may have arrived with the Indo-European Mycenaeans to the mainland of Greece, perhaps via Crete, an island which in the classical world seems to have been preoccupied with bulls and bull symbols.

The fifty daughters of Danaus were now threatened with an arranged marriage by the more powerful of the brothers, Aegyptus, and his fifty sons. The daughters quit Egypt and sailed to Argos, their ancestral home, pursued by their men cousins, who if not actually tauriform, had bull's blood and powerfully fertile inclinations. On disembarking the women found the country suffering from Poseidon's prolonged drought.

The fifty bridegrooms on arriving in Argos claimed their brides. Danaus, giving each of his daughters a long, sharp knife, urged them to murder their spouses during the wedding night. One of the daughters, Hypermnestra, chose to spare the life of her husband Lynceus – a vital decision. The rest of the daughters killed their husbands, decapitated the bodies, and buried the heads at Argos. Following the massacre, another of Danaus's daughters, Amymone, set out to find water and was intercepted and seduced by Poseidon, who in return for her favours showed her – or created for her – the springs near the marshes of Lerna, where Hercules and his companion Iolus later defeated the seven-headed Hydra.

The direct result of the nuptial killings and the burial of the heads, is the gift of water, presumably ending the drought.

While the myth can be interpreted as being about the Greek Danaides contending with Aegyptus over the claims to the marriage contract, why does one daughter spare the life of her husband, and why do the others decapitate the bodies and bury the heads? And why are there fifty daughters and fifty sons? To sire fifty children would tax even the lustiest of Olympian fathers, and the most fertile of mothers, even given the time.

Arthur Bernard Cook, Cambridge scholar and author of *Zeus*, regards the myth as a potent fertility charm,[2] which is likely, but fails to explain the curious details, while Professor G. S. Kirk suggests that the tale is an example of the 'single survivor' motif,[3] one of such devices common in folktales, and that there is no significance in the number fifty, being 'a standard group number'; there are fifty Argonauts, fifty Nereids, Priam the king of Troy had fifty wives, Hermes stole fifty of Apollo's cattle, Heracles slept with the fifty daughters of Thespius; Aesculapius lay with fifty amorous girls in one night — some more sceptical reporters allowed him a week for the task. In some societies, fifty is in fact a mystic number, but the choice here owes more to arithmetic and so is deliberate. It is rather like a classroom exercise — if fifty daughters decapitate fifty sons, all but one (Hypermnestra, remember, spared the life of her husband Lynceus) how many heads did they bury? The answer is of course forty-nine, being seven times seven and, like three times three, forty-nine is a number representing a powerfully symbolic concept promising boundless fertility and water.

The number seven implies the solar nature of the myth. The formula appears in other myths too, in the myth of the fifty women of Lemnos, who slaughtered all the menfolk on the island for reasons of their spouses' infidelity — all, that is, save one, when Hypsipyle spared her father Troas. Hypsipyle, who guided travellers to find water, managed to protect her father by smuggling him off the island, and in so doing provided the magic prime number.

The story of the Danaides, who brought water to arid Argos, 'the land of a thousand thirsts', reflects the concern of early populations living in a country poorly supplied with rivers and springs, where irrigation was essential; an acre of vegetation in full sunlight loses on average about 10 tons of water a day in summer.[4]

The ancient Mediterranean world would have known about, and no doubt envied, the fertility of the Nile delta, flooded by the inundation of the river every year at the height of summer, filling the irrigation channels, vital to the growth of crops.

There is a another, deeper layer to this myth. The Danaides arrived from the south-east by ship, their cousins following by the same route. Like the vessel of the Argonauts, both ships were symbols of the passage of the sun, arriving at the time of the rains in the autumn.

FIG. 22 The hand as a symbol of the sun.

The sun, both as a physical object in the sky and, in the abstract, a powerful influence on mankind, was over thousands of years gradually invested — through a process of sympathetic association — with human properties and characteristics. In the autumn and winter it was weak and old, in the spring it was compared to a child, like the infants Apollo, Hermes and Zeus who grew up in caves. It was alternately strong and virile, a celestial warrior, and vulnerable like a child or an old man. By analogy the winter sun was thought to be blind, like Samson, and shorn of its hair, or in danger of losing its head, as Esau and John the Baptist and the sons of Aegyptus lost theirs.

Such ideas, and the myths which they gradually formed, are extremely ancient and possibly originated in a common homeland in a northern climate. How far north, and exactly where, it is impossible to say, but the solar symbolism suggests a place where the sun in winter is low on the horizon, and at a time when autumn rains sweep in from a mountain range. In addition to its human attributes the sun might be imagined as an animal, like the horse or bison of the Ice Age caves, and like a stag, boar or bull. This was a useful form of metamorphosis because the animal could be sacrificed, as the animals in the caves may have been sacrificed. Perhaps man felt that he was participating in the activities of the sun, becoming involved in its influence. Sacrifice became a way of affecting solar power, to hasten the winter sun's journey to the underworld. By this it was hoped to induce the rains, to swell the rivers and encourage springs to arise. The decapitation of the forty-nine men and the burial of their heads is a means of describing how the sun 'loses its head' as it descends towards winter and the underworld, the time of sowing seeds, and promised fertility – the decapitation occurred on the wedding night, when the tauric men had sown their seed and were slaughtered, as the solar bull is sacrificed before the ploughing season. The decapitated head, regardless of whether it was human or animal, always represented the sun. And so, interring the seven-times-seven heads of Aegyptus's men of the Nile would hasten the rains and refresh the land that Poseidon had dried up. This is why the daughter Amymone is able to draw water from the spring at Lerna, as a direct result of the 'sacrifice' of their menfolk.

The myth ultimately relies on the power of numbers, on arithmetic in fact, because certain numbers were perceived as having a magical influence on the forces of nature, especially in regard to ritual. The Hittites of Asia Minor observed a rite in which they dug seven holes in the ground. These were then filled with water, wine, honey, oil, and milk. Then seven loaves of bread were put into each of the seven holes, as a means of encouraging productivity, as are all ritual buryings in pits.[5] What would this performance achieve, and how could it possibly be effective?

Here, the symbolism is both solar and phallic. If my interpretation of the number seven is correct – that it symbolises seven months of autumn and spring and the quickening of nature's womb – then the holes presumably represent the seven gestatory months of the year, when the earth has received the celestial semen, represented by the honey, oil and other liquids. The loaves of bread may be phallic, placed in the holes as analogous to copulation, but a more prosaic reason would suggest that the loaves are introduced to symbolise a good harvest.

This is a simple agricultural equation – burying votive symbols of productivity is like planting seed corn in the earth, but the burial of heads, animal or human, suggests a more potent and primitive origin. The forty-nine daughters of Danaus in fact collectively represent the great goddess Hera who, we may remember, by banishing her priestess Io, instigated the cycle of the myth, and whose cult was closely observed in Argive plain. At her

FIG. 23 Goddess of springs and rivers on an archaic Greek water vessel.

shrines in Argos, water pitchers were dedicated. It was the duty of the goddess of the earth to bring about and hasten the decline of the sun, for the rains would surely follow, and burying heads (and covering them with red ochre) was a solar ritual.

There is a postscipt to the tale of the daughters of Danaus. They were punished by Zeus for murdering their husbands, and dispatched to Hades where they pursued the endless and futile task of trying to fill a leaking pitcher with water. But the idea was actually beneficial. In Greece and elsewhere, perforated vessels were used in rainmaking rituals, and when it rained, rustic wits observed that Zeus was urinating through a sieve. A final clue remains.

The survivor of the sons of Aegyptus was Lynceus, whose name means 'keen-sighted', like the sun whose rays illuminate the darkness and from its lofty position can see from afar. Lynceus is granted a reprieve by Hypermnestra, the 'water-finder'. He is thus the solar hero who rises from the watery embrace of his spouse at the time of the winter solstice, to escape death and to quicken the life of the coming year, albeit at the expense of his brothers, who lost their heads.

Cracking the Codex

Earlier I mentioned the puzzle of the Maya's numbering system, of which certain features seem to have been recognised and shared by all the ancient world. During the nineteenth century, scholars began to investigate the strange proliferation of numbers contained in the codices – the sacred writings and picture manuscripts of the Mayas. Among them was Ernst Förstemann of the State Library in Dresden, where the manuscript now known as the Dresden Codex was kept, and which revealed a number system of astonishing complexity. 'Mathematics', wrote Förstemann, 'has rightly been called petrified music. We hear the music in this case from so great a distance that, though we perceive the full harmonic chords, we do not recognise the connecting and animating melody.'[6]

For the Maya, and for the rest of the ancient world, arithmetic held a fascination and a mystique and appeared to have powerful links with the natural world, through the progress of the seasons and the cycles of celestial bodies. In common with the clue of the forty-nine buried heads the Mayan numbers will reveal a remarkable equation. But first let us look at a celebrated number in Revelation (13.18), the 'mark of the beast' the number of man – 666.

When divided by two, the number 333 emerges which, if the digits are added together, gives us nine, one of the most venerated of symbolic numbers along with three and seven. What happens if the sixes are added together? The answer is 18, and one plus eight equals nine. Now multiply the sixes. 6×6×6 gives us 216, each number added together comes to nine. The next sum is 66 plus 6, which arrives at 72, and seven plus two equals nine. Multiply 66 by 6 and the result is 396, and these numbers add up to 18, 1+8 = 9. Multiply 3×6×9 and they arrive at 162, numbers which added together makes nine. Even when added, 396 plus 162 comes to 558, which resolves by addition into 18 (1+8 = 9). To modern mathematicians, this recurring formula is no more than a curiosity. It was familiar to the Greeks as an arithmetical formula known as 'casting out nines', and seems to have carried considerable weight in ancient societies where numbers were invested with a mystique.

The foundation text of the Hindu faith, the Rig-Veda, has 432,000 syllables, the number of stanzas 10,800; the number 108 occurs regularly in Indian tradition, and we saw earlier that there were 108 statues flanking the five gateways at Angkor. And of course they add up to nine. This number 10,800 is also the number of bricks in the Hindu fire-altar (a useful solar correlation) the Agnicayana, and the number given by the fifth-century Greek philosopher Heraclitus (On Nature 18) for the duration of Aion. The number 432,000 is also that of the Babylonian Great Year, so these ancient cultures each acknowledged the portent, primacy and potency of nine. Like six, number nine has a magic property of reproducing itself: twice nine is 18, and 8+1 = 9; three nines are 27, 2+7 = 9; four nines are 36, 3+6 = 9, and so on. It may be coincidence, but it was said of Sophocles that he coined or varied the construction of 1296 words, a number that adds up to 18, and 9.

Nowhere, it seems, was this mystique of numbers more developed than by the societies of Central America, and in particular by the Maya. Their priesthood was obsessed by numbers, which scholars have since deciphered from the codices and monumental reliefs. It may have something to do with their apparent preoccupation with ritual and order, which in turn probably developed out of fear. Their rituals were excessively cruel, with grotesque self-inflicted castigation, such as the gouging out of one's own eye with the sharpened end of a human thigh-bone, a possible product of propitiation to the water sun.

Mayan monuments were richly carved and decorative, stopping just short of florid, their art so strongly stylised with an almost unrelenting emphasis on symbolism. The pitiless, implacable Aztec and Maya priesthood, who in the service of religion sacrificed children (because their tears encouraged rain), flayed, decapitated and tore the heart 'like a raging tiger' from their victims, saw themselves as victims of the equally harsh rule of nature. They were constantly made aware of an acute dependence on rain (mention of drought looms large in their writings) and a total dependence on the maize crop.

Perhaps this is why the Maya developed two calendars – one a time-period, called a *tzolkin*, which consisted of 260 days, the other a 360-day solar year – as a way to hedge their bets on fate. The 260-day calendar, or *tonalamatl*, was purely astrological. It seems also to have been divided into quarters, relating to cardinal points of the compass, each quarter coming under the influence of one of the four rain gods, known as the Chacs.

Both calendars were based on a vigesimal, or 20-day system, giving a 20-day 'month'. The 360-day, or 'vague year', tried to dispense with the odd five days (regarded as unlucky) in the 365-day solar year. Why choose 360 days in preference to 365? By multiplication, 360 may be endlessly reduced to nine, and the 360-

day year was divided into 18 of these 20-day months, or *uinals*. This gave a *tun*, or year, of 360 days. Multiplication by 20 gave a *katun* of 7200 days; a *baktun* of 144,000 days; an *alautun* of 23,040 million days, and each will reduce to nine, if you miss out the noughts. In fact, the inclusion of the noughts, and no doubt their purpose, was to conceal what is really a simple equation. If you add the numbers together (36+72+144+234) you arrive at 486, which equals 18. Nine again. The addition or multiplication of these numbers always comes to nine. For instance, $36 \times 72 \times 144 \times 234 = 87340032$. Add these numbers and you get 27. Seven plus two is nine.

Förstemann suggested that the vigesimal system arose from the primitive method of counting the toes and the fingers. But why would a society lumber themselves with such an unsuitable method of reckoning the solar year? We can guess that they chose a shortfall year of 360 days because it reduces to the magic nine.

The obvious route to take now would be a 30-day month, which would approximate nicely to a solar year of twelve months – $12 \times 30 = 360$. Yet they choose a 20-day month of 18 months. Why? Was it because because 18 resolves to the magic nine? The Mayan priests relished the additional complexities created by computing the cycle of the planet Venus. Its passage around the sun amounted to a mean of 584 revolutions per year, a cycle that could be made to coincide with the solar year or rather, years: 5 Venus years equals 8 solar years, both amounting to cycles of 2920 days.

In their need to bring into harmony the planetary cycles, priest-astronomers worked out a period covering 37,960 days, which length of time is the equivalent of 65 Venus, 104 solar, and 146 calendar years of the 260-day cycle. Add these figures together and you get 315 which, not surprisingly, adds up to nine. This is one of the ways in which the Mayans arrived at such large figures. I suggest, however, that the numerical importance of the Venus cycle is much easier to calculate, and was probably known to the Babylonians at an earlier date. In the Fertile Crescent, the planet Venus was identified with Ishtar, and called Nin-dar-anna, 'mistress of the heavens'.[7] The appearance of Venus as the morning star for a period, and then the evening star for another period, is due to the planet's phases of invisibility, called the superior and inferior conjunctions, during Venus's circuit around the sun. This occurs when the view of Venus from earth is obscured by the sun – the superior conjunction – or when Venus is front of the sun – the inferior conjunction. At other times Venus appears in either the east or the west as the morning or the evening star. Venus's time-intervals are unfailingly regular. For 8 months and 5 days she shines in the east before disappearing for 3 months. Venus then reappears in the west, again for 8 months and five days. She then disappears again, this time for 7 days before reappearing in the east. The correct Venus period amounts to a total of 19 months and 17 days.

What occurs when we add these two numbers? The answer is 36, which leads to nine. 19 months and 17 days comes to a total of 549 days, which of course gives 18, and nine. Förstemann noted in the Dresden Codex the frequent appearance of a special number, 10404. It has the property of yielding nine through almost endless computations. $14040 \times 5 = 70200$; $14040 \times 11 = 154440$; $14040 \times 37 = 519480$. The Codex also showed certain numbers nestling in the coils of serpents, invariably a symbol of water.

The most important of all the numbers featured in the Mayas' mythology was the great figure of 1,366,560. It is, of course, a 'nine' number. Adding the numbers together produces 27, or taking them in pairs, $13+66+56 = 135 = 9$. Multiply the individual numbers and they arrive at 3240. The most awesome combination occurs when you multiply groups from the prime number 1,366,560: $1 \times 3 = 3$. $3 \times 6 = 18$ (9); $18 \times 6 = 108$ (9); $108 \times 5 = 540$ (9); $540 \times 6 = 3240$ (9). Or multiply 1×3, $3 \times 3 = 9$, $9 \times 6 = 54$ (9), $54 \times 6 = 324$ (9), $324 \times 5 = 1620$ (9), $1620 \times 6 = 9720 = 18 = 9$. But the 1,366,560 is also a product of several symbolic numbers: $260 \times 9 \times 584$ (the Venus cycle), or $584 \times 9 \times 13 \times 20$. It can be made to agree with the harmony of the Venus, solar and tonalamatl cycles, for 1,366,560 is divisible by 584, 365 and 260, and by the combined cycles, mentioned above (p.109), 37960, 36 times – a 'nine' number. In fact, this most prestigious number in Mayan chronology is really a date, which Förstemann has identified in the Dresden Codex with the day of the summer solstice in Central America.[8] At this time of the year, the four Chacs of the sacred calendar would hasten the hoped-for thunderstorms and the rains which would replenish the cenotes around the centre of Chichen Itza in Yucatan.

The point is, of course, that all this is fundamentally solar, because the numerical structure is supported by the foundation of three, the square root of nine, and underlines the immense importance of solar symbols in prehistoric thought and behaviour. The vital role of the sun in the lives of the Central and South American cultures, the Mayas, Toltecs, Aztecs and Incas, was intimately related to water, combined in their symbol of the 'water sun', and the personification of water from the skies in the resplendent figure of Quetzalcoatl, the feathered serpent. This preoccupation with celestial mathematics was as much as feature of prophecy and augury as were the oracular centres of classical Greece. The numbers system found its way into the calendar customs of the Roman Church, where in July, the seventh month, the Church commemorates the seven martyred brothers – the *Septem Fratres Martyres*. The martyred Saint Symphorosa and her seven martyred sons are commemorated on the 18th of July – and note that the 18 reduces to 9. There are the Seven Martyrs of Samosata on 9th December, and the seven virgin Martyrs of Ancyra on 18th May (9 again), not to mention the Seven Sleepers of Ephesus, 'walled up in a cave' and commemorated on 27th July (9); in the Koran the seven sleepers sleep with their eyes open for 309 years. They meet their martyrdom in different ways: one is flogged to death with whips, two with clubs, one is thrown over a precipice, and three are beheaded, like the sons of Aegyptus.

Although the myth of the Danaides who behead their husbands stems originally from the attentions of Zeus towards a priestess of Hera, it also contains the story of the conflict between the brothers Aegyptus and Danaus. In one sense, Aegyptus and his sons represent the masculine side of the family, while Danaus and his daughters are the feminine side. The bitter hostility between twins prompted the first murder, when Cain killed Abel because, according to Genesis, God preferred Abel's offering to that of Cain. Abel thus became the object of sibling rivalry, as was the case of Jacob and Esau, who were rivalrous while still in the womb. Jacob, 'the usurper, the deceiver', took hold of Esau's vulnerable heel and lamed him, as he himself was to be lamed by wrestling with the angel at Peniel.

In the myth of the Roman twins, Romulus and Remus, hostility was aroused over the division of land, and Romulus slew Remus on a ploughed furrow. The twin sons of Oedipus, Eteocles and Polynices, killed each other in a dispute regarding the right to the throne of Thebes, a city founded and built by another pair, Amphion and Zethus. In the myth of the Danaides, the theme of hostility passes to the children.

Sometimes this hostility is displaced. When the Spartan twins Castor and Polydeuces (Latin, Pollux) – the Dioscuri – engage in a fight with the rival twins Idas and Lynceus, Castor is killed, and Idas and Lynceus also perish. Polydeuces persuades Zeus to allow Castor to share his immortality, living half the year in the underworld, half in Olympus.

Sets of twins are an important feature in mythological social structures, and there are worldwide examples: Romulus and Remus, Eteocles and Polynices, Krishna and Balarama, Agni and Indra, Amphion and Zethus, Osiris and Set, Shu and Tefnut, Hengist and Horsa, James and John, Jesus and Thomas 'Didymus', whose name means 'twin'; Balder and Hodr, Yama and Yima, the Hindu Asvins, Florus and Larus, Neleus and Pelias, Quetzal-coatl (Aztec god of twins) his brother and enemy Huitzilopochtli, and many more.

In a study of twins the American folklorist Donald Ward notes: 'The worship of Divine Twins is a universal phenomenon, and the religious concepts, the functions, and the mythological themes associated with such pairs reveal a remarkable similarity through-out the world.'[9]

The meaning (or rather, the failure to find a meaning) for the Divine or Heavenly Twins provoked the Oxford classics scholar and author Lewis Farnell to declare that the cult presents 'more perplexing problems than perhaps any other chapter of Greek religion';[10] it was a subject which the Cambridge scholar Rendel Harris seems to have spent much of his life studying.[11] Harris's contemporary and friend, A. B. Cook, also at Cambridge chose to pass the buck, saying that he was not the right man for the job, especially since Rendel Harris had 'made the subject peculiarly his own'.[12]

Superstitions regarding the birth of twins may become confused with the myths and legends. Some tribes look upon twins with fear, and establish taboos by which the children and their mother are either banished or killed. The superstition that twins are the result of two fathers has certainly led to the idea that mythological twins had dual parentage – usually one is a god, the other a mortal, hence the parentage of the Dioscuri, 'Zeus's boys', is shared between Zeus and Tyndareus.

It is easy to suppose that the birth of twins could symbolise fertility, and that this may be the simple reason for their importance in mythology. In Botswana the bodies of stillborn twins were especially efficacious in rainmaking. The Zulu, Tswana and Kalanga used to kill one of a pair of twins, since their fertile powers were regarded as unstable, and were thought to provoke an excess of rain or drought.[13] This is a persistent association, and Rendel Harris notes how the mother of twins would be ritually drenched with water.[14]

Fertility, though, fails to explain some strange notions about twins in mythology. Castor and Polydeuces were famously born of an egg, when their mother Leda was approached and trod by Zeus in the form of a swan. The twins were not the only offspring of this bizarre union, for they had twin sisters, Helen and Clytemnestra, and several traditions claim a triad where twins are featured with a sister.

The Hindu Asvins, twin horsemen, have Usas, the dawn, or Surya the sun goddess, who mounts a chariot with the twins and orbits the heavens. Similarly, the Dioscuri, also twin horsemen, have such strong equine attributes that they are almost centaurs, and lead Helen home in a horse-drawn chariot. Yet again the horse appears as a meaningful symbol. Castor is a tamer of horses, and the horse theme is unmistakable in the names of the Saxon twins Hengist ('stallion') and Horsa ('horse', or perhaps 'mare') who arrive in tenth-century Britain in three ships.[15]

To their close connection with horses can be added a remarkable list of attributes and functions. The Dioscuri drive chariots, are builders, stonemasons, carpenters, and they manufacture ploughs. They also make balances, or scales – a curious pastime for a pair of warriors, yet no more curious, perhaps, than their association with childbirth, and the midwife goddess Kalligeneia. The Dioscuri climb trees, often in the company of their sister Helen, and their token plant is fennel or silphium. Their functions are to save from darkness, restore youth and vitality, protect in battle, act as physicians, to be patrons of the bridal chamber, to promote male fertility, and to protect travellers by land and by sea.

The Twins are associated with stars, oak trees, woodpeckers, the trident, double axe, honey and bees, and they spread dew around every morning. They are river gods, sea gods, rainmakers, sons of thunder and lightning, and sons of the temple threshold. They preside over disputes in law, and are avengers of perjury.[16]

Throughout their adventures they are never separated, and this is so firmly stressed that their sign in Sparta, where they were held in particular reverence, was two wooden uprights joined by a crossbeam – the *dokana*. The Asvins were also called *nasataya*, from the Sanskrit root *nes*, which means 'to unite' or 'bring together'.

Lewis Farnell listed a number of attempts by modern scholars to interpret the meaning of the Twins, suggesting that they were 'Sun and Moon, Day and Night, Morning and Evening Stars, the Constellation Gemini, celestial swan-men crossed with a strain of horses, and finally as personifications of the male sexual organs'.[17] Farnell was fairly contemptuous of this idea, yet it offers presentable evidence. According to the Rig-Veda, the Asvin twins are 'praised for placing the germ in all female creatures'. They can give virile strength to an aged man, and even give a child to the wife of a eunuch, and as we saw above, they are patrons of the bridal chamber.

The names of the Dioscuri, Castor and Polydeuces, might yield some clues. Castor means 'beaver' and is derived from the Greek *kastor*, and ultimately from the Sanskrit *kasturi* ('musk'), on account of the two pear-shaped anal glands from which was obtained the extract castoreum. This has inspired French etymologists to declare that, since castoreum was used for 'maladies of the womb' and the Dioscuri were protectors of women, the derivation was valid.[18] The name of Castor's twin, Polydeuces, must be taken into account. It means, says Robert Graves, 'much sweet wine',[19] but is derived from the Sanskrit *phal* and *phala* (both meaning 'fruit', and 'fruit-bearing'), which is cognate with *phal*, ('to swell' or 'ripen'), *phulla* ('testicles', and *bhal* ('strong'), a word which gave the name to Krishna's twin Balarama.

The idea of fruit, swelling, and strong, coupled with Castor's association with the musk glands might lend additional weight to the twins as symbols of the male testicles, as previously suggested. A scrap of European folklore says that beavers outwit their pursuers by tearing off their own testicles.[20] It is an intriguing theory, but Castor's name does indeed mean 'beaver', and is due to the fact that beavers are builders. They build lodges, and rafts, and dam streams. Beavers are aquatic, and can create large areas of watermeadow, swamp and lake, so their principal association is with water, and the seasons of the year. Perhaps there is a further association with Castor, or Kastor, in the Sanskrit word *kas*, meaning 'to shine'.

Polydeuces' apparent connection with fruit comes from the ripening effects of the sun at the end of summer, before the arrival of the rains, and probably explains why the Dioscuri and their sister are sometimes found sitting in trees, or within a hollow oak, because above all the oak is the tree of rain and storms. Castor is the tree of winter and springtime, Polydeuces the tree of summer and autumn, functions also found in the Mithraic torchbearers, Cautes and Cautopates. This is why the Dioscuri share their year above and below ground, and it is but a small step now to see that the symbolism of twins is solar – they are the two 'halves' of the sun's year, they are the sun in all its functions, while the 'sister' represents the third of the essential solar triad, but in essence she is the goddess of spring waters.

This contribution to mythology is part of the legend where the weak sun of winter gives way to his rival twin, the strong, white, youthful sun of spring – *bhal*, the strong, Balarama the 'white' versus his dark brother, Krishna, whose name means 'blue-black' and who dies after being shot in the foot by an arrow. In this myth, however, Krishna and Balarama die more or less at the same time, Balarama spewing the great snake Sesha from his mouth, the snake that represents water, the natural result of the decline of the sun. This is why Leda, 'dusky' Leda[21], the mother of the twins, couples with a white bird, Zeus as the sun in the shape of a swan. It has its distant parallels in the birth of Krishna and Balarama from the black and white hairs of Vishnu.[22] The division into the black and white halves of the sun is symbolised by the Chinese Yin/Yang, and the Black Virgins of the Roman Church whose association with trees tells of their time of the year, of the fruiting apple and oak. This blackness refers to winter, when certain goddesses, such as Demeter and Aphrodite bear the epithet 'black', when Cinderella sits among the ashes.

The theme of the rival twins is the theme of succession. The brothers often argue about the right to the throne, as the sons of Oedipus fought over the right to rule Thebes, the city of seven gates, the city of the sun and abundant springs, the springs of Oidipodia and Agianni which Cadmus created by stamping on the ground with his foot. The half-brothers Aeson and Pelias squabbled over an inheritance that was to lead to the saga of Jason and the Argonauts. The softening of the rivalry between Castor and his brother is perhaps why Polydeuces is simply 'a boxer' with a scarred face, and because he is the 'striker', or the 'pounder', like the smith with his hammer.

Within the theme of succession is concealed yet another meaning. One twin is always the weaker of the two, just as one is mortal, the other immortal. Sometimes the twins are described as one being red and hairy, the other smooth and white, the latter having feminine characteristics. Their rivalry often ends in death, as when Cain murdered Abel, and Romulus killed his twin Remus while laying the foundations of Rome. It is fair to mention that the identity of Cain and Abel as twin aspects of the sun had been perceived long ago by the surveyor and archaeologist Claud Conder, who decided that Abel represented the dawn. In the death of Remus we may find a clue. He was killed 'in a ploughed furrow' which indicates the time of the year as autumn, when the ground has been softened by the rains. I am guessing that this was when the Danaides slew their menfolk, for of the twins the feminine one is always the victor, the more powerful, the survivor. He is acting in the interests of the goddess of the earth, of springs and rivers, to bring about the decline and 'death' of the sun in autumn. This is why the names of Polydeuces and Balarama mean 'fruitful' or 'fruit-bearing' for they represent the fruits of autumn when the rains refresh the earth and impregnate the earth goddess.

So the Twins are builders, carpenters and ploughmen because these are the ancient trades so closely associated with fecundity, like the potter-gods and smiths, and the powers of sun and rain. The Dioscuri, who preside over the bridal chamber, 'make people' and restore lapsed sexual functions, but their true purpose was to increase prosperity of the land through the agency of fire and water, and this is why they were revered in Sparta, the most fertile plain in the Peloponnese and the entire Greek archipelago.

We know why they make ploughs, but why balances or scales? Rendel Harris declared that this must be a misprint, but there was no mistake – they make scales or balances simply because the balance has twin weighing bowls, joined by a balancing beam; several engravings from Etruria show the Twins joined at the head by a sort of pediment, emphasising their permanent union, for they are the two contrasting aspects of the same element – the sun. Their habit of wearing a star on their heads is relatively late, and comes no doubt from the development of astronomy, and in the recognition of the constellation Gemini.

Their other most frequent symbol was a pair of amphoras in the coils of two snakes, a clear indication that water was as fundamental to their identities and purpose as its opposite, fire. The twins combine these elements in their own particular way, as the heads of the sons of Aegyptus, and the water-vessels of the daughters of Danaus, represented the essential combination of sun and rain. They were the combined essence of fertility. Because the sun was all-seeing, and therefore all-knowing, the sun-god was a judge and presided over disputes in law, and so the Dioscuri punish perjurers, and turn their enemies blind, just as they help the blind to see, and the lame to walk. In assisting the lame, the Twins would surely be in much demand, because lameness was a curse suffered by not a few gods and heroes. The vulnerable heel of Achilles, the swollen feet of Oedipus, the twisted limbs of Hephaestus are among the most puzzling features of mythology. Yet the hobbling gods performed a vital and reassuring role in the ancient world.

CHAPTER 9

Crippled Gods

There are several folktales in which a hero, or a bird sent by a hero, seeks the waters of life, and in doing so often spills some water. The bird loses a tail-feather, the hero suffers a wound in the foot, or is mortally wounded. Symbolism is by nature theatrical, using a device to draw attention to something while at the same time disguising it – revealing yet concealing, playing a role, wearing a mask.

Sacred lameness in heaven, or on earth, carries a message. So it was with Hephaestus, who suffered broken legs on being thrown from heaven by his mother Hera, the wife of Zeus. Some say he fell into the sea, others that he fell on the volcanic island of Lemnos. The lameness of Hephaestus guides us towards a hidden aspect of his character, and of some importance in the understanding of mythology.

One interpretation, from the French writer Marie Delcourt, is that it represented the ritual wounding of the initiate to the magic arts,[1] for the smith-gods were magicians, Hephaestus was a goldsmith, an artisan who reputedly worked his forge, first on the volcanic isle of Lemnos, later under Mount Etna. This initiation would explain why the Cretan engineer Daedalus, who built the labyrinth and fashioned the wings which he and his son Icarus wore to escape the wrath of Minos, suffered the ritual wounding of having his tendons cut, as Zeus had his sinews snatched away during his terrible fight with the monster Typhon. The smith Vulcan, the Roman version of Hephaestus, was also said to be lame, and flaunted his lameness by wearing golden shoes.[2] The Scandinavian smith Wieland was lame, so was the Hindu god Varuna. The Chinese smith-god, 'The Great Yu', regularly performed a ritual dance on one leg.

Another theory claimed that the tale was a simple one of cause and effect. The archaeologist and mythologist Nils Martin Nilsson thought it was a tale of little importance, brought about by cause and result. 'Stunted limbs or severed tendons distinguish the smiths of mythology, and even today smiths still tend to acquire strong arms but weak legs by constantly standing hammering at the anvil. Men choose the trade for which they are fitted, and therefore under primitive conditions blind men become minstrels and lame men smiths. Accordingly, their god too is lame, and it is this fact which the myth seeks to explain.'[3]

These might be plausible explanations, if the deformity were peculiar to divine smiths, and it is not. Other limping figures, ignorant of the workings of the forge, or of magic arts, hobble across the stage of mythology: Acrisius, Orestes, Talos, Dionysus, and especially Oedipus, whose name means 'swollen foot' and upon whose shoulders the entire burden of psychoanalysis rests. And what about Achilles of the vulnerable heel, Bellerophon, Anchises, Mopsus the seer, the Centaurs Chiron and Pholus, and many more?

Interpretations inspired by psychoanalysis are less concerned with the phenomenon of deformity, concentrating on the sexual element. They include the suggestion that Hephaestus, when faced with the oedipal conflict with his father, chose to remain in the body of his mother, that is, in the symbolic earth-womb of his smithy, where he triumphs as the phallus-in-residence, with his assistants performing the function of a group of personified phalli.[4]

The theme was elaborated by the American sociologist Paul Friederich, in his book *The Meaning of Aphrodite*, where the smithy is the core of a powerful male symbolism 'that only the most inhibited imagination could deny; his bellows as testicles, his hammer as a phallus, the gold he works as semen, and the fire of his great forge as the lust of sex'.[5]

Clearly, the edge of Friederich's imagination is not dulled by inhibitions, and we might accept this description as having some substance were there smith-gods who could not have been prey to oedipal conflicts, since they were each born from an egg, good examples being the Chinese artisan Pan-Ku, and the Egyptian god Ptah, and in some versions Hephaestus himself, who was said to have been the issue of a virgin birth. No paternal conflict there. Nor was Hephaestus driven by the lust of sex, as Friederich suggests, with testicles like fire-bellows; he failed in his pursuit of Athena, and as the husband of Aphrodite was cuckolded by Ares.

The affliction of lameness spread beyond the Greek world. In

Hindu myth, Krishna was mortally wounded in the heel by an arrow from Jara the Hunter[6] – he had already survived a bite to his heel from the serpent Kaliya. The Celtic Bran was wounded in the foot by a poisoned spear.[7] The Egyptian Harpocrates, as the Greeks called the child of Isis who later became Horus, was stung on the heel by his uncle, Set, who had taken the form of a scorpion; and it was Isis who sent a snake to bite the heel of Ra. A scorpion, on behalf of Artemis, stung the heel of the giant Orion. A version of the death of Osiris has the god Set as a flea. It crept into the sandal of Osiris and fatally bit his heel.[8] In Christian legend the Devil, cast like Hephaestus from Heaven, limps his way to hell.

One clue that emerges from this list of sufferers is that they are all male. There are no limping goddesses, except in folklore where Cinderella loses her slipper, because women are usually the instigators of the deformity, as Hera crippled Hephaestus, as Isis lamed Ra, as Medea bled Talos and the Prioress bled Robin Hood, and Thetis, mother of Achilles, created his one vulnerable spot, and Aphrodite lamed Anchises.

Talos and Hephaestus have much in common. The death of Talos by the hand of Medea, or by an arrow, are two of several versions. Talos, the bull-headed guardian of Crete, was said to have been thrown from a height by Daedalus, but was transformed into a partridge by Athene or Aphrodite before he hit the ground. Why a partridge? The association may seem tenuous, but its purpose is to emphasise the condition of lameness, to draw attention to it.

Partridges, especially the chukar (*Alectoris chukar*), whose habitat includes Greece and Crete, perform aggressive and self-assertive sexual dance displays during courtship, accompanied by goose-stepping movements. The male chukar adopts a distraction-display when threatened, and feigns lameness, hobbling along the ground, pathetically fluttering and trailing one wing.[9] And so Talos is sometimes called Perdix, 'Partridge', which would confuse those of us who have read that he was a bronze bull, or a version of the Cretan Zeus or, more frequently, that his name means 'the sun'. There is good evidence to show that these mythological figures were created solely to express this deformity, even perhaps, in some strange way, to celebrate it.

Bellerophon, the equestrian hero who with Athena's help tamed Pegasus and rode forth to vanquish the monster Chimaera,

1. The 'Clootie' or ragwell at Munlochry on the Black Isle, Ross and Cromarty, Scotland. The practice of dressing trees and wells is very ancient. Trees were sacred to the goddess of springs and rivers, the strips of cloth symbols of feminine attire.

2. *Top left*: Stonehenge at sunset.
3. *Below left*: Silbury Hill near Avebury, Wiltshire, surrounded by water from nearby springs.
4. *Above*: Callanish, 'the Stonehenge of the North' on the Isle of Lewis in the Outer Hebrides.
5. *Left*: Calderstones at Allerton, Liverpool protected from weathering by a conservatory structure. The stones may represent 'male' and 'female' stones in a stone circle.
6. *Below*: Spinster's Rock, a dolmen near Dartmoor. Structures of this sort (found as far east as India) are usually erected near a water source.

7. The Persian goddess Anahita, who may
have become fused with the god Mithra,
later the Roman Mithras, an androgyne.
(British Museum.)

8. An important symbol in the long
development of religion, the lion-bull
combat (here a lion attacking a fawn)
probably originated in Asia Minor, and
led to the concept of Mithras slaying the
bull (opposite). A Greek bronze from
the George Ortiz Collection, Geneva.

9-10. *Above*: The Greek goddess Nike, a version of Athena, slaying a bull. The combined image of Anahita, Athena and Nike could have inspired that of Mithras (*below*). His flying cloak developed from Nike's wings.(British Museum.)

11. *Above*: Painted
terracotta Gorgon's
head. (British Museum.)

12. *Right*: Pagan-
inspired rites are still
celebrated by Druids
at Stonehenge during
the summer solstice.

13. *Above*: A painted terracotta mask from the Sanctuary of Artemis, Orthia, Sparta. The bearded mask was probably worn by priestesses of Artemis while performing a rain dance.

14 and 15. The Priory gatehouse and Nun Brook at Kirklees, near Brighouse, Yorkshire. According to legend, from the gatehouse window Robin Hood shot an arrow to mark his grave.

was thrown to earth by Zeus and lamed in the fall. Attempting to reach Olympus on his winged steed, he had set his sights too high, both socially and celestially.

Mopsus, the seer and prophet of the Argonauts, was bitten on the heel by a snake, while Jason their leader displays a token lameness by losing his sandal. Chiron the Centaur was wounded by Achilles, who was in turn struck on the heel by an arrow shot by the Trojan Paris. The name Paris is said to come from the Greek *piros*, meaning 'wallet',[10] but it could derive from *peros*, 'lame'. Why should a hero, a prince of the royal household, be called 'wallet' or 'bag'? Is it because a wallet implies a receptacle such as the womb? Paris has certain feminine traits.

Homer, in the *Iliad*, describes how Menelaus seized Paris's helmet by its 'much embroidered strap', and 'strangled his soft neck'. 'What are you doing on the battlefield?' demands Menelaus. 'Get back to the boudoir!' And so Paris retires from the field 'as if returning from a dance'.[11]

Variety was added to the theme of lameness in that it was not strictly necessary to be struck on the heel – the thigh would do, or the leg below the knee. Odysseus, described as red-haired, with a large torso but short legs, was wounded in the thigh (by a boar), and Telephus, as we saw, received a wound to his leg which eventually festered, while Adonis was gored in the thigh, also by a boar, and Philoctetes bitten on the leg by a water snake, or in another version by an arrow dipped in the poison of the Lernean Hydra.

For an explanation of the curious symbolism of the lame god we should look first to Hephaestus, a craftsman, a goldsmith and worker of fine jewellery, who spent the first nine years of his life in an underwater grotto. He was cared for by the Nereid Thetis, mother of Achilles, who rendered vulnerable her own son's heel. There Hephaestus worked his forge, and was widely regarded by the Greeks as a fire god, a status he shared with the Mesopotamian Gibil, the Hindu Agni, and the Cretan figure of Talos 'the sun' who, by the way, was also a craftsman. Talos is said to have invented the potter's wheel and the saw.

Just as the potter's wheel is a craftsman's tool, so the saw is the tool of the carpenter, who uses wood as the potter uses clay, as the 'carpenter of the insides' forms mankind. The carpenter, the potter and the smith who works his forge are metaphors, for the 'carpenter of the insides' was an epithet of the Mesopotamian goddess of childbirth, Ninhursag, and refers to the womb, to gestation and birth. As the potter uses clay, so mankind was thought to have been created from clay. The connection with this and the idea of prosperity is found in a Sanskrit word for carpenter, *vardhaka*, and prosperity, *vardha*, from the root VRS, 'to rain'. Another Sanskrit word for carpenter, '*tvashtri*', is also the name of the first-born god, Tvashtri, the creator of all living things. Was not Jesus a carpenter's apprentice? Yet Talos, said the Cretans, could also make himself red-hot, and clasped those who had incurred his displeasure in his arms, burning them to death in a deadly embrace, as did the Carthaginian god Moloch.[12]

There is little credibility in this story. Talos was a creator and protector, not a destroyer, and his qualities of fire are misleading – it was never destructive. The lame god or hero, thrown from heaven or struck on his heel by an arrow, or a snake, is the possessor of the foot with a special significance. Indra grabs his father by the foot and crushes him; Kumarbi catches hold of his father's feet before biting off his genitals. The suggestion was made long ago that lameness has solar origins, and represents the sun's decline towards winter, symbolised by the story of Samson, shorn of his locks and then blinded.

The interpretation is probably accurate, yet it has not been adequately explored, nor the wider implications realised, for it is intimately connected with water. The lame sun that limps towards the winter solstice confirms its deformity by the Sanskrit root PA, which gives *pada*, 'foot'; *padma*, 'lame'; *pani*, 'water'; but also *pur*, 'to burn'; from another set of 'burn' words comes *cudh*, 'burn'; *cush*, 'to dry up'; and *cuth*, 'to limp'.

The foot is a source of water; a spring burst forth from under the foot of the 'wild ass-man' Ishmael, from the footprint of Cadmus, from the hoof of Pegasus. A spring rose when Job stamped his heel on the ground.[13] A Roman legend tells of Bacchus dying of thirst in the Libyan desert, and appealing to Jupiter for help. He sent a ram which scratched with its foot on the hard, cracked soil, and a spring obligingly appeared. The ram is the sun, like the ram with the Golden Fleece, and votive models of rams in terracotta, mentioned previously, were made with only three legs and betray their solar identity. Surely there can be no clearer indication that 'three' is a number of the sun?

The ram who strikes a spring from the ground may be compared to the horse Pegasus, who created the Hippocrene spring by striking Mount Helicon with his hoof. Both animals represent the sun, which touches down and was thought to enter the earth during the winter when the rains arrive, and springs burst forth from the hillsides. In the previous chapter I suggested that man had gradually, over a long period of time, invested the sun with human attributes, strengths and weaknesses. The sun in winter was shorn of its hair, or blinded, or made lame. Some sense can now be made of the lame gods and heroes. Hephaestus is lame because lameness symbolises the sun's creative role following its winter journey. Having delivered the fructifying rains, his task is to warm the barren earth with the fires of gestation. Hephaestus is solar and works with fire and gold in the womb or labyrinth of the earth. This is why the Roman Vulcan wears golden shoes, because he follows in the footsteps of the sun.

In the earliest Egyptian creation legends the first appearance of the sun arises from a lotus flower, and with it the eight primitive water deities, frog-headed and serpent-headed. Horus, the son of Isis and Osiris, who took the form of a falcon because he was the all-seeing, keen-eyed sun, emerged from a lotus, as did the Vedic Prajapati, the Creator. The Sanskrit word for the lotus is *padma*, related to *pad* and *pada*, meaning 'foot' (Greek *pous*), from the root PA, 'to drink', giving *pani*, 'water'.

The sacred footprints of Buddha as the sun yielded lotus flowers wherever he walked. The foot, having five toes, gives the Sanskrit word *panca*, 'five' (and *pane*, 'hand'). The symbolism comes from the idea of the sun's footprints, and wherever the sun treads, plants grow, and springs of water appear. The sole of Buddha's foot, a sacred symbol, bears a sun motif along with seven swastikas. The white, many-petalled lotus floating on the dark waters was likened to the sun because the flower 'treads' the water and, more pertinently, the lotus flower blossomed in response to the sun's warmth. From the same root PA comes *pur*, 'to burn', one of the many solar words in Sanskrit. Sacred footprints are a feature of shrines and temples – the sandal of Perseus in Egypt; the footprints of Vishnu and Buddha in India and the East; Abraham's footprints in Mecca; the footprint of Christ at Aska, and on the summit of Olivet; Adam's footprint in the Haram mosque at Hebron.

The lameness of Hephaestus and all smith-gods symbolises that most fertile period of the year, when the sun is in its decline and hobbles through autumn, and the rains sweep in from the west to soften the hard earth for ploughing and sowing. In Greece, this period brings deep, low-pressure fronts and very stormy weather. The lame smith-god is the solar bull, or the ram during tupping time, the period of sexual activity among most horned animals, when he spills his seed on the earth, which he later quickens with fire. His seed is also the water that forms the clay with which he sculpts mankind. Remember that Hephaestus spent the first nine years of his life underwater.

The role of the smith gods originated in a primitive world where it was thought that the winter sun entered the earth and with its heat created life. This idea may seem decidedly incompatible with the fact that, in lands bordering the Mediterranean, and in the Near East, the sun stands high in the sky for most of the year. Yet the myths tell of the sun's period in the underworld, before being reborn at the winter solstice, a discrepancy which suggests that the myths were born in another time and another place and in a cold climate. The sun was the great limping workman whose helpers numbered seven and whose domain was deep in the caves, the tunnels and chambers of the earth, which the sun warmed and brought to life. This is why the cave was the sacred nucleus of so many cults and religions.

The creator god who drags his foot represents the sun in autumn, the limping orb of heaven that heralded the approaching winter. This may explain why Hephaestus, Talos, Bellerophon, and other sun gods were thrown from above, for the fall stands for the decline of the sun and the fall of the year. It is why Icarus, son of the engineer Daedalus who constructed waxen wings for their flight from Crete, plunged to his death when he flew too close to the sun. It is also why Harpocrates and Orion were stung by scorpions, because Scorpio rules the stormy autumn sky when the constellation Orion is most prominent in the south, and from the left foot of Orion springs the great celestial river Eridanus. It is why Jason the Argonaut loses his sandal fording a river, acting the role of the sun that limps through water during the rainy season, and why Philoctetes was bitten by a water snake, and Anchises lamed by a thunderbolt.

When Hera, the mother of Hephaestus, threw him from heaven into the sea, she had a good reason, because her main function was as a goddess of springs. At Argos and Samos, water played an important role in the ceremonies, when water jars or hydria were dedicated to the goddess. Excavations of a dump near the temple of Hera recovered 900 miniature hydrias from the seventh and sixth centuries BC.[14]

The goddess's task is to engineer the wounding or demise of the sun, or its representative in myth – the solar hero, be it Talos, Hephaestus or Icarus. In anticipation of the rains, the wound to the heel is accompanied by the symbolic spilling of water or other liquids. When the Sumerian shepherd D'uzu (the Babylonian Tammuz) is set upon by the seven gallu demons, sent by Inanna (Ishtar), his 'seven milk churns are spilled'.[15] When Odysseus reveals the scar on his thigh, caused by a boar, his foot accidentally knocks over a bowl of water.[16] When Talos dies, his vital fluid, his ichor, trickles out from his heel. In ancient Mexico, the god of the winter sun, Tezcatlipoca, reputedly lost a foot, or had one leg terminating in a snake,[17] a useful way of combining a solar symbol with one (the snake) representing water.

The death of the solar hero is often preceded by a period of wandering, because the sun was said to be a wanderer. Anchises, the Trojan prince who had been lamed by Zeus for boasting of his affair with Aphrodite, wanders a while before he reaches the port of Drepanon where he dies. Oedipus, now blind because he is the winter sun, and of course permanently lame, wanders with his daughter Antigone, whose name may mean 'in place of a mother'.

The story of Oedipus has always fascinated scholars – historians, mythologists, psychologists alike – due in part to its suggestive content of incest, parricide, suicide and such rich symbolism as the riddle of the Theban Sphinx. The Hungarian anthropologist Geza Roheim, in *The Riddle of the Sphinx*[18] (1934) attempted to interpret the myth through the study and analysis of dreams, in particular those of Australian aborigines (Roheim was also a Freudian analyst). It was of course Sigmund Freud who established the Oedipus myth as a foundation of our modern preoccupation with the self, with the mechanics of repression and the liberation of the psyche. In his book *Greek Fire* (1989), the Oxford classics scholar Oliver Taplin writes of the inexhaustible multivalence of Greek myth, and especially our fascination with the Oedipus story in this century, when it has been 'perhaps the most studied and alluded to of all Greek myths'. Ever since Freud, says Taplin, 'Greek myth has held a privileged place in psychology.' Freud saw in myths, and the legend of Oedipus in particular, a clue to our own psychic history.[19]

The idea that a growing child might nourish in his unconscious

mind the desire to get rid of his father, his chief rival for the
affections of his mother, perhaps eventually to possess her in a
sexual sense, this was the 'Oedipus complex'. It became the matrix
of psychoanalysis, which aimed to resolve all those problems of
guilt, repression and despair attendant to the desire, problems
endured by the lone figure of Oedipus Rex, the scapegoat for the
Greek psyche.

In *Oedipus the King*, Sophocles drew upon and dramatised an
original myth. In our age it seems to epitomise the search for the
self, especially to Carl Jung who saw in the tale the dark forces of
oppressive archetypes, which we have inherited and from which
we must free ourselves.

Why has the myth been so influential? Perhaps because it has
enabled us to indulge in our obsession with the motives of human
behaviour, although in its original form the story of Oedipus had
little to do with infantile sexuality as perceived by Freud, but it did
have the richly dramatic elements of murder, incest and mutilation.

Oedipus's father Laius was king of Thebes in Boeotia, his
mother Iocasta. Laius had been warned by the Delphic Oracle that
his son would kill him if he did not take steps to protect himself, a
common theme in the myths of royal succession. Laius cannot
quite bring himself to murder Oedipus, but instead exposes the
child, when he is only three days old, in Hera's meadow on
Mount Cithaeron, with an iron spike driven through his ankles[20]
(the names of both Laius and his father Labdacus have the
meaning of 'lame'[21]), much in the same way as Christ suffered a
nail through the feet at the Crucifixion. Hera's name has cropped
up once again, and we can guess that it was in her interests that
Oedipus was crippled, as she had crippled her son Hephaestus.

Oedipus was found by a shepherd in the service of King Polybus
of Corinth, another common theme whereby the sun-child is
nourished by animals, which the shepherd here represents. Grown
to manhood, Oedipus travels to his family home in Thebes and en
route accidentally bumps into his father, whom he fails to
recognise, at a place where 'three roads meet' – the road from
Daulis, the road from Delphi, and the road from Thebes. The spot
was known as the 'Cleft Way',[22] the cleft in the earth being where
the dying sun descends. They quarrel, and sure enough Laius is
dragged to his death, his foot caught in a reign from his own
chariot.

There follows the famous confrontation between Oedipus and the Theban Sphinx, who had brought drought to Thebes and dried up the city's many springs. Here is another example of a myth featuring a drought. The Sphinx is a version of Medusa, and poses a tripartite riddle: 'There walks on land a creature of two feet, of four feet, and of three; it has one voice, but sole among animals that grow on land or in the sea, it can change its nature; nay, when it walks propped up on most feet, then is the speed of its limbs less than it has ever been before.' The Sphinx has threatened to kill anyone who fails to solve her riddle. Oedipus answers: 'Man, who in infancy crawls on hands and knees, walks with two feet as an adult, but supports himself on a stick in old age.'

Outwitted, the enraged Sphinx flings herself over a precipice, and is dashed to death on the rocks below. One writer, the American psychologist Richard Caldwell,[23] complained that this was a curious and unlikely way for a winged creature to kill itself, but of course the leonine Sphinx was an aspect of the sun. She was a drought-demon, 'The Throttler' or 'Tight-Binder', which really means withholding or binding the needs of life – rain and fertility. The death of this creature with the body of a lion is comparable to that of the lion-faced Gorgon, and the leonine Chimaera; the agents of their demise – Oedipus, Perseus and Bellerophon – all share the same function. The city of Thebes, normally well-provided with several springs, was menaced by drought.

There are several versions of the Oedipus myth, principally from the works of Sophocles and Euripides. The incest theme, which inspired and was eventually to mislead Freud, is a later development, where Oedipus marries his mother Iocasta and on learning of her identity, blinds himself with a pin from her garment. This is certainly a fragment of early myth or folklore, employed dramatically by the tragedians (in Sophocles' *Oedipus Coloneus*), for it recognises in the figure of Oedipus the blind and limping sun of winter. One account of Oedipus's death says that he miraculously disappeared into the earth, following the path of the sun.

The children of Oedipus are solar too, for they are the warring twin brothers Eteocles and Polynices (fighting over the succession of the throne of Thebes), and the sisters Antigone and Ismene. While Antigone wanders with her blind father, Ismene is killed or sacrificed at the instigation of Athena, and where she fell the Agianni spring burst forth, known in antiquity as the Ismene spring or 'Cadmus's Foot', and the source of the river that bears her name.[24] The Ismenos river was also fed by the Oidipodia spring in Thebes, and the reliable water supply in the city (there were numerous natural springs supplying three rivers) suggests to me that here was the origin of the Oedipus cycle.[25]

The death of Laius is a variation on the theme of succession, and the added theme of incest is said by some authorities to be a later addition. The best account is by the German scholar Carl Robert, who in *Oidipus*[26] (1915) suggested that Oedipus's original mother was the earth goddess Demeter. Robert says this might explain the incest factor, as the son, born of mother earth, is naturally the husband too. This is why Osiris is the son and husband of Isis, why Attis is the son and lover of Cybele. Oedipus is a 'year-god' born in spring but dying in winter. Laius is also a year-god who must be killed in the struggle for succession. Parricide and incest are rooted in nature religion. Only when the god becomes human, says Carl Robert, and earth becomes a human woman are these deeds considered crimes.

The incest theme has perhaps a simpler meaning, and refers to the fertilising rains that impregnate mother earth. During the wedding of Cadmus and Harmonia, Demeter and Iasion, perhaps a version of Triptolemus, slip away and make love in a ploughed field. The time is autumn, and he personifies the solar phallus delivering its seed. When Hephaestus forces his attentions on Athena, he ejaculates on her thigh, but the semen impregnates earth, which gives birth to Erichthonious. Thus Athena remains a virgin yet is also a mother. These are pure nature myths, to do with seasons and the elements, and they gave rise to the themes of incest, and the idea of the virgin goddess. Iocasta and Athena both feature in the story because, of course, they are goddesses of springs, and the deaths of Laius, the Sphinx, Oedipus and Ismene confirm their function. The wandering heroes and anti-heroes became the stuff of epic legend, upon which the Greek dramatists grafted numerous adventures, but the bare bones of each legend belong to world mythology, and are universally recognised even though differing in detail.

Myth is a formula, a structure, and might usefully be compared to the structure of music, the universal language of the octave from which simple combination of eight notes, sublime harmonies and variations can be created. Neither music nor myth could be said to be the invention of one man, but the invention of mankind, and the formula of myths was gradually established in much the same way as music, lending itself to a great variety of stories. The formula is based upon the passage of the seasons, the birth and death of the sun, and the arrival of rain, and since natural phenomena are more or less universal, myths are but variations on a theme. They tell the story of man's dependence on the essentially unreliable, and often threatening, performance of nature, but myth never had anything to do − in its original structure − with the human psyche, and this is why Freud and Jung were wrong in their separate views on the story of Oedipus, although as a result of Freudian theory, the twentieth century has imposed its own interpretations on the myth. Successive cultures have each reinterpreted myths according to their individual needs. The structure of religions, with their emphasis on the spiritual, was a later development.

The spread of the mythic formula across the world shows a close relationship in the myths and legends of different cultures and societies. The legend of Jason and the Argonauts and the quest for the Golden Fleece migrated to far distant places. Folklorists such as Andrew Lang traced it − in its various disguises − from Finland to Samoa.[27] Lang, writing in 1893, described the legend on which the Argonautica was based as a story which has the widest circulation in the world, 'transmitted slowly from people to people, in the immense unknown prehistoric past of the human race'. Like the story of Cinderella, it was part of the folklore of practically every society on earth, and thus must have been based on something universally experienced, perhaps a collective anxiety or concern of early man. Myths, on the whole, attempt to resolve predicaments − usually drought and disease − perceived as life-threatening.

The essentials of the myth tell of a hero challenged by a hostile authority, usually a giant, to perform a number of seemingly impossible tasks. He achieves the impossible with the magical assistance of the giant's daughter, plus assorted helpful animals common to folklore. The adventurer elopes with the daughter and, chased by the giant, throws obstacles behind them to check his pursuit. They are eventually successful and escape. This tale is fundamentally the story of Jason and the Argonauts, who sail to Colchis at the far, eastern end of the Black Sea to retrieve the Golden Fleece.

The myth begins with a typically devious plot, in which the children of King Athamas, Phrixus and Helle, are ordered to be sacrificed to relieve a drought. Zeus intervenes, and provides a golden, talking ram upon which the fugitives make their escape. Helle loses her grip and drowns in the straits, thereafter called the Hellespont. She, too, is an aspect of the sun, her fall may be compared to that of Icarus, of Hephaestus and Bellerophon, and the three daughters of Erechtheus who leaped off the Acropolis. The ram takes Phrixus to Colchis. On the advice of the ram itself, Phrixus sacrifices it, and hangs its fleece by a spring sacred to Ares, guarded, of course, by a dragon, or serpent.

The direct cause of the launching of the *Argo*, from the port of Iolcus in Thessaly, was a familiar one of sibling rivalry, of emnity between solar twins or bothers. An incident had occurred in which the heir apparent, Aeson, had been deprived of his right to the throne by a half-brother, Pelias. In due course Jason arrives in Iolcus to redress the wrong to his father Aeson, and to reclaim the throne. En route, Jason had lost a sandal while fording a river, and is thus symbolically 'lamed', his crossing representing the successful course of the sun through the winter rains. The parable of Saint Christopher carrying the infant sun god Jesus across a river by night has the same meaning.

The tale contains a number of oracular warnings, including one to the usurper Pelias to beware of the arrival of a stranger with only one shoe. To get rid of him, Pelias sets Jason the task of bringing back the Golden Fleece. The voyage was initiated by Athena, who instructs Jason to include in the vessel a branch from the prophetic oak tree of Zeus from the oracular shrine at Dodona in Epirus, for the oak branch was special to the goddess of springs, and was used to induce rain.

Jason builds a ship, the *Argo*, assisted by Athena, and gathers a crew of fifty men to sail to Colchis. Members include two prophets or seers, Mopsus and Idmon, the keen-eyed Lynceus, plus the Dioscuri Castor and Polydeuces, and the twins Amphion and Zethus, not to mention such heavyweights as Heracles. One could reasonably claim that the legend of the Argonauts was based upon, and inspired by, twin symbolism.

The ancient tale was overlaid with all the rich trappings, involved plottings and clues of Greek mythology, including subplots which bring in the sailor's liaisons with the women of Lemnos, and the perilous route through the Clashing Rocks. The

Argonauts landed at Lemnos, where Jason marries Hypsipyle (the water finder) and the crew tarry for a year with the fifty Lemnian women, mentioned earlier.

Having sown their seed seven-times-seven (because Hercules stayed on board) the Argonauts set sail to face the ordeal of the Clashing Rocks, a fearsome hazard on their journey eastwards. The Rocks, either side of a sea passage, hurtled together like slamming gates, crushing every ship that attempted to pass through them.

Hera, or Athena, on behalf of the Argonauts, sent first a dove as a pathfinder, and the bird scraped through leaving only a tail feather behind. Waiting for the passage between the Rocks to reach its maximum width before rushing together again, the shuddering *Argo* followed, observing the dove's same accurate timing, and fled through, the crew desperately whipping the sea to a foam with their oars. With Athena's aid, commanding a fast wave to push the *Argo* forward, their passage was successful, the Rocks merely slicing off a part of the ship's stern – clipping its 'heel'. Later the helmsman, Tithys, dies, a contrivance which offers a second clue.

The *Argo* is a talking ship. The branch of the prophetic oak delivers warnings and does so three times – again, the solar number. Once at the start of the voyage, once at the passing of Tithys, and lastly on reaching their destination. The *Argo* thus represents the voyage of the sun. The episode of Clashing Rocks that clip the *Argo*'s stern symbolises the 'laming' of the solar ship.

This is perhaps the meaning of the white solar horse with a black tail. The voyage begins with the winter solstice, the death of Tithys symbolises the start of the sun's decline at the summer solstice, and the voyage terminates either at Colchis, or on reaching the home port of Iolcus, when the final prophecy is delivered at the winter solstice.

Colchis is ruled by King Aeëtes, whose father was the sun. Aeëtes agrees to hand over the Golden Fleece, but on condition that Jason successfully completes a number of difficult and challenging tasks, which include ploughing a field with two fire-breathing bulls and sowing it with the teeth of a dragon. Jason is aided by Aeëtes's daughter Medea, who falls in love with him and thereby becomes his accomplice, and it is she who completes Jason's tasks. She and Jason outwit the dragon, steal the Fleece, and are pursued by Aeëtes. Here, the Greeks add savage features of their own, but not without meaning. To delay Aeëtes, Medea performs a grisly sacrifice, killing and dismembering her brother taken as hostage, and casting his limbs behind her, which Aeëtes stops to bury and mourn. In fact, Medea embarks on an orgy of killing, dismembering and cooking Pelias, killing Talos on Crete by draining his heel, and finally murdering her own children by Jason, the most potent form of sacrifice imaginable. These are sacrifices to the sun, and occur during the month preceding winter.

We now have enough information to interpret the voyage of the Argonauts. The Golden Fleece, snatched from where it hung by a sacred spring, is a token and symbol of the sun. It is the fleece of a ram because, like the bull, the ram's sacrifice and death must be carried out to encourage the fertilising rains, to be released on reaching home. In this it is similar to the golden rain of Zeus. The entire saga is based upon the vital need to hasten the sun's decline in order to precipitate the rain and terminate the drought with which the tale began.

The *Argo* and all aboard her represent the fetching of the sun from the east and bringing it back, westwards, to its winter abode. The replacement of the usurper Pelias by Jason on behalf of his deposed father is the replacement of the old reigning sun by the new. The myth is loaded with such clues – the fall of Helle; the death of Talos the sun by the hand of Medea, acting for Jason, weakened like Robin Hood by being drained of his life blood. The name Argos, who built the *Argo*, means 'glittering, bright'. He was Argos Panoptes, or 'he who sees all', and Aeschylus refers to 'the all-seeing (*panopten*) circle of the sun'.[28] The instigator of the journey is Athena, or Hera, or both, because these goddesses of spring waters have a vested interest. The ram, like the bull, is their sacrificial victim. The presence of a ram is not essential to the myth; there were no rams in the original folk tale, but the Golden Fleece does, however, lend weight to the role played by the sun, representing as it does the ram's masculine task as the bringer of fertilising rains. Aeëtes, Medea, Talos, Jason and his lost sandal, the dash through the Rocks and the death of Tithys, the emphasis throughout on prophecy, the voyage of the *Argo* to the furthest point eastward, where the sun would rise, all lead to the conclusion that this saga was based on a primeval tale, common to all societies and all lands, about hastening the sun's journey towards the winter solstice.

The emphasis on prophecy, which originated in the idea of the all-seeing, all-knowing sun, is one reason why the voyage was instigated by Athena, aiding the solar hero Jason. This is why those who suffer wounds to the heel are often seers, such as Mopsus. The *Argo* is the boat of the sun, similar to the vessel that conveyed Ra on his daily passage, and the young man who must confront the father, elope with his daughter and win her hand, is the sun-god.

He is also Apollo, he is Mithras, Perseus, Heracles, and every solar hero who has aided and abetted the forces of nature's destiny. Jason's loss of his sandal at the start of the tale is really a microcosm describing the task that awaits him, and the sun's passing through the summer solstice. The father, Aeëtes, the 'giant' in the folktales, is threatening to prevent the sun's south-westward journey, and with it the fertility of the earth.

This was a genuine fear in primitive societies, even in the more enlightened ones. The Egyptians thought that Ra, in his boat, was nightly menaced and forced to do battle with the serpent Apep, who attempted to prevent his return. This is really the meaning of Zeus's fight with Typhon, in which Zeus's sinews are stolen.

Typhon, the offspring of one of Hera's less discerning liaisons, was almost wholly serpent, covered in wings and breathing fire, and so terrifying that the gods of Olympus fled to Egypt and turned themselves into animals – Zeus became a ram, Hera a cow, Dionysus a goat. Zeus, later in human form, grabbed a sickle and did battle with the monster. Overcome, he suffered to lose the sinews of his hands and feet, and thus lamed, was cast into a cave. Typhon hid the sinews under the skin of a bear, where they were later found by Hermes whose domain is the cave, and who restored them to Zeus. The solar references are all there – the ram, sickle, symbolic laming, the cave, and the bear; we may perceive in these symbols the basic structure of primeval myth.

The daughter of the giant, and Medea the daughter of Aeëtes, is in fact the sun and water goddess, who will return to ripen the crops, and watch over the annual rebirth of nature. She is the feminine half of the sun, Jason the male half. She may even be Jason's 'twin'. The tasks set for the hero are often of an agricultural nature – even though they may be sowing dragon's teeth.

Finally, the fate visited on so many solar heroes catches up with Jason, for he is now the weakened sun, the human representative of the *Argo* and, like John the Baptist, 'must decrease', as the sun decreases. The ship has completed its journey, and as Jason dozes under the stern of the Argo, a heavy timber falls from the damaged poop – and kills him.

Strictly speaking, and like John the Baptist, he should have been decapitated, or wounded by a boar. Perhaps the most dramatic and vivid example of this elemental symbolism, and a favourite theme of Greek art, is the fearsome face of Medusa the Gorgon whose decapitation, far from being an image of death, was essential to life.

CHAPTER 10

The Mask of Medusa

Who does not know the myth of Perseus and the Gorgon Medusa? The hero, aided and abetted by Athena, sets out to destroy the monster whose glance turned men to stone – it could even turn seaweed to coral. Perseus is armed with magical equipment: a cap to render him invisible; winged sandals from Hermes to ensure a swift getaway; a weapon, the arpe or drepanon, a sort of sickle-sword; an eye and a tooth, snatched from the three Graeai; the reflective shield from Athena; a bag called a cibisis to hold the head. Seven items in all, if you count the sandals as a pair, as one item.

This might suggest that the deed was done at the time of the harvest, in the summer, a view supported by the fact that Perseus uses the arpe (even though in some examples he uses a sword), and the cibisis was a bag to hold grain. Judging his aim by looking at her reflection in Athena's shield, Perseus sliced off the monster's head, as he would reap a head of barley. The hero stowed it away, and flew three times around the world, stopping off to rescue Andromeda, chained to a rock, from an advancing sea-monster. He also chose to reveal the Gorgon's head to Atlas, spitefully in my view, turning him to stone.

Were the higher gods immune to the Gorgon's stare, to her power to petrify them? It is difficult otherwise to comprehend how Poseidon, the Greek god of the sea, ventured to have an affair with Medusa, although it was said that long ago, she was beautiful. Perhaps he enjoyed the challenge, or was there something special about her that other goddesses lacked? Or was there something peculiar about him that he chose this grotesque winged female with the tusks of a boar and snakes in her hair? But of course this is myth, this is magic, and nothing is as it seems. She acceded to his demands, and their offspring was the warrior Chrysaor with his golden sword, and the legendary winged horse

FIG. 24 Sixth-century Attic vase painting of Perseus,
Medusa and Hermes.

Pegasus, both of whom sprang from the body of Medusa when
she lost her head.

Horses were sacred to Poseidon. He was 'the Lord of the
Horse', although when it came to honouring him in ritual fashion,
the sacrificed animal was usually a bull.[1] Poseidon was invoked as
Hippius, the protector of horsemen, and the reason for his equine
nature was said to be due to the sea, to the waves of 'white horses'
that crashed on to the rocky shores of Greece, and the thundering
herds of wild horses that may have led to his other epithet, 'the
earth-shaker'.

The claim that this title refers to his influence over earthquakes
should be considered. Earthquakes are not uncommon in the
Eastern Mediterranean, and Poseidon bangs his trident on the
ground in order to create springs of water. He does not appear to
be an agent of fire, however, nor of rivers of molten lava, and he
does not reside under a volcano – this is the domain of Hephaestus
and Prometheus. Yet he holds a trident, almost certainly a solar
symbol. In Vedic legend, the sun goddess Saranyu fashioned the
trident of Siva and the discus of Vishnu.[2] Remember that
Poseidon is one of a triad of gods, so that in part he represents the
sun, his companions being Zeus and Hades.

The Greek month Poitropios is dedicated to Poseidon, the month of December and the birth of the sun at the winter solstice. The connection with the sea was relatively late, his original function, says Lewis Farnell in *Cults of the Greek States* (1896), being to preside over springs.[3]

As a fresh-water divinity Poseidon could call forth water from a rock. Mithras was able to perform this trick, as was Perseus by plucking a wild mushroom. And so was Pegasus, who struck a rock with his hoof and created the Hippocrene spring on Mount Helicon.

While searching for water, Cadmus the Phoenician, the inventor of the alphabet, fought and killed a dragon to found the city of Thebes. This heroic act prompted the Ismene spring to gush out from Cadmus's footprint in the mud, as the Ganges was said to issue from the foot of the Hindu god of creation, Vishnu, when he took the form of a horse. We know that it was Poseidon who revealed the springs at Lerna to the Danaides, and so his watery nature is well-attested.

On a Greek coin the horse Scapheus is seen leaping out of a rock, burst open with his hooves, as a spring gushes from the rocky foothills of the mountains, and as Athena the horse-tamer and creator of horses, bursts from the head of Zeus, so the sun god Mithras was born from a rock.

One aspect of the gorgon Medusa, as Poseidon must have known, is that her parents were both sea creatures. Her father was Phorcys, or Medon, 'Lord of the Sea' (of which 'Medusa' is the feminine), a boar from the ocean, while her was mother Ceto, a sea serpent, perhaps the same one that menaced Andromeda.

Medusa's father endowed her with tusks, her mother with serpentine tresses, although some authorities say that the snakes were a late addition, and are absent from archaic representations of the head, or 'gorgoneion' as the apparition is called.[4] Also late is the idea that Medusa's glance turned men to stone – it was unknown to Homer and Hesiod – but became a popular folklore theme.

From a sample of seventy representations of the Gorgon, from Greece, Etruria and elsewhere, two-thirds have boar's tusks, but only a third possess the snaky coiffure, and the same number have a beard, so Medusa is perhaps androgynous. The most persistent feature, though, is the tongue, appearing in all but three of the sample. It hangs loosely like that of a panting dog, and from a mouth well equipped with fangs, and with the additional tusks. The mouth has a grin, almost a sneer, with the nose above it wrinkled like a snarling cat, actually a lion. The idea that the head is leonine has been proposed by several scholars, some suggesting that the Gorgon's occasional beard is taken from a lion's mane.[5]

The reason given for this choice is that a snarling lion is a frightening beast, thus suitable for an apotropaic mask. That the Gorgon's head, displayed on a shield, was a device to scare the enemy, is a plausible explanation. Jane Harrison, prominent scholar of Greek mythology at the end of the nineteenth century, claimed that the Gorgon had migrated to Greece from the East, as a mask only, and that the Greeks had thoughtfully provided Medusa with a body.

In this form she is shown with two sets of wings, a snake-belt, a normal female torso, and often in a kneeling pose which, for want of a label in English, we have adopted the German term 'knielauf', or 'knielaufschema', which is hardly translatable but seems to mean 'knee-running pose' and appears to mimic the swastika, a solar reference. It is in this form that Perseus met her, and there is an archaic seal from Cyprus, and others from Mesopotamia, which suggests that the legend is very ancient, pre-dating the classical period when the images of Medusa were so popular.

FIG. 25 A Greek gorgon and an earlier version from Assyria.

Before going on to study the Gorgon's mask, it would be useful to ask why Perseus features so strongly in this myth. He was a descendant of the house of Danaus, introduced previously in the myth of the fifty water-seeking Danaides who cut off their husbands' heads. He reigned over the fortified, royal city of Tiryns in the Argive plain, and had seven children by Andromeda. His mother was Danae, whose father Acrisius, learning from an oracle that his grandson would be the cause of his death (a frequent theme in myth) imprisoned Danae in a 'brazen chamber', where Zeus famously visited her in a shower of golden rain.

The detail here is significant. Why is the rain 'golden'? The answer is because the shower combines the two elements of fire and water, the sun and the rain which gives life to all things. Is Danae, then, a sun-goddess? Does her incarceration in the brazen chamber represent the period of the sun's captivity in the earth during winter? In fact like all goddesses, her primary function is to create springs, according to Robert Graves, but the name 'Danae' means 'parched',[6] so she represents the earth during a period of drought. Zeus's 'golden rain' both revitalised her and caused her to give birth to the solar hero Perseus. His name has been interpreted to mean 'destroyer' or 'cutter', appropriate for a hero with a sickle.

The fear of the aged Acrisius was that of the weakening solar divinity being supplanted by his youthful inheritor, yet when Acrisius freed Danae from the earth, and in so doing discovered Perseus, he could not bring himself to kill both mother and son, and instead shut them in a casket, and had it thrown into the sea.

This 'floating chest' is another common theme in myth, and owes its origins to the passage of the 'infant' sun through the watery months of winter. Osiris was sealed in a box by his brother, the Egyptian sun god Set, the red-pelted ass of the scorching desert, and thrown into the Nile. The infant Moses, whose face glowed like solar fire, was set adrift in a reed basket. Dionysus, Telephus, Sargon, Cyrus, Romulus and Remus, each had versions of a birth followed by a journey in a floating box or chest.

Yet not all these threatened children suffer a watery journey. In the example of Oedipus it was sufficient that he be exposed like Telephus on a hillside, a pin driven through his ankles. There have been several studies in the life-pattern of mythological heroes, such as Oedipus, Theseus, Perseus, and Jason the Argonaut, many of whom share similar afflictions.

In addition to being shut in a floating chest, some of them suffer a mysterious death at the top of a hill, as Jesus was crucified on the hill of Golgotha, as the sun symbolically dies on reaching its highpoint of the solar year, at the summer solstice. The chest

containing Perseus and Danae is washed up on the island of
Seriphos, and discovered by the fisherman Dictys.

Seriphos is one of the Cyclades, an island of caves and rocks
with little to recommend it except for its warm and potable spring
by the church of St Isisdorus, again the reference to fire and water,
and like the hot springs of Bath, is the place of the Gorgon. The
old coins of Seriphos bore Medusa's head – but then so did the
coinage of many Greek states, it was a popular motif. The choice
of Seriphos was perhaps because it is the nearest of the Cyclades to
Argos. For the purposes of the myth, the island stood for the
entire group of these volcanic islands, abounding in hot springs,
fissures and caves.

The Victorian traveller and archaeologist Theodore Bent,
exploring the islands in the 1880s, wrote of black, sulphur-
streaked blocks of lava, and steaming pools of water coloured
bright orange from iron oxide.[8] It was from here that Perseus,
grown to manhood, set out to find Medusa, to fulfil a boast that
he had made to the ruler of the island, one Polydectes, that he
would 'bring back the Gorgon's head'.

This head, then, is part boar and part lion, a lion with a
protruding tongue. When a feature seems puzzling it is often
helpful to seek supportive evidence, and in this case it is close at
hand. Practically every public drinking fountain, bath, or well, had
its outlet in the form of a stone or cast-metal lion's head, where
the water flowed over the tongue, and this device was to be found
throughout the Near East and the Mediterranean. Lion's head
faucets are still a feature of modern fountains.

Why the lion? One answer is provided by a simple comparison
– its roar was compared to the distant rumbling of thunder, and
thunder heralded rain. On ancient cylinder seals from Mesopotamia we see winged lions with water gushing from their mouths,
and to the people of the Fertile Crescent the storm bird, Imdugud,
was a huge vulture or eagle – but with the head of a lion (since
eagles do not roar).[9] The writer Simon Barnes, on safari in
Zambia, wrote in The Times that 'The true lion roar is not the
half-hearted snarl we know from Metro-Goldwyn-Meyer movies,
it is an altogether stranger and wilder sound, caught half-way
between a belch and a clap of thunder . . . you can hear a lion five
miles away.'[10]

This explains the name 'Gorgon'. It derives originally from the
Sanskrit root GA, which actually means 'to go', but yields gala,

'throat' and *garj*, 'to roar' (like a lion) and 'to thunder'; *gala* is also 'to flow' and is cognate with *jala*, 'water'. All are words related to the throat, to drinking, associated with *ganda*, 'jaw' and 'chin', and to our 'gargoyle' (which of course acts as a rain-spout), and allied words such as gully, gorge, gullet. A Lithuanian hag called Gylo is a swallower and devours.

FIG. 26 Lion's head from which the gorgon's mask was derived.

There is another reason, however, for the lion's head, and this is the animal's apparent likeness to the sun, and to fire. It is partly due to the tawny colour of the lion, but mainly because like fire the lion is fast, and like fire it devours. It also rules the animal kingdom as 'the King of Beasts' – as the sun rules the heavens. Agni, the Vedic god of fire, had an insatiable appetite and was a glutton.

The prominence of the lion as a symbol in antiquity was noted by folklorists and historians, and Staniland Wake in *Serpent Worship* (1888) refers to the connection between the Sanskrit *ar*, 'fire', and *ari*, 'lion', speculating that this may have been the original meaning of the Aryans as sun-worshippers, and probably the name Ares, the Greek war god who also represented the sun.[11]

A. B. Cook, in *Zeus*, mentions that 'Greeks and Romans alike, therein agreeing with the Egyptians and the nations of the nearer east, looked upon the lion as an animal full of inward fire and essentially akin to the sun. The lion on Roman military standards was interpreted as a solar emblem. The Mithraic sun-god was figured with a lion's face. The sign Leo was called "the house of the sun", and – be it noted – the sun was in Leo when Persephone was carried off."[12]

This is one of the reasons why lions were the companions of goddesses such as Ishtar, and why leopards, in place of lions, flank the statue of the Mother Goddess of Çatal Hüyük. The eagle, the vulture, and all flesh-tearing, devouring creatures were likened to fire because of their swiftness and voracity. This is one reason why the gyrfalcon personified the Egyptian Horus, son of Isis and Osiris. But there was another, more primitive and savage reason for the prominence of the lion. Here, along with the leopard, was one of the most dangerous predators, and the natural adversary of the bull, an animal equally powerful yet embodying a more pronounced virility.

In the lion, the prehistoric myth-makers perceived a vigorous 'twin' symbol of the sun, the predator that brought the bull to its knees, as the sun was brought to its knees at the onset of winter. Thus was the lion the agent of the fecund goddess.

The sanskrit root GA, then, refers to fire and to water, and this is why it yields so many seemingly disparate words, such as 'to shine' and 'to flow'; 'to swallow' and 'to roar'; also 'to seize' and 'to devour', which lead us to the gyr of gyr falcon, to the griph of griffin, and to gridh meaning 'greed' – a vulture is gridhra. The essence of all this, however, is the idea behind that of movement, the passage of the sun, the swift, protean shape-changing of water and fire, that we met earlier.

This by no means exhausts Medusa's many prominent and less than subtle theriomorphic features. She has the tusks of a boar and snakes in her hair, but she is also a horse, and she is androgynous. It is in the form of a horse that Medusa coupled with Poseidon. A temple pediment from Corcyra shows her hugging her offspring, the horse Pegasus. One especially archaic picture of Medusa appears on an amphora, or water vessel, from Boeotia in Greece, now in the Louvre. The scene depicts a rather rustic Perseus about to decapitate a gorgon-headed horse, and perhaps this was the version that attracted the horse god Poseidon. Above the horse we see a salamander, and to one side a plant wilting from heat.

The salamander was reputed to be able to quench fire because it is cold and wet to the touch, instead of dry and scaly like newts and lizards, and it is able to survive drought. Its presence in the scene suggests that heat is about to be tempered by rain.

The horse depicted on the amphora, with the Gorgon-head, is decorated with wavy lines, probably to represent rain, for the horse is a symbol of water. This is why it is sacred to Poseidon, and once again the representation is partly due to sound. The thunder of horses' hooves was likened to approaching rain, and explains why Pegasus was able to strike water from his hoof, an occasion that was also accompanied by a thunderstorm.

There is, however, another meaning to the symbolism of the horse and the equine Gorgon, for both represent the sun. In the Gorgon's case she is, in fact, 'withholding the horse' for it is only on her decapitation that her horse-self, her avatar as Pegasus, is released. We saw earlier that the horse was a prime solar symbol, the 'winged one darting from heaven'. This horse of the sun, in the late autumn, seems to touch down on the earth, when the rains sweep across the mountains to soak into the earth and rise as springs.

Now we can see why Medusa has boar's tusks. The boar was a water symbol too. Along with the lion's-head faucets we find those of boars, and the boar's head prominence in winter festivals was due in part to this being the rainy season. 'The boar,' says Robert Graves in *The White Goddess*, 'is the beast of death and the "fall" of the year begins in the month of the boar'.[13]

In *The Golden Bough*, Frazer mentions the boar's fondness for a watery environment: 'The places they love to frequent are the reedy marshes and thickets by rivers and lakes, and they swarm in the thickets along the banks of the Jordan from Jericho to the Lake of Gennaseret.'[14] They also frequented the marshes of the Nile delta, and the alluvial marshlands of the Euphrates – and still do.

In sites located around the eastern end of the Mediterranean, and in Asia Minor, votive clay effigies of boars were buried in pits, many apparently covered in stab marks.[15] These were not, as the archaeologist James Mellaart suggests, the result of sympathetic magic before hunting, to induce a good kill, but more likely to encourage rain, and promote a favourable growth of crops, for a buried head was a powerful talisman. As a descendant of the head-burying Danaides, we might expect Perseus to bury the head of

FIG. 27 Sacred boar from Rhodes. Boars' tusks were one of the features
of the Gorgon's head.

Medusa in some favourable spot, along, perhaps, with the forty-nine heads at Lerna, and this indeed does happen.

In some versions of the myth, Perseus buries the head either at Delphi, under the Omphalos, or in the Agora at Argos – the latter a more likely place since the Danaides were of course Argive rulers, and it was the spot they chose for the burial of their husbands' heads.

Here, the buried head of Medusa would influence the fertility of the plains of Argos, a preoccupation of the Argive dynasty, and of every society in the frequently arid lands of the Mediterranean. The association of heads with springs was observed near the Hippocrene spring, where three goddesses known as the Praxi-dikai had an open-roofed temple. They were represented by the head only, a peculiarity which, combined with their status as a triad, marks them out as the sun-goddesses of winter. The heads of animals – most probably horses – were dedicated to them.[16]

Here once more is this symbolic fusion of fire and water. Their existence as a triad implies their solar origins, their roofless temple adjacent to a spring encouraging the sun and the rain, reflecting the manner by which libations of water were ceremonially poured on to altar fires. I propose this to be the sole original purpose of libations, and of baptism too, the pouring out of liquid representing the rains that quenched the fires of summer's heat in the autumn, the prelude to the impregnation of the earth by plough and grain. Remember that John the Baptist was beheaded, and the head drenched with water symbolises the sun's descent at the end of the year.

I would like to stress that this symbolism was of vital importance to prehistoric man, who painstakingly developed it, for it allowed him to relate more easily to the seemingly capricious, wilful and mysterious behaviour of natural phenomena, in particular of the elements, the sun, wind and rain, supply of food and water, or the lack of it. That a horse or lion could be a representation of rain and thunder seemed perfectly reasonable, and it could be taken further, so that a horse might usefully symbolise the rainy season of the year, while its value as a sacrificial animal served to influence fertility.

In October, the eighth month in the Roman calendar and time of the first rains, a chariot race was held in Rome's Campus Martius, in honour of Mars, a sun-god. A horse of the winning team was ritually beheaded and divided into three parts. Different groups of team supporters competed for possession of the head, hung with loaves of bread.

The association with the eighth month is perhaps why Sleipnir, the horse of the Scandinavian god Odin, has eight legs, for this eighth month was the beginning of the fruitful season, a fragment of Indo-Aryan mythology can perhaps be traced back to Sanskrit word for horse, asva, and Asvina, the month October, and the word asta meaning 'eight'.

Poseidon, whose month in December witnesses the rebirth of the sun, whose emblem is the solar trident, was also 'rich in horses', for horses galloped like the crackling fire through a forest. Horses draw the chariots of fire carrying the sun gods. The Vedic sun god Surya's celestial carriage is drawn by seven mares, or a mare with seven heads – mares because they obey the feminine principle of the number seven.

In European legends, the chariot-horse of the sun, or of the sun hero, is sometimes a malnourished, crippled mare who is later mysteriously transformed into a shining white vigorous steed.[17] The change is solar, and describes the sun's growth and recovery from winter to spring and summer.

The decapitation of Medusa occurred in the autumn, and

induced the rains, a time of the year associated with the boar, and this is why she had boar's tusks. It is also why we find strong evidence of boar symbolism through prehistory – boars' jaws in graves, effigies in shrines and buried in the earth, for the boar brought the rain that supported life. The meaning of this most famous myth now becomes clear. Danae was the earth and water goddess presiding over a land stricken by drought at the end of summer, symbolised by Medusa. Impregnated by the thunder god Zeus, she conceives Perseus, who will destroy the drought-demon Medusa, liberating the water-horse Pegasus, to strike a spring, bringing relief to the parched earth, restoring her natural function and rule.

CHAPTER 11

The Evil Eye

When Perseus had beheaded Medusa with his sickle-sword he took the head and put it in his bag, the *cibisis*, and flew three times around the world – a solar number. Perseus was himself a solar hero, the lion who acted on behalf of his mother Danae (as Cronus acted on behalf of Gaia) and the goddess Athena, who in turn fertilised the earth, as she did with the misdirected semen of the fire- and sun-god Hephaestus. He and Athena symbolised the power that could influence the seasons.

The Gorgon's head, hideous though it may appear, was a symbol of life, but because the sun could also bring drought, despair and death, the head had its darker side. The earliest evidence of a malign Gorgon appears on the Ain-Samiya goblet from Mesopotamia about 3000 BC as a sun-rayed face. Another example, on the Khafaje plaque, now in Chicago, shows the stabbing of a sun-headed female by a proto-Perseus. In the middle of her forehead is a huge, single eye, the 'eye of the sun'.

Here is the evil eye that has run a course of superstitious belief throughout history, and retains its influence in the folklore of Mediterranean countries and the Middle East. There is a considerable body of scholarly work devoted to the phenomenon of the evil eye, notably by Frederick Elworthy (1895) and more recently by Alan Dundes who asks, 'What theoretical or underlying principle or principles, if any, can explain the whole range of phenomena believed to be caused by the evil eye, from the withering of fruit trees, to the loss of milk from cows to impotence among males?'[1]

The answer is found in the power of the noonday summer sun to cause life to wither and die. This is why the baleful influence of the eye can be countered by spitting, by baring the nourishing breast, making 'horns' with the fingers (the horns of the bull that bring rain) displaying a phallic amulet or making a sign with a 'phallic' finger, because all these things are sources of liquid and life – especially nourishing or fertilising liquids such as milk and semen, the latter being equated with spittle.

The power of the evil eye may explain why it was impossible to look at Medusa's face, and Perseus was obliged to temper her fiery gaze by using Athene's reflective shield. Only a hero of Perseus's inherited talents, as a descendant of Danaus who watered the plains of Argos, could defeat drought and the evil eye. In this, he reflects the triumph of the Vedic god Indra, the god of storms, who overcame the demon Vrtra, a huge boar, or in some versions a snake – in this case male. The name is derived from the Sankrit root VRS 'to water', from which comes the word for rain *varsa*, and from the Latin the word *ver*, 'a spring', and *verres*, 'a boar'. Vrtra's mother was Danu, meaning 'stream', and her son was also known as 'Danava' – 'Indra struck down the snorting Danava to release the waters'.[2] The myth has echoes of the medieval story of Beowulf, whose adversary, Grendel, lived with his mother in a lake.

It is pertinent to ask why it was that the great hero Hercules fought that fearsome serpent, the seven-headed Hydra, at Lerna, a feat that constituted the second of his twelve Labours. The question arises because there is a further aspect of the Gorgon's head that remains unexplained – perhaps her most famous attribute, the wreath of serpents in her hair.

FIG. 28 Hercules fighting the Hydra, a vase from Argos.

First, it should be understood that Hercules – or to give him his proper Greek name, Heracles – was, like Perseus, an Argive, and six of his Labours were performed in and around Argos. It is possible, and I make a suggestion here, that there were originally seven Labours only, and that all were located in Argos, because it lends support to a persistent feature that seems to be appearing in myth and legend, that of the fertility of the land and the almost numinous power of water.

For one thing, Argos was once the site of the great early civilisation of Mycenae which flourished in the late Bronze Age in the north-east of the Argive plain, and which certainly established many of the legends, and the dramatis personae, of Greek mythology. Argos was also the fertile land upon which the myths were able to develop.

The Myceneans, possibly the first wave of Greek-speaking, Indo-European peoples to settle in the Greek mainland, may have brought with them a developed fire-and-water mythology, similar to that of the Minoan civilisation of Crete where, like many islands in the Mediterranean, even today water is in short supply, and a continual problem.

Heracles restored the springs at Lerna, which Poseidon created for the Danaides, by battling with the Hydra, as Perseus confronted Medusa. He cut off the monster's seven heads and burnt each severed stump with a firebrand to prevent them from growing again. Observing the time-honoured Argive ritual, he buried the seventh head by the spring.[3]

Like Heracles, the Mesopotamian hero Marduk, having destroyed and dismembered the primeval, serpentine, gloomy mother-of-mothers called Tiamat, who rose from the abyss of the deep sea, cut off her head and buried it under a mountain, whereupon springs burst forth and water flowed, her eyes being the source of the Euphrates and the Tigris.[4] Once again we find that the burial of a head triggers a supply of water.

Among the Bantu societies, the rain god Pulu Bunzi is in conflict with the rainbow serpent Mbumba, here a male, who prevents the rains from falling until he is finally decapitated by Pulu. The head of Nkongolo, the rainbow serpent king of the Luba tribe, is buried under a termite mound – as Hercules buries the heads of the Hydra – his body under a river, while the mortal remains of the female serpent Lueji, are cut to pieces and thrown into a water jar.[5] The serpent that withheld the rain gradually evolved into the winged and fiery dragon, later to become a celebrated heraldic device.

The symbolism of the dragon is periodically taken out and dusted down for study by a variety of scholars. A recurring interpretation is that it represents chaos, or the triumph of the forces of light over darkness, of good versus evil. For the mythologist Walter Burkert at Zurich the dragon is a 'crystallisation of fantastic and demonic features'. He exists solely to provide a frightening and therefore worthy opponent for the hero to combat and eventually to destroy.

'He is a snake,' continues Burkert, 'because this is the most dreaded and hated animal, having resorted to chemical warfare long ago; he has a huge and devouring mouth, because being swallowed and eaten is a most basic anxiety of every living being; he may have wings, making him ubiquitous and unassailable; he may exhale fire, because this is the most destructive kind of energy known – his modern counterparts in science fiction wield nuclear bombs or laser machines.'[6]

Is being eaten by a snake a basic human anxiety? It is certainly an anxiety among frogs and mice when confronted by a serpent, but I doubt that it worried the Babylonians even though they lived in a territory populated by snakes and lions. Desmond Morris, however, says that snake phobia is still more prevalent than fear or dislike of spiders, perhaps because snakes are in the main more dangerous.[7] The biologist Balaji Mundkur, in *The Cult of the Serpent*,[8] says that it is man's elementary fear of snakes that prompted its adoption as a symbol. Leaning somewhat on Jungian principles, Mundkur suggests that we all have within us a deeply rooted ophidiophobia – an inherent fear of snakes – that penetrated into the psyche, fuelled by certain biochemical influences, which remains as a sort of permanent scar tissue on what Jung would term the collective unconscious.

In other words, being bitten throughout mankind's formative years (annually some 10,000 people in India alone are bitten, often fatally, according to the World Health Organisation) has resulted in an instinctive terror of snakes. This is misleading. Veneration of the serpent was never inspired by fear. 'By all among you who worship heathen gods,' said the Christian apologist Justin Martyr, 'the serpent is depicted as their great symbol and mystery.'

The archaeologist Marija Gimbutas was more emphatic, if not to say effusive: 'The mysterious dynamism of the snake, its extraordinary vitality and periodic rejuvenation, must have provoked a powerful emotional response in the Neolithic agriculturalists, and the snake was consequently mythologised, and attributed with a power that can move the entire cosmos."[9]

The conflict of the hero versus the monster is generally held to be about how human societies dealt with their fears by means of a mythology in which the hero is equal to, or superior to, the malign or threatening forces of nature – drought especially. Hence the fact that Heracles, whose adversary was the seven-headed Hydra, is a super-hero capable of great deeds of valour. This is a valid explanation, but to which must be added a less abstract reason.

The Hydra, although a water-snake, is actually the sun or a solar symbol because in astronomical terms it is a constellation that rises with Cancer at the summer solstice, heralding the period of fierce heat, and was thus viewed as a cause of drought. Stars and their appearance were thought to be the cause of climatic phenomena.

In art, Heracles is shown attacking the Hydra, not with a sickle, but with his famous club. The two weapons are not dissimilar, though. The club was made of oak, the oracular tree sacred to Zeus, the breast-like acorns of which symbolised the autumn rains. While fighting the Hydra, Heracles was repeatedly attacked on the ankles by a crab sent by Hera. We are told that she hated the hero because he was the child of an adulterous union by her husband Zeus, but Heracles was the epitome of the solar hero whose demise Hera needs to bring about in order to fulfill her natural functions. The crab, a further astronomical note, was the constellation Cancer, which rises with Hydra. Is this why the snakes in Medusa's hair were a late addition, because of the advances in astronomy and celestial imagery in the Hellenistic period?

The Greeks had adopted and improved upon the astronomical discoveries of the Babylonians, identifying a number of constellations of their own – Perseus and Pegasus being two of them, although the constellation Perseus as an astronomical symbol, may have migrated from Phrygia in Asia Minor. The shape of the stars form, I suggest, that curious item of headgear called the 'Phrygian cap', a motif probably agricultural in nature since the springtime constellation Perseus rises in time for the harvest in late April – or did in classical times. This was the old Caananite month of Abib, meaning 'ear month' or the month of ripening corn, appearing later in the Hebrew calendar as Nisan, corresponding to our April.[10] In some icons of Perseus and the Gorgon, the hero is wearing the Phrygian cap, dotted to represent stars like the spotted Hydra, as do the figures of Attis and Mithra, who each wears a Phrygian cap decorated with stars.

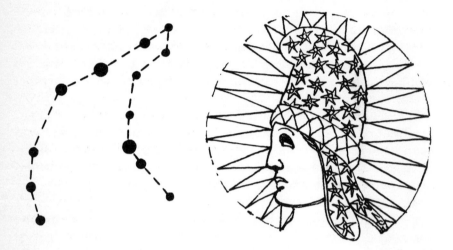

FIG. 29 The constellation Perseus, and Mithras wearing a Phrygian cap Reconstruction of a stone relic from Commagene in Asia Minor. Perseus rose in late April and set in October.

The Old Testament serpent in Eden has been identified by some scholars[11] as identical to Eve, comparing Aramaic and Hebrew words *havvah* and *heva*, meaning 'serpent', with *hawwa*, 'Eve'. (The role of Eve would be that of the goddess of springs, and her consort Adam, 'the red one', is the sun). The mythic elements in Genesis have long been recognised. The Oxford theologian, T. K. Cheyne, made the point that 'It is not the mythic basis but the infused idealism of the Eden story that constitutes its abiding interest for religious men.'[12] Cheyne, who edited *Encyclopaedia Biblica*, suggested that of the two trees in Eden – the tree of knowledge of good and evil, and the tree of life – only the tree of life was the original one, around which in art the serpent is often coiled (in a medieval window in York Minster, the serpent has a woman's head, suggesting perhaps a further identification with Eve). The story of Adam eating the fruit has its origins in the Babylonian myth of Adapa, forbidden by his divine father Ea from partaking of the food of life. Further mythic, and solar, elements in Genesis include the Deluge myth, also Babylonian in origin, the groups of twins, Cain and Abel, Jacob and Esau, Pharez and Zarah (Gen 38: 30), and the three patriarchs Abraham, Isaac and Jacob, allegedly entombed in the Cave of Machpelah in Hebron, Palestine. Genesis, as a primeval history of mankind, woven with a patriarchal history of the Hebrews, drew its material from a number of sources, its message idealistic, theological, and ultimately uplifting, but the creation legend was never intended to be taken literally. However, the close association between Eve, the tree and the serpent, symbol of the waters of life, might suggest that she was indeed the goddess of springs, and that the Fall of Man, like the fall of the sun, was her prime intention. If the tree was popularly the apple, it would have borne its fruits at the approach of autumn.

The symbolism of the serpent came from its similarity to the serpentine course of water — although snakes were and are taken up by various cults and religions as a prime symbol to represent all manner of things — healing, immortality, wisdom, evil, chaos, mendacity, and so on. The connection between the snake and water is found in the Sanskrit root SAR which means 'to flow', 'to move away', from which are derived sara, 'water', sarp, 'glide', sarpa, 'a snake', hence 'serpentine'. In Mesopotamia, the Euphrates was called 'the river of the snake'.

Throughout its long history as a symbol, the snake has been invested with a high degree of sexuality, particularly in reference to phallicism. Freud, who undoubtedly made sexual symbolism fashionable, referred to the snake as 'the famous symbol of the male organ', which prompted his disciple and biographer Ernest Jones to claim, unwisely, that 'most symbols refer to the male organ'.[13]

Freud went on to publish, in 1922, his study The Gorgon's Head, a fine example of Freudian Oedipal nonesense, albeit wonderfully inventive.[14] 'Decapitation,' he asserted, 'equals castration.' In one respect, Freud was correct. Castration was one way by which the vigour of the solar hero was weakened, but this was not Freud's view. The terror of Medusa is the terror of castration which threatens the boy on perceiving 'the terrifying genitals of the Mother'. This would have been frightening especially to Greek men, 'who were in the main strongly homosexual'.

Furthermore, the petrifying stare of the Gorgon, the 'turning to stone' represented the erection of the male organ at the sight of the maternal vulva. Perhaps Freud did not know that the Gorgon's stare also turned women to stone – such was the fate of the priestess of Athena, Iodama, when she caught sight of Athena's aegis, bearing the gorgoneion.

While there is much evidence of widespread phallicism in religions, it is less evident that snakes are phallic symbols, especially since they are generally regarded as female. The Hindu divinities of human fertility and sexuality, Mudamma and Manasa, were both cobras, and female.[15] Snakes were said to be associated with childbirth, or it was said that when a snake appeared it denoted pregnancy. The Aztec goddess Chiuacoatl, who presided over childbirth, was also known as the Serpent Woman, and had the head of a snake – as did Renenet, the Egyptian goddess of nursing and nourishment.[16]

The Maya goddess Ix Cheel – 'Lady Rainbow' – presided over childbirth, sexual intercourse, medicine and water, and she wore as her headdress a knotted serpent. If anything, snakes were likened to the vagina due to their ability to constrict, grip, and swallow their prey whole; in Babylonian myth, the great serpent, the mus-hus–sa, was known as the 'wombsnake'.[17] There are, however, sufficient examples of carved stone phalli, decorated with snakes, to suggest that they were seen as one and the same.

Apart from the Babylonian boundary stones, or kudurrus, displayed in the British Museum, I know of several huge stone phalli in the museum at Lagos, Portugal, decorated with the serpent caduceus symbol. Yet the association is due, I think, to the fertility of rain, which the female snake was thought to encourage.

The idea is ancient and widespread. The rainsnake as a concept of natural fertility migrated with peoples across the globe. 'The progress of the sacred serpent from Paradise to Peru is one of the most remarkable phenomena in mythological history,' wrote John Deane in The Worship of the Serpent[18] (1833). The snake is perhaps the most prominent religious symbol throughout Mesoamerica, where the success of the maize crop depended on the summer rains; a prolonged drought in the ancient world practically guaranteed starvation.

'The Maya people were as much in thrall to the mighty thunderclouds of summer as the Egyptians were to the annual rise and fall of the Nile.'[19] Hence the prevalence of the snake in Maya art, and the respect paid to the god Quetzalcoatl, who combines

the plumage of the quetzal bird of the rain forests, with that of the
snake, probably the *crotalus* rattlesnake, or cascaral.

The snake is also found among the tribes of North-Western
Australia where Undugud, or the 'Rainbow Serpent' – who
appeared at the beginning of time as a pregnant woman –
symbolises everything from the blood of circumcision and menses
to rain and rivers, but in other parts of the continent the Rainbow
Serpent is either bisexual or masculine. In Japan the thunder god
was a serpent; the Naga cobras of India controlled rain, while the
Hopi tribe of North America invoked rain by performing
serpentine dances.

The direct association between snakes and the fertility of crops
is seen in reliefs of the Greek agricultural figure of Triptolemus,
who broadcasts seed from a winged chariot pulled by two giant
pythons, the hubs of the wheels featuring lion's heads; sometimes
his chariot is depicted with only one wheel – the wheel of the sun.
In borrowing such details to decorate and embellish mythological
scenes represented in art, the Greeks (like other cultures before
them) were reaching back over thousands of years, to the early
stages of agriculture.

FIG. 30 Demeter and Triptolemus.

Triptolemus gets his name from the Greek *tripolos*, meaning 'thrice-ploughed',[20] which has a sexual inference: in Babylonian myth, Gestinanna, goddess of the vine (because her time of year is the autumn when grapes are gathered and the seed is planted), compares her body to a plot that needs to be tilled, the ploughman chosen for the task is Du'zu, later Tammuz, who like Triptolemus is an aspect of the sun. In fact 'thrice-ploughed' really means that the furrows were ploughed by the sun, because the sun in winter comes to earth. We saw in a previous chapter how the sun is the phallus that penetrates the earth. A seal shows the sun-god Shamash, whose hands are scorpions (the constellation Scorpius) ploughing a furrow with a plough drawn by a serpent, guided by a lion in the service of Ishtar.

The lion-serpent combination, common to both Greece and Assyria, means that the sun ploughs in company with the rains of autumn, for snakes bring rain, and if the sun is shining the two elements are combined to create the rainbow serpent. The 'seed' sown by Triptolemus is not corn, but rain, or perhaps he sows both corn and rain. He is often seen in the company of Demeter and her daughter Persephone.

Demeter, identified with the Roman Ceres, is the corn mother, but she and Persephone really represent the seasons of the solar year. Persephone, whose attribute is the gold-red fruit of the pomegranate tree that ripens in the summer; Demeter the ears of wheat sown in the autumn and harvested in April. Both goddesses represent water. It played an important part in the cult of Demeter, and there were provisions for water in all of her sanctuaries, such as that of Demeter Potnia by the Strophia river at Thebes.

Persephone, picking flowers in midsummer, is 'raped' by Hades. She is swallowed up by the earth near the spring of Arethusa at Syracuse in Sicily, as the earth dries up and becomes arid through the heat of summer. Demeter laments for her, as the women lament and weep for Tammuz, 'son of the fresh waters', and the soil becomes a barren wasteland. Snake-haired like Medusa, Persephone lives in the underworld as the consort of Hades until the autumn, when she returns as the cave-dwelling, horse-headed Demeter Melainis, 'black' Demeter, the goddess of the winter rains, when from his python-drawn chariot Triptolemus broadcasts his corn.

Spiral bowls in the form of a snake, perforated with holes,

probably as a means of invoking rain, were made in the east
Balkans at the end of the sixth millennium BC. These Balkan potters
were in turn referring to a symbolism already ancient, while today,
tribes in Botswana believe that certain large rainsnakes live on the
tops of hills and draw down water from the clouds.[21]

The whole point of the veneration of serpents in cults and
religions is that they were seen as life-enhancing, not because they
sloughed their old skins and so were 'reborn' (a favourite theme of
modern religious groups and cult movements) but because they
were thought to procure rain. The serpent was adopted as a
symbol of health (retained as the motif of the modern medical
profession) and the Greek god of medicine Aesculapius, son of
Apollo, takes the form of a serpent. Diseases were – and in many
parts of the world still are – prevalent during the dry season from
the end of May to October. In the eastern Mediterranean, the
rainfall period runs from late October to late April with the
chance of a few light showers in May, although I have known it to
rain in August. In medieval England, the Black Death was the
precursor of seasonal plague conditions which were to persist for
centuries; summer was a season to be feared, while the rains
promised a return to a healthier environment.

As a symbol of fertility the snake was valued right across the
Mediterranean world. Twin snakes make up the herald's winged
staff, known as the caduceus, carried by Hermes. Its shape forms
the sun, producing the combination of fire and water, sun and
rain. Hermes is the divine herald, the 'psychopomp' or conductor
of souls to Hades, the go-between, his route passing from the
upper to the lower world.

Hermes probably began as a primitive deity of caves, represented as an upright stone, or herm, which may have associations
with stalagmites. He was really a symbol of the sun entering the
earth, which is why he is phallic, and associated with Aphrodite as
a combined androgynous being – the hermaphrodite. The
caduceus illuminated the way below, as the golden bough of
Aeneas penetrated the darkness of the underworld, and so Hermes
is a solar guide, a herald, and as a go-between became eventually a
god of merchants.

The caduceus is a version of the Egyptian, and Mesopotamian,
winged disc, the disc of the sun combined with vulture's wings, in
the company of two uraeus snakes. The power of symbols is
augmented by association: since snakes symbolise water, and water

is a product of, or encouraged by, the winter sun, the snakes also represent the sun. The African and Australian rainbow serpents are a symbol of celestial fire and water. This is a further reason why the seven-headed snake has to be decapitated, just as the sun is decapitated in the form of snake, horse, gorgon.

The goddess Athena, who aided Perseus in his successful bid to vanquish Medusa, wears by tradition a serpent-fringed cape known as the aegis, although the wearing of it was not entirely her prerogative – it was sometimes worn by stormy Zeus, and by the thunderous god of war, Ares or Mars, whose serpent guarded his spring at Thebes. The aegis, when vigorously shaken, produced a thunderstorm and was regarded by Virgil as part of the rain-maker's paraphernalia.[22]

'Aegis' is said to mean 'goat-skin' from the Greek word *aig*, stem of *aix*, 'goat'. The fact that goats, along with other ungulates, are particularly fertile and sexually attentive during the rutting season that corresponds with the arrival of the rains, may have led to this idea. However, the scaly cape, with its border of snakes, is clearly not a goat-skin but a snake-skin, snakes being far more frequently seen as the companions of Athena than are goats.

Athena wore a small image of the gorgoneion on her aegis, and it is said that it was she who tamed Pegasus; in some representations she wears an image of Pegasus on her helmet. Those who were not Argives spread the rumour that Perseus had nothing to do with the decapitation of Medusa, and that it was Athena herself who had done the deed. Her role is similar to that played by Ariadne, who assisted Theseus in his adventure with the Minotaur. Ariadne was perhaps the Cretan goddess (see Fig. 7) whose twin snakes and bared breasts symbolised life and nourishment. The drama of the hero versus the monster was always played out in the dark shadow of the goddess.

CHAPTER 12

Day of Blood

There is sufficient evidence now to see that the Gorgon, in all her forms, was an extraordinary multiple symbol of fire and water. She represents the 'water sun'. This is why in every single example of the gorgoneion her head is perfectly circular, for Medusa is entirely solar; her tongue hangs out because the land is parched, but the gaping jaws of the lion and boar promise life-giving water, which it was hoped would arrive in time for the sowing.

The Gorgon's hanging tongue is an indication of time, and it points to the end of summer when the land is in dire need of the refreshing rains. This is why she has boar's tusks, for the boar is the animal of winter. Perseus decapitates her to free the horse Pegasus, who will in turn release the waters from the earth with his hoof, and in so doing refreshes the parched Danae, whose distress started the ball rolling. Perseus also liberated the warrior Chrysaor, the young, virile and fertilising sun like the phallic, sword-bearing warriors engraved on rocks in Scandinavia. His name means 'golden sword' or 'falchion', and he represented fire, as Pegasus represented water.

Chrysaor has been a puzzle to students of the Gorgon myth, but his identity can be explained as the 'twin' of Pegasus and as such his adversary. The myth may have its origins in Phoenicia, where the river gods Chrysorrohoa and Pegai often appeared on the coins of Damascus, and evidently had a great part in the religion of the city.[1] Chrysaor is the lion born of the leonine Medusa, as Pegasus is the offspring of their father Poseidon, Lord of the Horse. The divine figure born with a sword is the sun. The solar Mithras rises from a rock brandishing a sword, and he too was emphatically leonine.

Here we discover the meaning of the action depicted on the archaic Beoetian amphora where Perseus decapitates the Medusa-horse with the solar head. In this version, where the wilting plant and the salamander indicate the end of summer, Medusa is a victim of sacrifice. In the ancient world, the head was the essence of all fertility, whether it be human (as with the Danaides) or equine, leonine, porcine. As we have seen, the head represented the sun, because like the sun it had the power of sight, was the seat of wisdom, and the saliva it produced was the source of water – like the boar's jaw – and the decapitated head in folklore was able to utter prophecies.

The possessor of the head was thus gifted with fruitfulness, good luck, fortune and power, not simply because it turned enemies to stone, but because it ensured a supply of water and benign fire to encourage growth, which is why Athena wears the gorgoneion on her aegis. After the Roman festival of the October horse, the teams fought for possession of the sacred head decorated with loaves.

It seems that horse-sacrifice, in which the horse was beheaded, was endemic among the Indo-Europeans. The Vedic Hindus observed a ritual in which a black or white horse was set free to wander for a year – as the sun itself and sun heroes notably 'wander'. The animal was accompanied by a priest (or in the *Mahabharata* an entire army) until it returned home at the end of the year, whereupon the horse was ceremonially beheaded with a sacred scimitar, or sickle.[2]

According to legend, the head ascended to heaven, while the carcass was burned on the altar fires – the process was known as the *Asvamedha*, 'horse sacrifice'. The *Asvamedha* had the same purpose as the decapitation of the October horse – the sacrifice of the solar animal hastened the fertilising rains. It was beheaded after Easter, and before the arrival of the south-west monsoons. Following the sacrifice, the rain drum and trumpet were sounded, and the king and queen were drenched with holy water.

The Gorgon is principally female because she represents the goddess's interest in the earth's fertility, and the revival of springs of water, and this is why the gorgoneion is worn by Athena. Medusa's beard, evident in many examples of the gorgoneion, refers to the androgynous nature of the sun. Her solar identity is further evident through the existence of her two sisters, who form the essential triad, and would otherwise be superfluous. Their names suggest their solar and equine nature: Stheno, 'the Strong', and Euryale, 'the Wide Leaping'.[3]

They were immortal, her two sisters, because they represent the winter solstice, the sun which though weakened now begins to regain its powers, and so never dies. Medusa, however, is the sun of the summer, 'decapitated' and thus weakened and mortal.

The myth pivots on the theme of decapitation and the act of Perseus in wielding his sickle. The sickle, or arpe, or drepanon, is a further clue to the meaning of the myth. The arpe used by Perseus is in fact a conventional sword but with a curious spur on the blade, not much use as a weapon for beheading victims, and impossible to sheathe.

Yet when Cronus notoriously emasculated his father, Uranus, he used a sickle, provided by his mother, Gaia, who instigated the crime. For the benefit of readers unfamiliar with this Greek creation legend, the earth mother Gaia coupled with her son Uranus to produce the race of Titans. Uranus imprisoned them within the body of Gaia, by embracing her in continuous sexual congress. In revenge, and to free herself of his attentions, she handed a sickle to her youngest child Cronus, with the command that he emsaculate his father while he slept. How Cronus achieved this, since he too was one of the imprisoned Titans is not made clear. Nor does it really matter. The action depends on the castration, where the drops of blood give birth to the Furies and the Meliae, the ash-tree nymphs. Cronus threw the genitals into the sea, from which was born the goddess Aphrodite.

To Greek poets and recorders of myth, such as Hesiod, the story was typical of creation legends, full of blood, mutilation, fire and sex, and it hardly needed explaining. To Socrates, interpreting myth demanded abundant leisure (which he surely possessed) and a 'vulgar curiosity'. But the origins and meaning of such myths were, as we say, 'lost in the mists of time' and seemed to defy interpretation.

The young god Attis unmanned himself with a sickle, sufficient examples to show that 'sickle' equals castration and decapitation. Why, then, this curious emphasis on an agricultural implement? Does it indicate, perhaps, the time that the decapitation of Medusa took place, in the late summer and early autumn? Yet this is the time of seed sowing, not harvesting. In antiquity, the Greeks harvested their barley at the end of April, their wheat in May – or at the morning rising of the Pleiades on 11th May. The first rains began to fall about mid-October.

This castration theme has provided a rich source of theorising for those who lean towards Freudian interpretations, theories both plausible and attractive – if one believes in the doctrine. Richard

Caldwell, in *The Origin of the Gods*, drily remarks of the Greek creation legend that 'psychoanalysis should have something to say about a myth in which the first father marries his mother and is then castrated by his son'.[4]

Pursuing a similar vein, Alan Dundes writes, 'The castration of the father by the son would, like the virgin birth, be an ultimate expression of the son's repudiation or rejection of his father.'[5] Theories about the purpose of castration in myth and religion are in general subjective. Burkert says that 'castration puts a man outside archaic society in an absolutely irrevocable way; being neither man nor woman, but "nothing", he has no place to go. He has no choice but to adhere to his goddess.' The act makes apostasy impossible. Burkert sees it as the conflict of opposites, inversion and reversal, the primordial hunter's situation involving killing and guilt.[6]

Motives suggested by other authors include asceticism, fecundation of Mother Earth, male envy of the female, and the like. Several cultures share a creation myth where the sky and earth are forcibly separated, among them Egypt, Greece, Babylonia, and Palestine. In Hebrew legend, Cham or Shem 'the black' mutilated his father Noah;[7] the sky god Baal Shamaim – according to the first-century AD Syrian scholar Philon of Byblos – was mutilated by his son, and the blood from the wound coloured the waters of the spring and river sacred to him; it was a common story in the Bible lands.[8]

The story of the insatiable sky-father Uranus and the put-upon Gaia was recounted by Hesiod in the *Theogony*, and it reveals that the classical world did not grasp the true meaning of the myth. Professor Kirk explains the act of castration as a folktale device, 'an ingenious solution to the problem of how to prevent the sky god from continuous mating with the earth'.[9]

The sickle, or reaping hook, is a vital clue to the plot because it was Cronus's main attribute. The name 'Cronus' may derive from the Greek *kuros*, meaning 'circle' or 'bent'; he possessed the power of a rainmaker. As the Roman Saturn he was a grim figure, invariably veiled, and his celebrations, the Saturnalia, took place in December. He is variously titled *megas*, 'abundance', and *ankulometes*, 'crooked'. Cronus has puzzled mythologists because of his contradictory nature, and his curious festivals.

The Greeks called theirs the Kronia, while the Romans had their Saturnalia, which began on 17th December and lasted for seven days. It was thus timed for the winter solstice. As to his contradictory character, he is known on the one hand for human sacrifices, and on the other is remembered as the god of the Golden Age, ruling the Islands of the Blessed. Hesiod, in *Works and Days*, called Cronus 'the king of heaven' in whose reign mortals lived like gods, 'untouched by work of sorrow' and to whom death came 'as sleep'.

In *The Case of Cronus*, the Dutch writer H. S. Versnel reviews these ambiguities, where Cronus is both god of an inhumanly cruel era without ethical standards, and yet the king presiding over justice, abundance and happiness. 'Such violent opposition within one and the same divine ambiance calls for an explanation. Explanations have been proposed, of course. They generally boil down to a denial of the seriousness of the contradictions.'[10]

At the Rhodian festival of the Kronia, a condemned criminal was given wine to drink, then slaughtered. A month prior to the Saturnalia, Roman troops observed a rite in which one of their number, chosen by lot, 'went about in public with full licence to indulge his passions and to taste every pleasure, however base and shameful'. When his time was up, the soldier cut his own throat and expired in his own blood 'on the altar of the god whom he personated'.[11]

The Saturnalia was to become the widely enjoyed Catholic carnival that began on the feast of Epiphany, its medieval equivalent the 'Feast of Fools' presided over by the Lord of Misrule. The feast had its parallels in the Babylonian Sacaea when slaves ruled their masters, and a criminal became king for the duration of the festival, but was afterwards put to death. The Roman festival in December was similarly a celebration of reversal when everything is turned upside-down, where slaves were waited on by their masters, played dice with them, and were encouraged to drink wine, where women play men's roles, and men dressed themselves as women, and presents were exchanged – a custom preserved in our Christmas celebrations. The sexual reversal may be found in our seasonal pantomimes, where the principal 'boy' is played by a girl, and the 'dame' by a man.

Modern scholars have interpreted this reversal, or conflict of extremes, as a way of neutralising the potential aggression and discontent of the oppressed – the criminals and slaves. Versnel's own interpretation is that Cronus is primeval chaos personified, in its dual aspect of freedom as joy and freedom as threat, and that unlimited euphoria cannot exist in reality, nor must anarchy be tolerated.

In both the myth and the rite, celebrants are reminded how the legitimate anarchy nears the limits of the allowable. The Lord of Misrule flirts with violent disorder, but reminds us that it must not subvert either the law or the structure of society.

This is elegant reasoning, and a valid contribution to our understanding of the conflicts in society, but the origins of Cronus are to be found in the physical rather than the philosophical world. Cronus, who is sometimes portrayed as Janiform, heads facing in opposite directions, is in fact the dual aspect of the sun. He is primarily the sun of death, of winter, appearing as Chronos, 'time', or Death with his scythe – 'The Grim Reaper'. Frazer says that of the names given by people to the seasons, Cronus was called 'winter'.[12]

This is why he appears veiled, and why he is celebrated by reversal, for the sun reverses after the winter solstice, and why he is a rainmaker. His festivals are solar, and take place at the time when the sun turns in its path to head north again towards the summer. Cronus is both the god of a Golden Age and of the dark days of winter.

Because Cronus rules over the winter, his weapon, the bill-hook or sickle, symbolises the tusks of the winter boar – 'the animal of death in the fall of the year'.[13] Ancient symbolism drew heavily on the image of the boar. The boar unmans, emasculates, the sun as it approaches winter, after the sun has delivered rain to the earth, and must now become female to fertilise the seed with solar heat.

It is the time, just following the rising of Virgo in late September, when Aphrodite rose from the sea. The king who must die at the Sacaea, the Kronia and the Saturnalia, is in fact Uranus, the great celestial solar bull, and it is he who Cronus emasculates, as he in turn will suffer a similar fate at the hands of Zeus, who will likewise meet his end on the island of Crete, gored to death by a boar.[14]

Adonis was savaged by Apollo or Ares in the guise of a boar;[15] Anceus, son of Poseidon, a winemaker (because he is a Dionysiac figure of the grape harvest in autumn) was likewise savaged by the boar of Calydon in September.[16] Odysseus had his thigh torn by a boar.[17] Osiris was ripped into fourteen pieces by Set as a boar;[18] the Phoenician Aleyin died when Mot, perhaps his twin, attacked him having shape-changed into a boar. This animal as an instrument of death was also a force of life and fecundity: the Hindu creator Prajapati took the form of a boar[19] which emerged from the primeval waters and created earth. Boars were of special interest because they symbolised the masculine principle and were regarded as especially virile on account of their numerous offspring. Rudra, who became the phallic Siva, rides a boar.[20]

The weakened or dying sun of winter, regarded by many as a bull, still had a task to fulfill, and this was to release seed to fall as rain and bring about abundant fertility. Having done so, its task then becomes a female one – that of germinating the seed. And so the emphasis is now placed on the female role of the androgynous deity; when Uranus's genitals were cast into the sea, there arose Aphrodite, whose landfall was the rocky shore at Paphos in Cyprus, and who presides over the fertility of the earth. Her name is derived from *aphros*, 'foam', because she powerfully represents the element from which she was born.

As the sun passes through water during the season of the rains, it undergoes a sex-change: the sun is 'male' before entering the water (the genitals of Uranus) at the winter solstice and female (Aphrodite) afterwards. It is firstly male because it delivers the celestial semen at the season of sowing, and in phallic terms was thought to penetrate the earth in its decline towards winter. The sun in winter was symbolised by the human phallus, painted in red ochre and buried in the earth.

The goddess Aphrodite seduced the Trojan prince Anchises, who boasted of the affair and was lamed by Zeus as a punishment. Anchises eventually died at Drepanon, a name meaning 'sickle'. Here was the solar hero, unmanned or 'weakened' by the powers of the goddess of love who was also, of course, a goddess of springs and rivers. The curious idea that Aphrodite was worshipped in Cyprus in the form of a woman with a beard comes from the recurring notion of the bisexual god, a figure derived from the sun which was thought to change its sexuality – Aphrodite was, after all, the product of her father's genitals.

The act of castration 'unmans' the virile deity, and he becomes possessed of female characteristics, as the eunuch develops breasts and undergoes a change of voice. This is why the festivals of Cronus witness the acts of cross-dressing, why Heracles exchanged clothes with Omphale, why Odysseus spent seven years on Circe's isle, and why Achilles was attired as a girl as he played among children, and why the prophet Tiresias was changed by Hera into a woman for seven years.

The bisexual nature of these solar figures will explain why Mithras and those wearing the Phrygian cap were suspected of being effeminate, and they include Attis who of course castrated himself; The sex change took place at the decline of the sun and the setting of the constellation Perseus in late October, the star group that perhaps inspired the Phrygian cap, mentioned previously.

Attis was the consort of the Anatolian mother goddess Cybele, and is represented as a solar figure who rides a cock or a lion, and who castrated himself with a sickle under a pine tree because the evergreen pine was the winter goddess's tree. The Mithraeum at Roman Carrawburgh, Northumberland (Procolitia), had a hearth fed with imported Mediterranean pine cones, and a bowl of pine-cone charcoal. All those strange, androgynous gods out of Asia Minor – Attis, Adonis, Men, Mithra and Sabazios, wearing the floppy Phrygian hat, display pine cones to show their devotion to the Mother Goddess.

Attis's employment of the sickle, like Cronus's, further indicates the time of the year as winter and the approach of spring. Attis is the combined agent or priest of sacrifice, and his own victim. He performs his act of self-mutilation to imitate the passing of the sun from male to female. Having impregnated the earth (Cybele) he now encourages the quickening of the earth's fecundity; all the eunuch priests in service of Cybele and Artemis have castrated themselves in support of this solar symbolism. It survives in the androgynous garb of the Christian Church, and the sexual abstinence of its clergy.

An icon shows Attis lying under the tree, between his spread legs a sickle and his shorn testicles, along with various animals – a cock, horse and bull. In performing this act of self-sacrifice, he simulates the predominantly feminine side of the sun and so encourages the spring rains essential to the crops and the harvest. In Upper Mesopotamia, if spring showers in March are only moderately abundant, wheat and barley grow to a great height. Across the eastern end of the Mediterranean, spring rains in March bring the crops to maturity, and late March through April was the time of the barley harvest. This is why the rite of the Dies Sanguine, the 'Day of Blood', was held in March.

The myth of Cronus and Uranus does lead to incest (as

suggested by the 'Oedipal' theorists) but Cronus eventually unites with his sister Rhea, and not his mother. The offspring of this celestial pairing was, of course, Zeus, who in turn succeeded Cronus. He was hardly the epitome of fatherly devotion, this savage god who devoured each of his children as they were born – an act famously portrayed by Goya – all except for the last child Zeus, when Rhea with belated concern substituted a stone which Cronus promptly swallowed. The swallowing theme was long ago explained by the Sanskrit scholar Adalbert Kuhn – who pioneered the study of Comparative Religion – as winter swallowing the sun.[21]

The incest theme that runs through these myths merely underlines the fusion of the sexes and that of the sun with the earth, and the celestial bull with the goddess.

There exist several very late versions of the Gorgon's head where she appears as a classic, normal head, but with the same furrowed brow that we find in the gorgoneion at Bath.[22] In almost every example the head is horned, like a bull. Thus she combines the lion and the bull, the male and the female, the androgynous character of the sun, with all its fertile powers. This metamorphosis should not seem strange, for there was an ancient precedent – the Assyrian horned lion with the tail of a scorpion, embodying the fertile qualities of the dark months of the year before the winter solstice.

The theme of castration was a primitive and effective way of describing the sun's bisexual nature, rather than the later concept of the hermaphrodite, and the boar presented itself as a useful agent of destruction. Adonis, of almost feminine beauty, was gored to death by a boar by the spring of Aphrodite at Af'ka, and his brief reign from the winter to the summer solstice was observed by women who put out fragile plants on rooftops – 'the gardens of Adonis' – to mourn the sun's waning powers of fertility, as in Babylonia they wept for Tammuz.

Death by the goddess's spring invariably symbolises the decline of the sun, whose seasonal descent invigorates the earth's waters. There is another aspect of this Adonis-type myth, where the boar gores its victim 'in the thigh', euphemistically castrating the sun's representative to effect the vital sex-change. A version of the death of King Saul says that he was 'crushed with stones between the thighs' before being decapitated.[23] Achilles, on the field of Troy, spears his adversary Hector in the thigh.

In Arthurian legend, Anfortas the Fisher King is castrated by a
lance or fiery spear. Valiant knights are wounded – like Adonis –
by a spring; one has his head cut off and thrown into a well. A
female guardian of the Holy Grail drove a cart drawn by stags and
carrying 152 severed heads to King Arthur's court.[24] These
medieval tales of severed heads, wounds to the thigh, watery
places and malevolent queens are all the legacy of very ancient
solar ideas, as is the castration of Uranus by Cronus, the self-
mutilation of Attis, and the unknown fate of Osiris's lost member,
swept away by the rising waters of the Nile.

The sun, having discharged its male seed must work in the earth
in the role of a female to gestate its progeny. The Egyptian sun-
god Atum-Re was called 'The Great He-She'[25] in recognition of
his dual nature, after he had 'performed a mutilation on himself',
while the goddess Mut, one of the Theban divine triad, depicted
as a lioness or a vulture, was correspondingly ithyphallic.

This is why the Hindu fire god Agni swallows the semen of
Prajapati and Siva, and the energy, or '*sakti*' of Agni, is female.
Agni, in fact, is an aspect of Parvati (whose symbol is the vulva or
yoni), the wife of the phallic god Siva. We know that his seven
assistants are all goddesses, as Hephaestus has seven golden robots,
also female.

The element of bisexuality is found in the childhood of
Achilles, who is decidedly solar, and who dressed as a girl and
played with girls: cross-dressing is a device to indicate the
feminine aspect of of the hero's normally manifest masculinity.
Dionysus dressed as a girl. Heracles swapped clothes with
Omphale. Odysseus spent seven years on Circe's Isle. We saw that
Paris was ordered off the battlefield of Troy by Menelaus, and told
to 'get back to the boudoir'.[26]

Apollo's femininity is less crudely etched but nevertheless well-
defined, and by the same token his sister Artemis is determinedly
virginal, pursuing a man's role as a hunter but also as the Nemesis
of the autumn stag, or bull. It is often hard to tell the difference in
representations of Apollo and Artemis – both carry a bow and
quiver of arrows, and as Robert Graves suggested, it may be that
they were twins, or fused into a single, androgynous figure.

The bisexual influence is again an ancient concept. The
castrated priests of the Mother Goddess cults, having performed
their self-mutilation, were given women's clothes to wear. Let's
not waste any time with the theory proposed by Bruno

Bettelheim and others that men, through envy of feminine creative powers, usurped their role. 'It proves,' declared Bettelheim, 'that men were willing and ready to make themselves into "females" in order to share women's superior powers.'[27] It proves no such thing.

The idea that the original creator was androgynous was deeply rooted in the imagination of many societies, but the concept is primeval and comes from the idea of the androgynous sun. This is simple nature symbolism – the bull precipitates the rain, the springs burst from the ground and nourish the newly emerging life, as do the breasts of the Mother Goddess. Water, as well as the sun, is thus both male and female.

Terracotta models of bulls' heads with female breasts below the horns predate 5000 BC.[28] At Çatal Hüyük in Asia Minor shrines displayed rows of breasts modelled in clay, juxtaposed with bucrania.[29] Hapi, a god of the Nile, whose head is crowned with water plants, has pendulous breasts, and so do some figures of Zeus. Among the Aboriginal Australians the male rainbow serpent Kumanggur has breasts,[30] and in each of the foregoing examples the breasts denote nourishment from spring waters while the male element denotes the fertility of rain.

This is the real reason why Zeus swallowed his first wife Metis, becoming effectively androgynous, probably an essential characteristic of all primitive deities, although in the more sophisticated deities of developed religions, the bisexual elements may prove hard to identify. Not so among remote tribes, however. In the 1930s Joseph Winthius, a Catholic missionary and ethnologist (the professions are not mutually exclusive), studied the Gunantuna tribe of New Guinea and wrote down their tribal songs. All but one had a meaning 'so crude that he felt obliged to translate them in Latin rather than in his native German'. Winthius concluded that the primitive mind is pervaded by sexuality, and his main discovery was that tribal religion appeared to originate in the belief of a bisexual god, a view that was heartily opposed by the ethnological establishment of the time, but one which Winthius defended with a passionate conviction.[31] Recently the ethnologist Hermann Baumann has traced the spread of this concept across the globe, delineated by areas occupied by agricultural rather than hunting societies.[32]

Baumann doesn't venture an explanation, having failed to perceive the overriding solar symbolism, but cites many examples among the shamans of the arctic regions. Shamanism, practised in religions where priests (shamans) claim to interpret and influence events through their relationship with otherworld spirits (often in the form of snakes), seems to exist principally where environments are especially harsh, for example in arid regions of Africa ('witch doctors') and in the Siberian tundra. The shaman's ritual paraphernalia is usually a drum, decorated with seven pendants, his or her vestments hung with snake designs and plaits.[33] The drum and the seven snakes point to sun and rain, and we would expect the number seven to be influential in an area so needful of the sun's warmth. The Ostyak people believe that a goddess, seated on a seven-storey celestial mountain, writes a man's fate, as soon as he is born, on a tree with seven branches.[34] A mammoth-ivory plaque decorated with a seven-turn spiral, with three snakes engraved on the back, dating from about 16,000 BC may be the earliest example of number symbolism, and is certainly the earliest example of a spiral in art.

Shamans were often transvestites, or had undergone a sex change. This may have been the result of a powerful Mother Goddess cult, extant among north Eurasian peoples, presided over by a solar triad of goddesses – Mother Earth, Mother Water and Mother Fire. Thus the shaman identifies with the feminine solar principle, concentrating all aspects of the elements and the environment into one being; the harsher the environment, the more intense (and mystical) the representation from the shaman, who was then more able to conduct spiritual intercourse between the members of his tribe and the spirits who controlled their fates. Medicine men serve a similar function, not unlike the Apollonine oracles of ancient Greece.

The main function of the shaman, indeed his raison d'être, is as a healer of the sick, in the course of which he undertakes his visionary journeys. This is comparable to the trance-states of the Pythia at Delphi, presided over by the healer Apollo, and the many other intermediaries between the petitioner and the god or goddess.

Identification with the female generative forces of the sun may also explain the notorious subincision wounds of the Australian Aborigines, where a lateral and deep cut is made along the length of the penis, probably in imitation of the vulva.[35] It was a system which ensured a closer bond with natural forces in the comparably harsh environment of the arid Australian bush. The copious blood from the subincicion wound was allowed to soak into the earth, like the blood of the effeminate Attis. This crude surgical operation was not infrequently fatal, and conducted to the sound of the whirring bullroarer, a shaped wooden slat attached to a long cord that imitated thunder, and was employed in the ancient world as a rain charm.

The purpose of subincision, I suggest, was to establish androgyny and permanent identification with the solar powers. The bisexual imperative has appeared in a less dramatic fashion throughout history in farming communities where cross-dressing takes place during ploughing and sowing, and at the time of the harvest. Sir James Frazer noted how male harvesters in rural communities wore women's clothes, or women wore men's clothes, often with a black mask. As the final sheaf was cut, the reaper would be drenched with water. 'Sometimes a black mask is fastened on the reaper's face and he is dressed in woman's clothes; or if the reaper is a woman, she is dressed in man's clothes; a dance follows.'[36]

Usually, however, the person drenched with water is a girl attired in leaves. In the place of a girl a sheaf of corn is dressed in a woman's clothes and drenched with water. In the more arid regions of the ancient world, rain in spring was essential to the success of the harvest in late March through April.

All these creator gods with marked, feminine attributes are also able to perform as male donors of seed. Agni is regularly called upon to produce rain. Isis becomes impregnated by the seed of Osiris prior to his death at the hands of Set, who casts his genitals into the Nile. Osiris, now 'female', descends to the underworld.

The sun that is the great celestial bull releases its seminal rains to fertilise the earth; the sun that represents the quickening powers of the womb to encourage the growth of animals and plants in the springtime, is female. This formula, performed annually by the sun between the summer and winter solstices perhaps explains the well-known nursery rhyme,

> Jack and Jill
> went up the hill
> to fetch a pail of water.
> Jack fell down
> and broke his crown
> and Jill came tumbling after.

The rhyme and its variations must be very ancient, and has puzzled those who picture the couple climbing a hill to draw water from a well, an arrangement that would defy physical laws. According to the folklorist, mythologist and hymnist Baring-Gould, 'Jack and Jill' can be traced to Scandinavian lore, where it is shown to be a rhyme featuring a pair called Bjuki and Bil, who are related in some way to the moon.

Perhaps there is another explanation, where Jack and Jill combine to make the androgynous sun, whose ascent 'up the hill' towards the summer solstice is followed by its fall towards winter, when it 'fetches water', and the pail is spilled.[37]

The role played by the smith-gods involves more than the annual fertilising of the earth. They assist in the creation of mankind, which was seen to require skills comparable to those of the male artisans in society, the architects, builders, carpenters and plough-makers, the men who dig the irrigation canals, the herders, the fishermen. Tvashtri, the Vedic creator god, whose name means 'carpenter' and who, like Ishtar, was a 'carpenter of the insides', seems to share his remarkable skills with an equally remarkable group of craftsmen – the cabinet-makers of Sorrento.

According to the travel writer Norman Lewis, the craftsmen of this southern Italian town, famous for marquetry, maintain a tradition whereby the eldest sons become surgeons, having developed extreme manual dexterity through the practice of their trade. One of their members, suitably a dwarf, became a gynaecologist, whose inherited nimble fingers were well suited to the task of working in the female pelvic cavity.[38] For the divine smiths, however, creation in the womb of the earth needed masculine as well as feminine effort, the swing of hammer on anvil. This is why the female creative role was the task of the artisan gods.

The womb is a source of heat, analagous to the potter's kiln and the baker's oven, and also to the forge, but a magic forge in which life was created. Their benefactor and overseer is, fittingly, a woman, and one appropriately in male attire – Athena, who presides over the work of potters and smiths and who sometimes sits in her owl-form on kilns and ovens. At the command of Zeus, Athena and Hephaestus formed Pandora. The smith-god moulded the clay and Athena clothed her.

The kiln is allied to the forge, but a magic forge in which life was created, worked by a solar artisan-smith, whose helpers numbered seven. They were cast as dwarfs because they laboured in a confined space, the womb of the earth, like the Seven Dwarfs who helped Snow White. They too worked deep in caves underground, in a diamond mine, seeking treasure which is comparable to the wealth and progeny of the womb.

These magical dwarf assistants that toil in the earth appear in the mythologies of many societies. They are the Hindu Ribhus, sons of the mare Saranyu, brothers of the twin Asvins, who assist Tvashtri in fashioning Indra's thunderbolts. In Teutonic myth they are the Nibelungen who guard a treasure hoard. In Crete they are represented by the supple-fingered Dactyls who taught the smelting of iron, while the Cabiri of Lemnos were marine deities worshipped in Asia Minor and throughout the Near East.

Most seem, in one way or another, to be associated with water in addition to metalworking because of the creative combination of water with fire; the Telchines of Rhodes; the Palici of Sicily, twins who first arose from two lakes of sulphurous water; the Corybantes and the Curetes, all appear to have some connection with the sea, as does the master smith Hephaestus.[39]

In ancient Mexico, rain was controlled by four gods, the Chacs, who lived in a cave with four chambers, and were assisted by dwarfs. Their task was to dispense rain from jars, filled by four huge storage casks, further possible evidence of how lore has spread westward from the Old World.[40]

Throughout central Africa, dwarfs are thought to be aquatic and nature spirits, and share with twins this same mystique of fertility. In Loango the king is obliged to travel through his realm, in order to be accepted by the spirits of the earth, by playing the role of a sacred cripple – the sun. And we find, too, the same emphasis on the number seven, the seven months of nature's gestation: Ogun, blacksmith god of the Yoruba of western Nigeria has seven names, is made up of seven parts, and is represented by seven, fourteen or twenty-one smith's implements of iron.[41]

In the Mesopotamian myth of Atrahasis, the goddess Mami makes fourteen clay wombs, seven of which will create men, and seven of which will create women.[42] Creation myths focus on the skills of the potters, who make men of clay, but the inert substance lacks the spark of life, the heat of gestation. This is why the master-craftsman Prometheus, 'the trickster', steals fire from the forge of Hephaestus, smouldering in the stalk of the giant fennel plant. Prometheus stole from heaven the solar powers of springtime. Prometheus is the sun itself. He is 'the forethinker', the sun on its climb towards the summer solstice, while his weaker brother, Epimetheus, 'the afterthinker', is the sun in decline. This is a dynamic relationship between twins, and a persistent theme in the great pageant of ancient mythology.

Nature symbolism is remarkably inventive and visually striking. In India, the god Balarama obligingly demonstrates by disgorging from his mouth a snake with a thousand heads.[43] India, with its somewhat stoic and fatalistic view of life, insists that its myths are at least entertaining. How else could they have created the pot-bellied, elephant-headed Ganesa, and the violent black-faced Kali, with her four arms, her tongue reaching her waist, dancing on the severed heads of men? Krishna was the favourite of the gopis, or milkmaids, and because they were cow girls, he is revered as the young bull. As his time came to decrease, Krishna retired to the forest to die, accompanied by his twin brother Balarama, the seventh son of Devaki, where he was shot in the heel by the hunter, Jara (*jar*, 'to reduce' or 'to wear out'). Krishna referred to himself as 'time', but his name means 'black'. It comes from the root KRS and *krsna*, 'black' or 'blue-black'.

Krishna and Balarama were said to have been formed from two hairs, plucked by Vishnu from his own head – one hair was white, the other (*krsna*) black. Why is Krishna black? John Robertson, writing at the turn of the century for the Rationalist Press, decided 'It is fallacious to assume that any one cause can be fixed as the reason for the attribution of this colour to deities in ancient religions'.[44] Scholars proposed various explanations, including the idea that blackness referred to the hidden sun at night; or the blackness of sky and rain, or of the earth, or because Krishna was 'a god of the black-skinned natives'. Blackness, however, refers neither to caste or race. Is it because he represents rainclouds which gather during the winter months when the sun declines? That Balarama represents this particular season of the year might be guessed from the claim that he was 'wine-drinking', a curious partiality in a country not noted for its vines. Balarama is the effeminate twin identified with the goddess of springs and the number seven, and is a version of Jara. It is in fact Balarama who kills Krishna, the lion that slays the bull.

The blackness of Krishna (like the Black Virgins) refers to the darkness of winter, and the underworld where the sun is thought to be going. The 'black' sun is the dying, weakened sun, while Balarama is the 'white', strong sun of revival. They are the divine twins. Balarama comes from the root BAL, another 'burn' word, which also gives *bhal*, 'to shine'.

This 'deformity' of the sun perhaps explains the animals with black tails appearing in myth and legend. Indra's steed had a black tail; Indian tribes in America have stories of deer with black tails burned in a fire and dogs or wolves that obtain fire by tying burning brands to their tails.[45]

We can now understand why Melampus, the earliest prophet known to the Greeks, and the seer at the oracular shrine at Olympus is 'blackfoot'. His mother was Melanippe ('black mare'), and he was the ancestor of a line of Argive kings and prophets including Amphiaraus ('very sacred') who, as the winter sun, was swallowed up by the earth. The word that gives Melampus's name – melas – was not used to convey blackness caused by dirt, but in describing a dark complexion.[46]

Achilles, delivering an invocation to Zeus before Troy, refers to the priests of Zeus, the Selloi, at the Oracle of 'hard-wintered Dodona', who had 'unwashen feet' and slept on the ground. This passage has puzzled interpreters of Homer's *Iliad*, in which it appears, but the reference is solar. The Selloi slept on the ground with their black feet as the sun sleeps on the ground during winter. Melampus and the Selloi were forecasters of rain and thus of fertility. The invocation before Troy, made by a solar hero to the prophets of the sun, by the prophetic oak at Dodona, was no doubt in the hope that Zeus and the Selloi might forecast success in battle.[47]

The idea of forecasting rain – or forecasting anything – bears with it the implication and the hope that the desired phenomenon will in fact occur, especially if the agent or catalyst is possessed of special powers – the magic foot, the visionary gifts of the seer, the trance states of the shaman, those who apparently have access to the other world.

Could this motif of blackness, and the 'unwashen feet' of the Selloi, go some way to explain the meaning behind one of the world's most celebrated folktales, the story of Cinderella, who sits among the ashes, as the Selloi sleep upon the ground? At the end of the last century, the folklorist Marian Rolfe Cox, on behalf of the Folklore Society, investigated and made a collection of all the variants of the folktale *Cinderella*.[48] She reached a total of 345, and suspecting this was a mere fraction of the whole, decided that enough was enough.

Cox's book *Cinderella* was the only major study until the publication in 1951 of Anna Birgitta Rooth's *The Cinderella Cycle*, and just over thirty years later, Alan Dundes's *Cinderella: A Folklore Casebook*. The most recent study, in 1989, is Neil Phillips's *The Cinderella Story*. One more work must be included, Harold Bayley's odd but absorbing book *The Lost Language of Symbolism*, published in 1912, drawing on Cox's references, and a collection of Gnostic watermarks from French papermakers. It doesn't sound like a best seller. It wasn't, but after nearly a century it still has a following, and remains in print.

No fairytale heroine has merited such attention and popular exposure. The worldwide dissemination of the original tale, and probably the reason for the variants, allowing for cultural preferences, is due to its antiquity. The story reputedly had its source in China, in the ninth century AD, but is decidedly older. Its popularity in the West came about with Charles Perrault's *Cendrillon*, published in 1697, the story drawn from oral tradition and shaped with French finesse. It took its place in European folk literature with three Grimm variants, but the original Perrault contains all the favourite details – the Pumpkin Coach, the Fairy Godmother and Rat Coachmen, and the glass slipper or shoe.

There have been many attempts to interpret the Cinderella story, not the least by writers with some leaning towards psycho-analysis. Grimm's version of the tale is called 'Aschenputtle', or 'ash pussy' which Dundes compares to the Latin *puta*, and *pudendum*. Several writers have suggested that Cinderella expressed penis envy, menstrual envy, mother's 'magic phallus', and oedipal conflicts.[49]

The writer Angela Carter decided that *Cinderella* was 'all about women and interfamilial rivalry and how girls and mothers hate one another'. This interpretation is supported by the views of Bruno Bettelheim, who plumps for sibling rivalry in his book *The Uses of Enchantment*.

He sees this as the main topic of the story, along with penis envy, castration anxiety, menstrual anxiety and, being a good Freudian, the Oedipus complex.[50] A more sober point of view was taken by Norbert Glas, in 1946, who said that the story was about 'the purification of the soul and the conquest of evil'.[51]

Freud pointed to the resemblance between the Cinderella theme and that of *The Three Caskets*,[52] where the tale pivots on a threefold choice – familiar in Paris's awarding the prize to one of three goddesses; the Prince choosing Cinderella in preference to her sisters; Psyche, chosen by Eros, has two jealous sisters. The theme provided the basis for Shakespeare's *King Lear*, where the king demands the evidence of love from his three daughters; in *The Merchant of Venice* Portia has to marry the suitor who makes the right choice between three caskets – one of gold, one of silver the third of lead.

Emphasis on the number three provides the story with a solar meaning. But is there also, perhaps, a phallic element here? The story is too familiar to warrant going over in detail, the Prince gives a grand Ball, the sisters are invited but poor Cinderella remains behind, sitting among the ashes; the Fairy Godmother (perhaps a sort of Athena), provides a magic coach (usually transformed from a pumpkin, to represent the sun), and Cinderella finds herself going to the Ball in a gorgeous dress. The Ball takes place three nights in a row, and on the third night the heroine forgets the curfew. She dashes away as her clothes turn to rags and the coach changes back into a pumpkin. In her haste to get away she loses one of her slippers (as does Jason the Argonaut). The Prince retrieves it, and so on.

In the original Chinese tale, the slippers are made of gold, but in the process of time, and migration, they become glass. Only in six of Cox's 345 variants are the slippers actually made of glass; in other tales they are silver, satin or silk. The Chinese gold slippers allow a solar identity, and so do many of Cinderella's epithets, where she is 'the fire blower', and the 'whipper of ashes'.

Indeed, her solar character is hard to ignore or deny. In a Scandinavian version she lives in a cave with seven maidens for seven years and takes three days to get out, a theme which may be compared to the creation legends. She is 'The Princess in the Mound', but in Portugal she lives in the bottom of a well. She is the seventh of seven daughters. The Indian Cinderella is 'The Seventh Wife in the Dungeon'. She hides in a 'golden chest' or is 'thrown into a briar bush'. Cinderella 'shines like the sun', and has a series of wonderful dresses – usually in threes – that are the colours of the dawn, she wears 'a dress like flame'.

Her name may related to the Latin *clara*, 'clear', or 'to shine'. She is also called Lucy in some versions, where she may be robed in black, her face blackened with soot or ashes.[53]

Cinderella climbs a staircase to the Ball in a shimmering dress like the sun, and is joined by the Prince who dances with her. She must observe the midnight curfew because it represents the midsummer solstice. She falls, loses her slipper, and is thus symbolically lamed. She takes her lowly place in the ashes of the hearth, as the Japanese goddess Amaterasu retires to her cave. She is asked 'How are you?' And Cinderella replies, 'As in winter.'

Only by retrieving her shoe, against the competition of her two sisters can she regain her rightful position as the sun-goddess, now married to the Prince who had been 'madly in love' or 'sick with love' because, of course, the sun is the ideal healer of sickness.

Nearly every commentator has alluded to the female genitalia, for which the shoe or slipper is a prime symbol, and she alone is destined to wear the shoe now held by the Prince or his deputy. There can be no doubt that many of her forms reveals bisexual characteristics found in solar myths. Thus the Prince on possession of Cinderella's shoe takes a female role, while Cinderella proffers her foot to fit it into the shoe. This role reversal is the same as that of the harvesters who swap clothes and wear black masks.

There is good reason why this classic fairytale is chosen as the subject for Christmas pantomimes. It is the direct descendant of the Roman Saturnalia held in December and its focus on role-reversal. The pantomime is a development of the harlequinade and the Italian commedia dell'arte, possibly introduced to England by the Grimaldi family of clowns in the late eighteenth century. The pantomime Prince Charming is played by the 'principal boy', traditionally acted by a woman, while the Dame and Ugly Sisters are played by men.

Cinderella's masculine identity may be seen where she lives in a golden bull, a golden chest, or a horse. She is 'no bigger than a little finger', fits into a candlestick, wears a mouse-skin or a cat's skin. Her identity as the tree goddess, like Artemis, appears in versions where she is 'Maria Wood', 'Woodencloak' or 'Wainscot', or she fits into a hollow log or wooden sheath. This feature may be compared to a Phoenician figurine of a goddess placed inside a hollow tree, the goddess encouraging the rise of sap, or of water to hasten life.[54] Cinderella as the archetypal sun and water-goddess is 'the giver of liquid life', and three streams of milk spring from her breasts or mouth.

When she speaks, pearls and gems pour from her lips; she loosens her hair and shakes out showers of pearls like rain. This very descriptive symbolism of the feminine blessings of nourishment could equally apply to the delivery of semen from the solar phallus – the three streams of milk, pearls falling from the lips.

Cinderella seems related to Ishtar, for both wore wonderful robes and passed through seven gates or curtains. Cinderella is the sun-goddess whose blackness refers to the fertile period of rainfall (as Dona Labismina, she is born with a snake around her neck; her fairy godmother is a sea-serpent), the period when the earth is ploughed and receives the seed. She may in this sense be related to the Black Virgins of the Catholic Church, for three drops of milk appeared to St Bernard from the Black Virgin.

Several goddesses were on occasions black. Aphrodite was black. Demeter, mare-headed, and having retired to her cave, was Demeter Melainis, 'black'. Her blackness was said to be rage, whence she was called Erinys 'fury', at having been covered by Poseidon as a horse, but she was black, horse-headed, and living in a cave to celebrate the seed-sowing, for Demeter was *par excellence* the goddess of crops. Persephone, Demeter's other half, is closely associated with the pomegranate, the golden-globe fruit and a symbol of the sun. She eats 'seven seeds' of the pomegranate and because of this was obliged to remain in the underworld for a season, as Cinderella lives under a mound, or in a well.

Cinderella, with the divine, sooty face, is the black goddess – Isis, Demeter, Aphrodite, Cybele, Anat and Ishtar, call her what you will – emphasising the feminine side of the androgynous sun, later joined to the solar hero in marriage when the year-cycle begins again.

CHAPTER 13

Goddesses of Death

The frequent apocalyptic references to drought scattered through myths shows that such events were a perpetual cause for concern. Indeed, it was a catastrophe demanding human sacrifice, one of the sternest measures imaginable. Such was the case where a father is obliged to sacrifice the first person he meets on making a solemn vow to a deity.

In the myth of Lophis, a father commits himself to a sacrifice in return for the cessation of a severe drought. The Delphic Oracle instructs him to slay the first person he meets on returning home, which of course turns out to be his son.

The father mortally wounds the boy with his sword, and where the dying Lophis ran in a circle, imitating the dying of the sun, there arose the springs of the river named after him.[1] This can be compared with the self-sacrifice of Callirhoe of Calydon, who stabs herself to death over a spring of water,[2] which thereafter bore her name, and of Maiandros, who threw himself into the river later named after him.[3]

Water-inducing myths served to relieve anxiety, and were also a form of insurance when acted out in a ritual. Thus it was hoped that the threat of drought was diverted by regular animal sacrifice, supposedly commanded by the goddess whose function it was to provide water. This is suggested by a scene on a Minoan seal showing a griffin, agent or 'priest' of the goddess, killing a stag over a sacrificial altar.[4] Another seal shows a bull's horns surmounted by a water vessel, and on the reverse of the seal the bull has been mortally struck by a spear.

Here is the equivalent of the spear of Athena, or the arrow of Artemis, and it tells us why the goddess of fertility is often shown in martial attire, not because (in Athena's case) she is the city protectoress of Athens (although that is certainly one of her functions) but because she is the nemesis of sacrificed men and animals.

Athena was a goddess of wisdom, of arts and crafts. These gifts contrast strangely with her appearance as Athene Promarchos, goddess of war, with her spear and shield. A virgin, and called by Athenians 'kore', 'the maiden', she was the favourite child of Zeus. She sprang from Zeus's head with a mighty shout and became the most influential of Greek goddesses to preside over Athens. But why? Does her name offer any clues? Tracing the source has led some scholars to the Indo-Aryan word *vadh*, pronounced with a soft 'd', more like 'th', so that 'vath' allows the first syllable of 'Ath-e-na'; the suffix *na* is non-Greek.

Vadh means 'to strike' and derives from the root VA meaning 'wind' and 'to blow'. It is related to *vach*, 'voice', and *vadana*, 'mouth', all suggesting Athena's shout or war-cry. Now, Vach was the 'Mother of the Vedas', goddess of poetry and eloquence, and the Minerva or Athena of the Hindu pantheon, so we seem to be on the right track. She was identical to Sarasvati, goddess of wisdom, of springs and rivers, so Vach was a water goddess.[5]

Vadh can also mean 'to sacrifice', and it leads to a subordinate or alter ego of Athena, the goddess Nike, who sacrificed bulls, and

FIG. 31 Birth of Athena from Zeus's head, aided by Hephaestus.

who was worshipped in the temple of the Winged Victory, dedicated to Athena-Nike, on the Acropolis in Athens. Greek *nike* means 'victory' (cp. Latin *vincere*) but it comes ultimately from the Sanskrit *nicah* 'to humble' or 'subdue', cognate with the meaning of 'violent and warlike'. This is why Athena wears a warrior's helmet (and sometimes a cap made from the head of a lion, the goddess's tutelary beast) and carries a spear.

It is Nike who appears in art as a winged figure carrying a jug or amphora, or a dish from which she pours water on to a blazing thymiaterion or altar. What she does, in effect, is to subdue the sun, here a fiery altar, elsewhere a bull, occasionally a ram. She seems also to be a version of Mithras, kneeling astride the bull and stabbing it in the neck.

In art, the figure of Nike became progressively more and more masculine. This appears on the Parthenon pediment, and by Roman times she has become almost totally androgynous, with male headdress and features, and would seem to have been fused with Mithras, much as Athena became fused with Pallas ('youth') as Pallas-Athene. It is reasonable to propose that Athena became an androgyne with Perseus, for Perseus and Mithras share many common features. Nike crowns heroes with the evergreen laurel wreath, sacred to Apollo. She is also depicted in a kneeling posture, like figures of the Gorgon, which Nike exactly matches.

What these heroes and goddesses do, in effect, is to terminate the harsh rule of the summer sun. The due process of nature will terminate it anyway, but in the unpredictable climate of the Mediterranean and the Near East where expected seasonal rain may fail to arrive, drought could mean starvation, and so the hero or heroine who overrules the sun, and prevails over the climate, is the victor, crowned by the goddess whose fertility is restored and guaranteed.

This martial aspect was the feature of all goddesses, because in order to discharge their primary duty, and encourage the arrival of water, they must bring about the death of the sun, in fact 'kill' the sun, and sacrifice the celestial bull, the solar representative. This is why Athena was 'the striker', the victorious martial goddess of Athens who, with her aide Nike, triumphs over want, and defies the drought that threatens the land. It is she who presides over the olive trees, and waters them, and ripens them with the sun, for the Athenians relied heavily on their olive crops, the only product that they exported in significant quantities.[6]

FIG. 32 Athena, aegis and a gorgoneion.

Farnell proposed that one of Athena's titles, 'Tritogeneia', means 'born near water', because legend says that she was born by Lake Tritogenia in Libya.[7] She sprang from the head of Zeus as the Ganges springs from the head of Siva, or the Nile flows from the mouth of Ra, as water gushes from a limestone fissure, and as the sun appears from the mountain peak, and this is why Hephaestus the goldsmith and fire-god was assigned to the task of liberating her, splitting Zeus's head open with an axe.

Athena's other well-known attribute was the owl, and not just any owl, but a particular species, the Little Owl, *Athena noctua*. In *Zeus*, Cook suggests that this may be due to the fact that the Acropolis in Athens was a favourite haunt of owls, where they nested in the rocks (the German name is *steinkauz* – 'rock owl'), and that Athena was herself the rock of the citadel.[8] The reputation of Athena for wisdom (her mother being Metis, or 'counsel') made the owl her natural associate.

Other goddesses can also lay claim to the owl as their familiar. The Mesopotamian Lilith was accompanied by lions and owls and is featured with the wings and legs of an owl; *Athena noctua* has a sub-species 'Lilith'. So Athena and Lilith share the same bird. Lilith, like Hecate, was a manifestation of the earth during winter, the months of darkness and rain. She was the 'night hag' responsible for the demise of the sun.

Perhaps this is why she is accompanied by owls. A clue to the meaning of Athena's owl might be found on Athenian coins, where the head of the goddess has an owl on the obverse side, and the bird is grasping a thunderbolt while perching on an upturned amphora, or water-vessel. Some small bronzes from Athens have twin owls on a thunderbolt, or perched on the branch of an olive.

This image points to the owl as being Athena herself, performing her duty of bringing rain and prosperity to the olive groves. In Palestine, the military surveyor Claud Conder noted that 'comical little owls are always found in olive trees', and he mentioned a 'fine olive grove, amongst the trees of which sat the little "boomehs" or Athenian owls only some ten inches high. By day their peculiar cry, a sort of mew, is the only indication of their lurking place, but by night their big eyes can be seen in the branches.'[9] The olive tree, and the resident owls, were both representations of Athena herself.

The Little Owl is diurnal, hunting by day and night. It has dual or 'twin' habits, and is therefore like the sun of summer and winter, suggesting that it is especially gifted with solar foresight, while the scowling, beetle-browed appearance notable in this species intensifies the piercing brilliance of its eyes. Because the sun was all-seeing and far-seeing, solar power was thought of in terms of wisdom and prophecy. This ancient idea probably led to the foundation of all oracles, and oracular shrines, and it is perhaps why the bright-eyed Little Owl – and indeed all owls – were thought to be wise and prophetic. The owl's ability to see in the dark calls to mind the Greek seer Teresias, whose blindness gave him prophetic 'vision'; an owl perched on the speartop of King Pyrrhus of Epirus, and foretold his death.

Athena's duty, and that of all goddesses, was to hasten the arrival of winter and rain; the goddess Anahita controlled Persia's rivers, and was customarily attired in a coat of thirty beaver skins. Springs and rivers are usually female because they arise from the female earth and provide nourishment, especially important among pastoral societies in hot climates, where there is a need to water cattle every day, and to fill the irrigation channels that water the fields.

The worship of Hera, Artemis and Demeter – especially Hera – was associated with springs. The goddess who averts famine and disease is the saviour who triumphs over death, and is yet paradoxically a destroyer. The destructive nature of the goddess nevertheless had a creative purpose, a purpose which reflects the importance of the myth of the daughters of Danaus who provided water to the parched land of Argos, the myth that began with the wrath of Hera.

According to Sir James Frazer, the Phoenician goddess Astarte, became under the Greeks, and later the Romans, the goddess Fortune or Victory.[11] The Romans called her Fors Fortuna and the Greeks Tyche. In fact, all these goddesses perform similar duties. Nemesis, Tyche, Athena, Nike, Fortuna, Victory, they bring about and celebrate the death of the bull, and crown the victor with a wreath. They have, however, a somewhat ambivalent nature, for like Nemesis their gift of water and bounteous produce (goddesses often carry a water vessel or a cornucopia spilling its fruits), is overshadowed by death.

Myths often carried to excess the aggressive character of the goddess. The Egyptian Hathor was determined to destroy mankind in a bloodbath of destruction until Ra intervened and got her drunk by flooding the earth with beer. The Hindu goddess of destruction, Kali, wading in blood, her tongue hanging to her waist, is adorned with a necklace threaded with the human

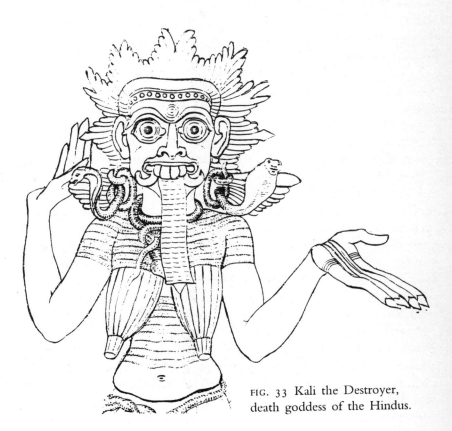

FIG. 33 Kali the Destroyer, death goddess of the Hindus.

skulls of her victims. The Sumerian goddess Gestinanna, later Ishtar, was portrayed with an assortment of weaponry, but sometimes as a dragon destroying by fire and flood, filling rivers with blood and the Phoenician Anat was 'ferociously cruel and bloodthirsty'.[12] The Greek goddesses such as Aphrodite and Athena seem benign by comparison.

Forming a relationship with a goddess invited disaster. Aphrodite, though the celebrated epitome of love and desire, was famous for her rages, her outbursts of anger and her curses. When the Trojan prince Anchises discovered that he had spent the night with Aphrodite, who at first had appeared to him in disguise, he was mortified, fearing that she would rob him of his manhood, and that he was condemned to live 'strengthless'. As it turned out, his fears were well founded. He was lamed by a thunderbolt from Zeus for boasting to his friends, and revealing the identity of his lover. The Babylonian hero Gilgamesh spurned the advances of Ishtar because, he said, she brought misfortune to any creature, human or animal, with which she was associated. The goddess's malign reputation was perhaps the reason why Theseus prudently deserted Ariadne on Naxos. Even the remote British goddess Sul of Bath was said to have been a deity of vengeance.

Nemesis and her sacred griffins were 'inescapable' while Tych's name, which first appears in Homer's Hymn to Athena, comes from the Greek stem *tuchanein* 'to hit the mark',[13] as the goddess's spear strikes home, as the griffin seizes the stag, or as Nike stabs the bull. On a Babylonian seal 'a bull is slain immediately in front of the rain spirit, a precise demonstration of cause and effect.'[14]

To understand Nemesis's function, we need to take into account the state of the land after a long, hot summer. The watercourses are dried up, and only the major rivers, such as the Acheloos, are still flowing. The springs are dry, and the cracked earth cries out for the long-awaited rain, whose appearance is generally preceded by the decline of the sun.

The creatures chosen to represent the sun, and in particular the sun in its decline – the bull, the ram, the stag, the horse, sometimes the boar – must be brought to book. Their demise must be swift and sure if the rains are to begin. And so the water-goddesses Nemesis and Nike send their griffins and lions to attack the bulls and stags; this is why the griffin is the mortal enemy of the horse.

Cult statues of Nemesis, and representations on coins, show her with various attributes – a solar wheel, a crown of stag's heads, griffins, a tree branch bearing apples, snakes, cornucopias. These signs indicate season, the time of the year, autumn, when the sun is weakening, and stags grow their antlers, and branches are heavy with fruit.

Here was the source of the Roman cult of Diana Nemorensis, the curious succession of its priesthood, and the subject with which Sir James Frazer began his monumental work *The Golden Bough*. This is how Frazer describes the ancient ritual, which took place in a grove near the Temple of Diana by Lake Nemi near Aricia, where the priest of Diana kept an almost ceaseless vigil, drawn sword in hand, ready to defend himself:

> In the sacred grove there grew a certain tree round which at any time of the day and probably far into the night a grim figure might be seen to prowl. In his hand he carried a drawn sword, and he kept peering warily about him as if at every instant he expected to be set upon by an enemy. He was a priest and a murderer; and the man for whom he looked was sooner or later to murder him and hold the priesthood in his stead. Such was the rule of the sanctuary. A candidate for the priesthood could only succeed to office by slaying the priest, and having slain him, he retained office until he was himself slain by a stronger or a craftier.[15]

The legend said that the victor could claim the title of Rex Nemorensis, the King of the Wood. There was a stipulation that the challenger must be a runaway slave, who would declare his intentions by tearing a bough from the tree. This 'Golden Bough' was traced by Frazer through world myth and folklore to its final identity in northern mythology as the mistletoe on the oak that killed the Norse god, 'Balder the Beautiful'. The green and gold plant, said Frazer, embodied the life of the thunder and lightning god and indeed the life of the king himself, the reason why he defended it so stoutly.

The myth of Balder is entirely solar, and relates how the goddess Frigg, Balder's mother and northern counterpart of Hera, journeyed through the world, imploring all things on earth – plants, trees, rocks, rivers, animals – never to injure Balder. Thus Balder was rendered invulnerable – almost. Frigg had overlooked one seemingly unimportant plant, the mistletoe, which was to bring about his death. Here is the well-tried formula, similar to the myth where Thetis renders Achilles invulnerable except for his heel: a fragment of this ancient idea survives in the myth where Balder's horse is lamed.

The young and radiant sun god is killed by his enemy, the cunning Loki who resembles the Egyptian Set, and slays Balder by making a spear of mistletoe wood, appropriately a winter plant. Also appropriate is Loki's involvement of the blind and aged god Hodr, whom he employs to throw the seemingly innocent weapon. The blindness of Hodr is a further symbol of the sun's nemesis — winter.

Balder, who must now descend to the underworld, is later brought back to life, as the sun returns in spring. Here we have the vital triad — the goddess, the agent and victim, although in this example it has become a quartet with Loki sub-contracting to the blind Hodr. It is possible that Loki is a version of Frigg herself. He has been identified as the subterranean fire (the sun in the earth in winter), regarded as female and producing vegetation and warmth.[16] In fact, all the participants are perhaps versions of the sun — Frigg, Loki, Hodr and Balder. A statue of Balder by the Swedish sculptor Fogelberg, although admittedly a nineteenth-century work, shows the god as a figure of almost feminine grace and beauty, the northern Apollo. The idea that the sun god should be slain by a blind brother, who represents winter, had been proposed by John Robertson over eighty years ago,[17] and Robertson further draws attention to a ninth-century legend that the Roman soldier Longinus, who wounded Christ at the Crucifixion, was also blind. Does this suggest, perhaps, that the blind Longinus is winter, who gives the *coup de grâce* that kills Jesus, the sun god?

The runaway slave in the grove at Nemi was the challenger because of all the positions in the ancient world, his was the most lowly, the future of an absconding slave the most threatened. Therefore he had nothing to lose. By killing and replacing the solitary king and taking his sword, he would become ruler of the grove. The branch, torn off the tree, did indeed represent the demise of the king, for this legend too is solar, and symbolises the succession of solar rule, and the Rex Nemorensis is the bull who must die, the slave the agent of the goddess Nemesis, with her apple branch and stags.

Nemesis is virtually the same as Diana Nemorensis, whose branch is the oak, and who in turn is the same as Artemis of

Ephesus, whose remarkable mammalian statue is richly-endowed with animal symbolism. Her rows of breasts are worn as a pectoral, and they have recently been interpreted, not as breasts, but as the scrota of bulls sacrificed to the goddess, or even as 'apples, pomegranates, pears or almonds'.[18] Closer scrutiny of the statue shows, however, that above the breasts Artemis wears a necklace of acorns, from which the breasts were certainly derived, a suggestion made by A. B. Cook.[19]

The oak was of the species *Quercus ilex*, the holm or holly oak, the commonest oak tree in the Mediterranean, an evergreen whose foliage survives the harshest winters, and whose acorns particularly resemble the human female breast. Oak is a feminine word in Greek. The acorns ripen and turn golden-brown in the autumn, and are still used as a food by Mediterranean peoples, especially in Spain.

When the thunderstorms rolled across the Aegean, eastwards over Ephesus, the glistening rain-wet 'breasts' of the ilex tree were the gift of the goddess who presided over these months of rain and fertility – Artemis, Diana, Nemesis, Fortuna, and all those other goddesses of plenty, accompanied by their stags, lions, horses and griffins.

On coins, Artemis holds a bow and arrow and an oak branch, or is surrounded by river gods, and it seems that the entire figure is meant to represent an oak. Her hieratic pose is like a tree, her forearms held out at right angles to her body like branches, the hands open to receive the beneficial rain, the trunk of which carries further seasonal clues – bees and flowers. Displayed above the pendulous acorns is a crab, denoting the second half of the year, the period after the summer solstice when the constellation Cancer the crab rose with Leo. (See frontispiece.)

On either side are lions, and above the crab a solar wreath held by two Nike figures. (Further indication that the oak is a tree of late autumn comes from the belief that oaks are especially prone to being struck by lightning, or that rain can be produced by stirring a pond with an oak branch.) The late summer to autumn theme is continued above the temple where the statue is crowned with an oak in leaf. A relief on the base depicts the sacrifice of the bull, whose demise brings nourishment and fertility and so completes the symbolic cycle.

The branch of a tree, whether it be the olive of Athena, the oak of Artemis, the pomegranate of Aphrodite, or the apple of Nemesis, was an instrument of thunder and rain, and thus appropriate to the goddess. Helen, sister of the Dioscuri, was called Helen Dendritus, or 'Helen of the Tree'. The arboreal theme tells us why Artemis Orthia resides in a willow, for willows are water loving and her temples were by water-courses; at her cult festivals, devotees wore Medusa masks to encourage rain.

It has been noted that the curious Black Virgins of the Catholic Church are connected with trees. The Jungian analyst Ean Begg, in his book *The Cult of the Black Virgin*,[20] plunges into mysticism and the Gnostics, by way of the Tarot, and feminism and the Great Goddess, to explain the Black Virgins as the dark latency of our own essential nature, and a manifestation of lost feminine wisdom. Are they not black because their time is the winter, and the approach of winter is heralded by the tree fruits of autumn? All tree cults were intimately connected with water and springs.

FIG.   34 Terracotta gorgon mask from the Temple of Artemis in Sparta.

Artemis of the willow (and perhaps of the plant artemisia, or mugwort, worn as a charm), was the huntress whose companions were stags, yet who turned the innocent hunter Actaeon into a stag to be devoured by his own dogs at Parthenius, whereupon a spring burst forth from the rocky ground, enriched by his blood. This theme is central to the entire complex of myths: Actaeon is the stag, or bull, the autumn victim who must be killed, that the springs be filled by the rains.

This is why Nemesis really does mean 'retribution' or to put it more acurately, unavoidable fate. A few Minoan seals show a stag being struck by a branch. It combines the image of the goddess's victim with her emblem of the fruiting branch of autumn which presages the stag's sacrifice. Frazer did not, I think, fully grasp the meaning of the branch, for it was Diana's weapon, and Frigg's weapon in the hand of Hodr, and the symbol of her power, the power over the stag or the bull, which brought about their sacrifice.

It represented the death of their human counterpart, Rex Nemorensis, the King of the Wood, at the hands of the usurper-slave, who is in fact the agent of the water goddess of Lake Nemi. It identifies too the famous oak club of Hercules, the hero who represents the lion in combat. A coin from Tarsus shows the lion killing the bull juxtaposed with Hercules's club.

The branch torn from the tree in the grove at Nemi, the fruits of which herald the rainy season, the sun's decline and contact with the earth, is the Golden Bough, whether it be oak, apple, sycamore, willow, olive or mistletoe. Frazer identified mistletoe as the branch that killed Balder, but it may just as easily have been the oak of the northern forests, for the branch that the Trojan hero Aeneas carried with him to the underworld was the oak, or perhaps it was that rare phenomenon, the mistletoe growing on the oak. Like the caduceus of Hermes, it illuminated the way, for Aeneas was a solar hero, his descent to the underworld an act of seasonal fertility.

The tree, and especially the tree by a spring, was the embodiment of the great goddess of life and death. Perhaps this will confirm why Athena was represented by the Little Owl, simply because as Claud Conder noted, they favour olive trees. Adonis was born of a tree, when his future mother was changed into a myrrh tree, and in the tenth month the trunk burst open and the infant Adonis came forth. Nana, mother of the Phrygian

Agdestis, was made pregnant when she ate a pomegranate. In Semitic myth, the goddess Al-Ozza resided in a sacred acacia, and both she and the goddess Al-Lat were worshipped as trees.[21] A clay effigy of Astarte was discovered in Cyprus placed in a tree trunk – there was a close connection between Cyprus and Phoenicia, where Astarte-Cybele and Adonis were worshipped. We have already seen how Cinderella was enclosed in a wooden sheath, or wore a petticoat fashioned from a hollow oak tree. In *The Song of Solomon*, the Fair Shulamite is 'enclosed with bonds of cedar'.

I should emphasise the importance of the role played by the goddess in the structure of myth. The actions of the Scandinavian Frigg, of the Egyptian Isis, the Greek Demeter, where the goddess mourns the death or disappearance of her child, or lover, hides the true fact that she was deliberately responsible for their demise, as Ishtar destroyed the young god Tammuz, and all those she loved. The goddess was equally capable of rewarding those whom she favoured, as Victory crowns the conquering hero with a wreath, a crown of bay laurel, *Laurus nobilis*. The wreath is a symbol of her tree, of the goddess herself, and evolved into the crown worn by royalty; that it could also symbolise death is perhaps shown by the crown of thorns placed upon the head of Jesus before the crucifixion.

In a recent book on Arthurian legends and the Knights of the Grail, John Darrah compares the scenes of combat to the rite at Nemi.[22] In the medieval romance, a hero such as Sir Gawain challenges an adversary, the Green Knight, to fight. Is the knight green because he is the tree goddess's champion? The battle invariably takes place in a forest glade, by a sacred tree near a spring or fountain. The accounts of ritual beheadings are an important feature in these tales, as is the Waste Land or Waste City – in other words, winter.

The stories also feature a Lady or Damsel, who will become the victor's prize. Gawain wins the hand of Orguelleuse, 'the Proud Damsel', who demands that he fetch a twig from the tree before she will consent to sleep with him. The damsel is of course the universal goddess, for whom Anfortas, the Fisher King, suffered castration by a fiery lance. Arthur, the Maimed King with his grievous wound, is carried to the magic isle of Avalon, the isle of apples. The twig broken from the tree was presumably an apple, the fruit of which, like the golden pomegranate, was a symbol of the sun, and therefore sacred to Nemesis.

FIG. 35 The goddess Nemesis with her branch, the fruit
indicating the season of the year.

The goddess's thirst for blood, particularly bull's blood let during sacrifice, and water, fertilised the earth which the goddess represented. In every sacrificial rite it was thought, as mentioned above, that the victim should always be acquiescent. The Pythia, who uttered the oracular responses at Delphi, affirmed that the sacrificial animal 'that willingly nods its head, I say you can rightly sacrifice it after a libation'. To get a goat to nod its head willingly, cold water was sprinkled over its body to make it shiver.[23]

The need for the victim to be humbled or subdued was not in order to appease the guilt of the sacrificers for killing a sacred animal, but to acknowledge that which actually took place. The victim, symbolising the sun, was weakened and subdued; the ritual merely observed natural events.

The solar bull as victim of the water goddess features in one of the most famous of all myths, that of Theseus and the Minotaur, the bull-headed son of King Minos of Crete, where remnants of bull-cults are still to be found.

In essence it begins when King Minos, whose name links the story and the location with the prehistoric Minoan civilisation of Crete, asked Poseidon to send a bull from the sea for him to sacrifice. Poseidon obliged with a pure white bull, but Minos could not bring himself to slaughter it. Affronted, Poseidon (or some say Aphrodite) caused Minos's wife Pasiphae to fall in love with the creature. If the structure of the myth seems crudely contrived, with its element of bestiality, it may be due to its very primitive origins. Sexual intercourse with the bull (a probable manifestation of Poseidon himself) is engineered with the help of Daedalus, a craftsman whose name has some connection with the word delta, related to 'womb'.

He builds a wood and leather cow in which Pasiphae conceals herself, and which the bull is encouraged to cover to deliver his semen. The offspring of this union is the Minotaur, a human male figure with the head of a bull. At Minos's request, Daedalus then constructed a complex lair for it. This was the labyrinth of seven passages or windings into which seven youths and seven maidens, every nine years, were thrown as a tribute, to be devoured by the labyrinth's resident, ignoring the usual preference of bulls for a diet of grass.

Enter Theseus. He is assisted by Ariadne, a goddess whose Minoan origins were themselves anteceded by earlier, oriental influences. She famously provided a thread which Theseus used to help him find his way in and out of the maze. We might do well to consider Pasiphae and Ariadne as one and the same.

The hero groped his way into the labyrinth, naked except for a lion-skin, just as Heracles wore his lion-skin, and carried the sacrifical sword. Ariadne and Athena wait outside the labyrinth while Theseus struggles with the Minotaur, which is depicted on a coin with ears of wheat sprouting from its tail (as is the bull of Mithras). Thus the true purpose of the myth is revealed: the goddess through her agent strikes the great solar bull in its cave. The labyrinth is the cave of the sun, the womb of nature with its seven cells or passages. The Minotaur's death simulates the fructifying solar power which is active during the seven months of the sun's residence in the earth, all directed towards encouraging rains, without which the crops would fail. After slaying the Minotaur, the hero hurries away with Ariadne, and they rest on the island of Naxos, where they find refuge for the night, and Ariadne falls asleep. Theseus steals away since he is aware that any close encounter with a goddess is always dangerous, and often fatal.

The hero now took the short sea route to Delos where Apollo was born, and in the company of the seven young men and seven maidens rescued from the Minotaur, he took part in a complicated measure called the Geranos or 'crane' dance, performed around a keraton or altar of bull's horns, a dance said to imitate the windings of the labyrinth. Here is a further seasonal clue added to the myth. Cranes migrate south across the Aegean during the autumn months and, according to Hesiod, their cry was a signal to the farming communities to begin ploughing; seasonal references are a vital part of all solar myths.

The legend of the Minotaur and labyrinth was discussed a century ago by scholars, among them Cook and Frazer, well aware of the solar symbolism. The general opinion seems to have pointed to the labyrinth as a dancing ground for a sun-dance, with Cook deciding that the Minotaur was a Cretan prince masquerading in a solar rite.[24] At the end of the eighteenth century, the antiquary Payne Knight suggested that the Minotaur in the labyrinth was similar to the Hindu symbol of the lingam of Siva in the yoni of Prajapati. The analogy of sexual congress is apt, for the myth is concerned with the process of fertilisation, but of the earth by the sun, not of human kind, yet the weight of modern interpretation leans heavily on human psychology.

The value of mythology as a source of inspiration is considerable. It has enabled successive generations to exploit the versatility of the original tale in the light of their own preoccupations, performing a beneficial service. While the original meaning of the myth has lost its validity, the underlying, dramatic structure continues to provide a solid foundation – it was, indeed, the foundation upon which religions first were built.

The modern view is that the Minotaur represents the dark side of the personality. Oliver Taplin mentions this in *Greek Fire*. 'If we all have within us a dark beast which threatens to consume innocence and rationality, we need to be able to go down into the labyrinth, to confront this side of our humanness, and to return. Must we kill the half-human, or can it be civilised? – or is that mere sentimentality? Whatever the answer the persistence of Greek myths may have something to do with their blending of the human and the monstrous, the heroic and the degrading, the pure and the erotic.'[25]

The Greeks, in order to explain the strangeness of this Cretan myth to themselves, made the Minotaur into a predatory monster, whereas he was in fact a victim of sacrifice. Even in Greek art he appears the injured party. The figure of the Minotaur can be identified with with Talos, also Cretan, the strange bull-man (made by Hephaestus) of bronze, who guarded the island, ran around it three times daily, and threw stones at strangers. Talos had, it was said, a single vein running through his body which reached to his heel, where it was stopped by a pin to prevent his life-blood running out. The pin was removed by Medea, whereupon Talos promptly expired. We cannot doubt that Medea was the goddess (perhaps a version of Ariadne) and Talos, like the Minotaur, her bull sacrifice.

Why, then, if Talos was usefully employed guarding Crete, did Medea pull the plug, so to speak, and cause him to expire? Because Talos is the solar bull whose released fluid or ichor (Gk. *ikhnos*, 'footprint') running from his heel is spring water, and by her action she hastens the weakening of the sun which heralds the rains, and so reveals the contradictory nature of the earth goddess who by her seemingly hostile behaviour in fact encourages fertility. Crete, in common with all the rocky islands of the Mediterranean had, and still has, severe problems with supplies of water. Majorca, in the Balearic islands, is obliged to ship water in from mainland Spain, itself suffering from a prolonged drought.

The myth of Talos has echos in the legend of the English folk-hero Robin Hood, who was bled to death by a woman's hand.

Although we cannot claim with certainty that Robin Hood was not an historic figure, the features in the legend ideally meet the requirements of the classic pattern of the doomed and sacrificed hero; it is not correct to say that 'The early tales of Robin, indeed the cycle as a whole, are without myth and magic', for the entire legend is based upon ancient mythology.[26]

Robin Hood is first mentioned in *Piers Plowman*, about 1377, and in the medieval manuscripts, such as *A Gest of Robyn Hode*. He is portrayed as a yeoman, whose followers were 'seven score young men', and Robin seems to have been associated with a seven-ringed maze or labyrinth. He does battle with an enemy, Sir Guy of Gisburn, a knight who wears the hide of a horse 'top, tail and mane', and whom Robin beheads with his sword at the height of summer.

Here again are the ancient links. Is he also Rex Nemorensis, king of the oak groves of Sherwood forest? Legend associates Robin with a sixteenth-century 'Robin Hood's Well', and there are other later wells that bear his name. Like Hercules, who wears the clothes of Omphale, Robin Hood changes clothes, not with a woman, but with a potter, an ancient symbol of the creator, the pot symbolising the female principle. The most durable part of the legend, however, is the death of the hero, who leaves his band of outlaws and travels to Kirklees Priory near Brighouse in Yorkshire to be bled as treatment for a fever.

The 'physician' is Robin's cousin, the treacherous prioress, a version of Medea and the water goddess's holy representative, who produces the 'bleeding irons' and pierces a vein, or perhaps an artery. Like Talos, Robin bleeds to death, and to make certain of his demise, he is attacked by the prioress's lover, Sir Roger of Doncaster, 'Red Roger', the griffin or lion, who stabs him in the side, as Mithras stabs the bull, as Jesus is speared by Longinus, and as Osiris is slain by the red-haired Set, and Balder is killed by Loki. The medieval ballad tells us how at first the blood ran thick and red, but was later thin and watery, just as the blood from the wounded Jesus was thinned by water.

Robin goes of his own accord to meet his fate, as does Jesus, and so he obeys the requirements made of the sacrificed bull, to submit willingly. He refuses to condemn the prioress, as Jesus forgives them that know not what they do. Although the legend of Robin Hood is dearly held to be pure English folklore, the essential structure is nonetheless oriental.

The setting for the oldest versions of the legend is not Sherwood Forest, but Barnsdale near Wakefield, along the course of Watling Street and the river Aire. Is it a coincidence that this was the centre of the Danelaw? Robin Hood may have been a product of the Viking rule, if not actually imported by the invaders. 'Robyn Hude' has been traced to the Scandinavian horse god Odin, or Woden, Balder's father.[27]

'Hood' or Woden, may be derived from an Old High German word *watan*, 'to gush out', and Robin from Robert, itself connected with the Old High German *hoppe*, 'horse', cognate with Greek Hippos. From this comes the hobby-horse, once paraded at Odin's festivals, central to the Morris dances with their Maid Marian and Robin Hood. There is another clue that Robin may be a version of the Norse god Balder, for the nineteenth-century antiquary John Brand mentions that Balder 'perished through blindness and a woman',[28] as of course did Samson through the agency of Delilah.

Like the weakening and dying of Krishna, the legend of Robin Hood, who wore the attire of a potter, and is thus allied to the artisan creators, accurately describes the death of the solar hero. Weakened by fever, he journeys alone and westward, simulating the declining sun.

The association of Robin in folklore with the Morris men may go some way to explain their ritual dances. Traditionally, there are six dancers with blackened faces and swords, the seventh a captain, and a fool or hobby-horse. The dancers complete their measure by interlocking their swords in a 'rose' or 'nut' – it is held high, a symbol of the sun. The fool is symbolically beheaded, or 'falls down dead', but is resurrected after being 'locked' three times by the swords.

The black-faced 'Moors' or Morris men are performing a sun-and-rain-dance and bring about the death and revival of the sun with their wooden weapons. They are the seven black-faced months from autumn to spring that witness the death and revival of the sun, the hobby-horse, who brings rain. Here, the rituals of rustic observances are very close to myth because, of course, they are nourished by the same spring. A popular feature of the English rustic festivals is the maypole, around which villagers dance. Although thought by many folklorists to be a phallic symbol, the maypole is more likely to represent the goddess's tree, possibly the rowan tree (mountain ash) or the hawthorn.

From a window in the Kirklees Priory gatehouse (now derelict), and by a stream called Nun Brook, the dying Robin looses an arrow to mark his grave. In myth the act would create a spring. The weakening of nature's powers during the march of winter and the decline of the sun was compared to the loss of blood, yet the loss served to nourish the earth. Like the myth of Lophis with which this chapter began, the hero perishes through loss of blood. Death was an essential precursor to the renewal of life, forming the iconography and symbolism of both Mithraism and Christianity.

CHAPTER 14

The Lion and the Unicorn

Death in the service of the virgin goddess was the origin and inspiration of several great examples of symbolic art. I have in my possession a rustic woodcarving, said to be Sicilian, depicting St George impaling a dragon with his spear. A tiny female figure stands behind him, perched on the rump of the saint's horse. I take this to be the Virgin Mary, or perhaps the princess Cleodolinda, menaced by the dragon, and rescued by the saint. St George is Perseus, 'the destroyer', who rescued Andromeda from the sea monster, or Heracles fighting the Hydra, or Zeus and Typhon, or Gilgamesh and Tiamat, an archetype described by Joseph Campbell in his book *The Hero With a Thousand Faces*.

Following his combat with the dragon, which he decapitates with his sword, St George baptises the princess, pouring a vase of water over her head. The saint is later martyred, and like the dragon is beheaded. The legend includes the conversion of twenty thousand people to Christianity, when St George – one of the Seven Champions of Christendom – baptises all of them in one day. We are not told what happened to St George's head; perhaps it was buried by the spring from which the saint drew water for the baptism. The mythic elements in the story – the hero, the monster, decapitation, water, might suggest that the princess is a double of Athena, or Ariadne, 'the striker', performing her duty encouraging rain, or water from springs.

It says much for the importance and tenacity of this symbolic group that it has crossed the frontiers of space and time to become an emblem of Christianity, and of St George the patron saint of England, while Athena has her counterpart in the martial figure of Britannia. Heraldry appropriates archaic symbols, recognising their imagery of power and influence, which is why they are so widely employed by ruling families and royal courts.

A favourite motif of heraldry, reaching its present form as the lion and unicorn, flanking the shield on the royal coat of arms, has gradually evolved from a symbol generally referred to by scholars as the 'lion-bull combat'. It is an image where a lion attacks a bull, straddling the kneeling beast and biting deep into its neck or shoulder. The symbol seems to have been so important to the mythology and religion of the ancient world that literally thousands of examples, with variations, were carved on seals and gemstones, especially in Minoan Crete.

The art historian C. G. E. Bunt was one of the first to discuss the ancient use and long development of this theme. 'The extraordinary persistence of the subject through fifty-five centuries of symbolic art would lead us to surmise that it has its origins in something deeper than mere fancifulness – something far more important to mankind than the mere record of a natural antipathy between two animals.'[1] Bunt does not venture an opinion on the nature of this deeper meaning, except to suggest that the animals might have been borrowed from ancient astronomy – the lion was Leo, the bull Taurus.

A Phoenician gemstone of chalcedony, made about 1400 BC, engraved with this 'lion-bull combat', has a griffin in place of the lion, and a stag instead of the bull. Just below the stag the engraver has included a tiny Medusa head, minus tusks and snakes, a simple sun-disc with a stuck-out tongue. This is the gorgoneion that Athena displays on her snakeskin aegis, while on her shield there is a motif showing the fight between the lion and the bull.

In the conflict between the two adversaries the bull is invariably acquiescent, the stag a helpless victim. It is subdued by the aggressor and collapses on its forelegs, adopting, like the Gorgon, the *knielauf* or kneeling pose that is faithfully represented in

FIG. 36 Lion-bull combat symbol, from a Greek coin, c. 500 BC.

hundreds of examples, attesting to its importance and to its antiquity. There can be no doubt that the artist who engraved this tiny cameo, more than two thousand years ago, knew exactly what the scene meant, for he included the Medusa head in the design, a vital clue which emphasises the purpose of the action.

In their search for an explanation of this curious scene of a lion killing a bull, many scholars took their cue from Bunt's theory that the origins were to be found in the heavens – the lion representing the constellation Leo, while the bull was Taurus. Leo rose in the hottest period of the year, and the bull was thought to be lunar, partly on account of the crescent shape of its horns; therefore the scene represented the triumph of day over night, the sun over the moon. Or that the lion of day slays the antelope, or bull, of the night. Here was a sensible solution, why bother to look any further? The triumph of day over night was an unfailing and reassuring phenomenon, but hardly one that threatened mankind, or required celebration through symbolism. There had to be a more practical reason for this scene, which was so widespread throughout the Mediterranean and the Middle East, and a favourite motif of the engravers of coins and seals.

Recently the German historian Willy Hartner, suggested an astronomical explanation with a practical value. Hartner claimed that the lion-bull combat represented the sky in February in 4000 BC when the constellation Taurus was setting, with Leo exactly at zenith, high above. This would signal the start of the springtime sowing of barley in Babylonia and of the agricultural year.[2] An objection to Hartner's theory, and that of the lion of day versus the bull of night, is that the combatants are not always lions and bulls, but often griffins and stags, as in the above cameo, and other animal combinations.

One of the earliest examples, on a lapis-lazuli seal, shows lion-headed eagles biting the rump of a man-headed bull. Another has a lion attacking a boar, a leopard or panther attacking a bull, two lions and a bull, two lions and a stag, a lion and an ibex, two griffins and a deer. There are also wolf-headed lions and sphinxes, birds and dogs. They cannot all be constellations rising or setting at propitious moments.

The most unlikely aggressor, in place of the lion, and on several seals, is a dolphin. While the dolphin could possibly represent the constellation Delphinus, which rises with other 'watery' constellations in winter such as Capricorn the goat-fish, and Aquarius the water-carrier, it does not mark the time of any significant agricultural event.

In some examples the victims are struck by a spear or arrow, flung by griffins or dolphins directed by robed priests.[3] And so the the astronomical theory has too many variables, and is not really sound. If this symbol represented, as Bunt thought, something deeper and more important for mankind than natural hostility between animals, what could this 'something' be?

FIG. 37 Phoenician gemstone – a griffin attacking a stag.

Some clues to the answer might be gained from archaic examples, especially those from the Minoan culture of early Crete. On a seal, a figure generally called a 'genius' or 'demon', attacks a bull, and in another example uses a knife to stab a deer. Both are without doubt versions of the combat scene. These genii are curious composite figures of lions attired as a bees, but the combination was not strange to the ancient world, where dead lions and bulls were thought to generate bees from their carcasses – the biblical story of Samson is but one example.

Bees were sacred to Demeter, and to Artemis of Ephesus whose priestesses were called *melissae* or 'bees'. The lion-bee genius of Minoan religion, killing the bull or stag, was an attribute of the goddess. The symbolism of the bee came from the observation that honey was a form of nourishment, just as the breasts of the Mother Goddess gave nourishment. Honey, the sweet, golden mysterious nectar ('mysterious', because it was not known how bees produced honey, it was simply 'the food of the gods'), was in fact the nourishment bestowed by the sun upon the solar hero or god, because bees (and butterflies) appeared in response to the sun's springtime warmth. The Cretan birth goddess Eileithyia has an amphora of honey dedicated to her in an inscription from Knossos.[4] This is the reason why bees emerged from the body of the solar lion, enabling Samson to feed his parents – 'and out of the strong came forth sweetness'.

The same was true of bulls. It was widely supposed in the ancient world that if you buried a bull in the earth, its decomposing carcass would in the course of time generate bees, which eventually found their way out through the horns, because the bull was a symbol of the sun – indeed, it embodied all the sun's generative and fertilising properties.

This is simple nature-symbolism. The fact that nobody had ever observed bees emerging from bull's horns did nothing to confound the belief. It is a strange idea, and may have its origins in caves, where wild bees often built their nests: the word 'hive' is ultimately derived from the Sanskrit *kupa*, meaning 'cave'. In John Masters's book *The Deceivers*, set in India, the fugitives escape through the intervention of a swarm of cave bees, which attack their pursuers. The great solar bull of Mithras dies in its cave, as does the Minotaur in the labyrinth. Could this be the connection? The bull, symbol of the sun, buried in the earth during winter, generates bees in the spring, which emerge through its horns. It is a tenuous connection, I admit, but the combined symbol of the bull and the bee is very ancient. Perhaps the idea came from India, where in the Vedas a celestial cow delivers ambrosia or honey. In the Scandinavian Eddas a cow's horn supplies mead. In Greece, the infant Zeus was fed on honey in a cave, as were Apollo and Hermes.

The lion-bee genii, who hold libation jugs of honey over the sacred tree which grows out of the horns of a bull are in effect priests or agents of the nature goddess, whose provision of the sun's nourishment encourages life. One of these genii, on a Minoan seal mentioned above, strikes the victim with a knife, and with this action tells us the meaning of the combat scene.

It represents the sacrifice of the bull by the goddess whose priest does the deed, symbolised by a variety of creatures such as the lion and the griffin. The griffin is simply a composite creature that in effect concentrates some of these attributes – having the body of a winged lion and the head of an eagle.

The griffin was also an agent of the Mesopotamian goddess Ninhursag, deity of the foothills of the Zagros range of mountains where there is rainfall and where the wild cereals of wheat and barley were first harvested, and where agriculture, 'the Neolithic revolution', began. Ninhursag, the 'Lady of the Mountains' was equated with the Sumerian Inanna and the Semitic Ishtar. She was goddess of springs, of grain, and the goddess of birth who helped to shape mankind, one of the many potter-metalworking-craft deities of oriental origins. Ninhursag controlled the lion-headed vulture Imdugud, the Babylonian storm-bird, she is the goddess of death who commands the lion or the griffin – her agent – to attack the bull or the stag.

The bull's role in the religious rituals of early societies was that of the prime sacrificial beast. The purpose of sacrifice has been much argued over because rituals vary considerably. One of the most deeply entrenched and persistent theories, with its origins in nineteenth-century anthropology, was that of totemism, or the belief in a group or clan having a common and unifying symbol, usually an animal, with attendant rituals and taboos. Walter Burkert refers to an animal god, identified with the sacrificial victim, being consecrated and eaten.[4] This had been the view of Robertson Smith, who saw sacrifice as a form of communion, man ingesting the vital force of the consumed animal. The animal is surrogate for the god, and each type of animal represents the chosen sacrificial victim of each god – bulls for Zeus and Poseidon, stags for Artemis, animals all inherited from the hunter tradition where they were the totem of the tribe.

It is easier to accept this theory in the example of the prehistoric sanctuary at Eridu, a relic of the Mesopotamian Ubaid culture, where the altar was found littered with fish bones six inches deep. But then Eridu was the holy city dedicated to the water-god Ea, whose influence and power was immense.[5]

This was not totemism but water symbolism. In fact totemism, as a significantly important social structure, was an invention of nineteenth-century anthropologists, much as structuralism was an invention of Lévi-Strauss and twentieth-century French intellectuals, their intention being to perpetuate, rather than penetrate, the myth of mythology.

The awe in which the bull was held by early societies may have been partly due to the size of wild cattle, especially the aurochs, *Bos primigenius*, which stood some 1.3 metres high, almost a third larger than our present-day domestic bull, and had huge horns.

The bull was frequently the emblem of the thunder god, of Adad, Zeus, and Jupiter Dolichenus, who stood on the back of a bull waving an axe in his right hand. This led Sir James Frazer to decide that 'The combination of the bull with the thunderbolt as emblems of the deity suggests that the animal may have been chosen to represent the sky-god for the sake not merely of its virility but of its voice; for in the peal of thunder primitive man may well have heard the bellowing of the celestial bull.'[6] In fact exactly the same symbolism as that of the roaring lion, and the pounding hooves of the herd – either of horses or of cattle. 'Let the heaven, the tawny bull thunder,' says the Rig-Veda in a poem to the storm gods.[7]

The animals and gods that bring rain can be found in the Sanskrit root VRS, 'to water', leading to *varsa*, 'to rain', and *vrishan*, 'rainmaker' (Indra, Varuna, Jupiter Pluvius, and Zeus Hyatous 'the rainy'), with allied words *vrisha*, 'to impregnate' (*vrishana* is 'penis') and *vrishabha*, 'bull'. The Latin root also gives *ver*, 'spring', and *verres*, 'boar'. In Persia the Zend word *gaya* means 'bull', and also 'soul' and 'life'.

The bull is one of the oldest of religious symbols, perhaps older than the serpent, but not older than the bear. Bulls' horns have been found embedded in the walls of houses of the Natufian period, 9000 BC. These would have been from the wild aurochs, harder to bring down than goat or gazelle, needing much communal effort. The symbolism attached to all aspects of the bull should now be clear. Strong, vigorous, fast and virile, and the most powerful of game and domestic animals, it symbolised the qualities of the sun, but more especially the character of the seasons. To the ancient pastoral societies, the equation was simple and straightforward: the rain impregnated the mother earth as the bull impregnated the cow, as the ram fertilised the ewe.

The rainy season followed the decline of the sun, the sun 'on its knees' like a sacrificed and dying bull. Thus the bull and the ram became symbols of the sun, and we find terracotta models of bulls and rams with three horns, or three legs, acknowledging the symbolism of the solar number.

In the springtime the bull with the golden horns ushered in the year. In the autumn the weak and 'dying' bull, the sacrificed bull on its knees, signalled the start of the rains, the rain was the tauric semen that fertilised the earth, and hastened the crops of wheat and barley. Ancient astronomers, observing a group of stars that rose and set with these seasons, named the constellation after the great celestial bull. To the Sumerians the fertilising rains were compared to semen – one word of their language stood for both.

The bull on its knees, or on one knee as it was often shown in art, will explain the concept of birth from the thigh or knees, which forms a substantial part of a work by Richard Broxton Onians, which he published in 1951 with the somewhat formidable title *The Origins of European Thought About the Body, the Mind, the Soul, the World, Time, and Fate.*[8] Onians produces evidence to show that the source of generative power, of 'seed' in the body, was believed by ancient societies, and the Greeks in particular, to come from the body's liquids, from blood, semen, saliva, sweat, tears, from fat, and especially from the marrow in the bones, and cerebro-spinal fluids. These fluids were compared to the natural sources of life-giving substances, such as blood and water, oil and wine, and the sap of plants. 'The vital sap of the human body,' says Onians, 'was spoken of in terms of plant life.[9] Life is liquid, while dryness is death. The plant, through lack of water withers and dies, like the human body and the soul.'

Where the life-bearing fluids were located in the body, their point of issue was to be found in the head, the jaw, the skin; but the most puzzling feature was in the belief that the knees were a source of generation. Onians decided that this is due to the fact that the joint-cavity of the knee is the largest in the body, and that the fluid contained in the joint, its true function not being known in the ancient world, was seen as the seed or generative fluid of life.

We know, however, that the anatomical dissection of humans was not carried out among the physicians of the ancient world, physicians such as Galen, although they presumably identified parts of the body from the bones of mortuary practices. The concept of birth from the knee must have been very old even by classical times, appearing in Sumerian with the word *birku*, which meant both 'knee' and 'penis'.[10] This strange idea was also influential and fundamental, as Onians appreciated, to the origins of myth and symbol, in fact to the origins of European thought.

Consider the related words for 'knee' − in Greek, *gonu*; in Latin, *genu*, *genus* and *genitalis*, giving 'generate', and 'generation', and 'genesis'. There are also the related Greek words *genus* and *geneion* for 'chin' and 'jaw' (and *genus* for 'race'). The Russian word for 'knee,' *koleno*, also means 'generation'. In the Hurrian language, the genitals were euphemistically referred to as 'knees'. 'The knee', says Onians, 'was thought in some way to be the seat of paternity, of life and generative power, unthinkable though that may seem to us'.[11]

The comparison was prevalent among the Celts and others, '*Le mot désignant le genou au sens de génération chez les Celtes, les Germains, les Slaves, les Assyriens.*'[12] The Latin poet and satirist Lucilius equated *gens*, 'knee', with *genus* meaning 'testes'. That the act of birth should be displaced in thought and language from the womb, or from the penis, to the knees, once again suggests that it has more to do with the fecundity of nature than of humankind. I should stress that the concept is very ancient and primitive, comparable in its simplicity to the belief that man was formed from red clay. What, then, triggered off the development of this strange idea, that the knee was a source of life?

Impregnation was brought about by the solar bull in the throes of death, metaphorically on its knees. The leg, thigh, foot and heel, then, are indications of fertility, and also of femininity. We are told that in Hindu legend Aurva was born from the thigh of his mother Vamora who had, after all, the necessary physical endowments for conventional birth.[13]

Birth from the knee is close to the idea of birth from the thigh, and again there are clues to be found in the relationship of words such as the Latin for thighbone, *femur* and *feminis*, so 'engenders'. The German word for 'thigh' is *schenkel* (our words 'shank', and 'shin') and the related word *schenk* means 'to bestow' and 'to give', particularly in relation to liquid. *Schenk* means 'to pour out', 'to fill'. This supports, albeit distantly in time and space, not to mention language, Osiris pouring out the Nile from his thigh.

Life is generated by the womb but, equally persistently in myth, in legend, in folklore, it comes in liquid form from the knee and thigh. Remember that Odysseus, wounded in the thigh, kicked over a bowl of water. The thigh is also the place of delivery in the androgyne – the god Dionysus was born from the thigh of Zeus.

It is a curious fact that the thighbone, the longest bone in the human body, in bovids and horses, was revered by the cave-dwellers of the Palaeolithic era, along with an equal admiration for the skull and jawbone, a veneration for these bones continued throughout the Bronze and Iron Ages. It is a fact that leads us to a remarkable discovery.

Through the process of synthesis in observation linked to language, the hoof and foot became the symbol of water and thus of fertility. Onians suggests that the horny, ungulous material of the hoof was compared to the horns of bovids, the horn being a source of plenty.[14] That the heel was also charged with fertile powers is shown by the belief that veins ran from the heel to the thighs, genitals and kidneys. But we are here concerned with birth from the knee, and it has nothing to do with the kneeling posture, or the 'spreading of the knees' while giving birth.

As I have pointed out, fertility in myth is related almost entirely to the fertility in nature, in the earth and the heavens, rather than in mankind. Therefore, the 'knee' does not refer to human knees, except by analogy, but to the kneeling attitude taken by the dying bull – the *knielauf* or kneeling posture of the sacrificial victim. In a cave on Mount Parnassus, where devotees offered the knuckle-bones of sheep and goats, archaeologists have recovered some 25,000 knee joints.

More precisely, the knee of the sacrificed animal refers ultimately to the kneeling sun in winter (comparable to the limping sun), when it had sunk to its lowest point in the sky during its yearly passage. The winter solstice was the start of the new year, when life is generated, when everything is born anew. The sun, remember, was thought figuratively to possess physical characteristics because, like animal symbols, it made it easier for mankind to relate to the more abstract influences of the elements.

It is possible that the kneeling animal was the initial idea responsible for the development of the four-footed swastika and the three-legged triskeles. The entire leg of the bull – shoulder, shin and foot – became a potent symbol in the ancient world, and was regarded as a source of life; to release water, the god Mithras stabs the kneeling bull in the shoulder.

The remarkable fact is that the birth of nature, following the winter sun and its rebirth in spring, took precedence in human thought over human birth. Nature ruled – a reflection of the primitive conditions of life, at least in view of today's philosophies, and the powerfully egocentric status of modern society. Birth could be controlled by human action (evidence of infanticide in prehistory is well documented), whereas the force of nature, and destiny, were beyond man's control. In prehistory nature was at the best of times a formidable adversary, and in desperation (particularly during long periods of famine), man reconciled and related to his struggles by creating objective symbols. At best, the symbols enabled him to relate to, and perhaps resolve, his anxieties.

The foot, and especially the heel, the long bones of the leg and the knee-joint, with the scapular in animals, were symbolic agents and votive objects in the creation of rain and spring water, and therefore of life. It is a mental connection and symbolic equation of great antiquity, from and during a time when the influence of the essential elements took priority over any other consideration.

The great Argive sun-hero Hercules, whose eponymous constellation sets in mid-July, was also known to astronomers as 'The Kneeler'. His death is curious. Hercules put on the poisoned tunic of the centaur Nessus, and felt as though he were consumed by fire. He made himself a funeral pyre of pine trees on Mount Oeta, and died in the flames, although some say that Zeus conducted him to Olympus. Death on a pyre is an appropriate end for a sun-hero, referring as it did – rather prematurely – to the decline of the sun after the summer solstice. He died by the horse, for centaurs are of course part equine.

The ritual sacrifice of an animal, in a temple and conducted by the priesthood, became a central part of developed religions everywhere, and its main purpose was that of propitiation, of asking for favours and begging clemency of the god or gods. Its aim was to appease, and prepare the way for divine intervention in the lives of the people.

Sacrifice was an intrinsic part of the structure of religion, but it developed out of a much simpler requirement – that of nourishing the land. The victim was killed that its vitality might encourage the onset of rain. Sir James Frazer noted several examples in Africa and in India where black bulls and goats were sacrificed as rain charms.[15] The rites are still carried out in Botswana, where the killing of an ox by the grave of a chieftain is a rainmaking ceremony in times of drought. The animal must be black to resemble rainclouds.[16]

Though the origin of these rites was a fundamental yet simple and straightforward appeal to nature, the need to inspire awe and respect from the worshippers led to the complexity of ritual and the formation of an intricate hierarchy and system of belief. Power is maintained through the rigid observance of an exclusive, formal, and often arcane ceremony, although audience participation is, of course, an essential feature of most religious observance.

Mountain and hill tops were the most regular spots chosen for shrines where sacrifices were performed, the 'High Place' of the Old Testament. Archaeological evidence of bull sacrifices comes from Minoan Crete, where 'a great number of bones, mixed with ashes, come from peak sanctuaries or mountain shrines . . . bones mixed with figurines and other offerings in the ash layers. Sometimes bones, mixed with ashes, were thrown into rock crevices or chasms. The same practice, of throwing offerings into crevices, is also attested for caves.'[17] Some of the animal remains, as we might expect, included the jawbones of boars, along with inverted concial cups – a cup turned upside-down thus spilled its watery contents into the earth. The purpose of this was to induce rainfall, because precipitation is greatest on mountain and hill tops, the mountain top is the abode of the rising sun, and also because the death of the bull encouraged the advent of rain.

The mountain abode of the weather-god seems to have been universal in the East where, for example, the Ugaritic Baal was god of the mountain peaks. For the Greeks, the home of the gods was Olympus, a name that means 'mountain'.[18]

Bronze Age people in Sardinia worshipped a bull-god in circular temples built over a sacred spring, and associated with the cult of a sacred pillar, which may have received libations of water from the spring.[19] The purpose of libation was to enact, in symbolic ritual, the 'wetting' of the sun by timely rains.

FIG. 38 Acheloos spewing water – a version of lion–bull combat.

Sir Arthur Evans witnessed the survival of a cult in Bulgaria where a libation of wine was poured over a Roman altar while rain was prayed for (because the wine, like Beaujolais Nouveau, would have been ready at the time of the rains) and according to Claud Conder, the shrine at Mecca was partially abolished by Mohammed, leaving only the holy black stone originally dedicated to the water-goddess Allat.[20] Seven stones once surrounded the shrine which regularly received libations of blood. Mostly, though, libations were of water or oil.

Bull's blood was used to fertilise fruit trees in Greece and Crete, diluted with enormous quantities of water.[21] In Sicily, a bull's carcass was thrown into the well or spring of Kyane (or Arethusa) at Syracuse for the same purpose that in Rhodes horses were sacrificed by being thrown into the sea – again, a symbolic 'wetting' of the sun as a rain charm.[22]

When in the later development of anthropomorphosis the celestial bull took on the form of a human god, to become, for example, Dionysus, sacrifice took on a savage and almost secular aspect. Dionysian cults may have originated in Asia Minor, and came to Greece by way of Phrygia and Thrace. The descriptions of the orgies, where women became possessed by a frenzy of savage lust that descended into cannibalism, and went roaming about the countryside devouring man and beast, are to say the least of it excessive.

This rending of the flesh appears in the myth of Agave, daughter of Cadmus and a follower of Dionysus, who in a state of intoxicated madness, tore her son Pentheus apart. There is a story that the reliably sceptical philosopher Bertrand Russell once offered to supply a live bull to the classical scholar Jane Harrison and her colleagues at Newnham College, Cambridge, if they would demonstrate how it could be torn to pieces with their bare hands.[23]

There were reputedly certain rites where a human male victim, dressed as a stag, was hunted, killed and eaten, and a similar fate meted out to children in the service of the 'God of Raw Flesh'. The priestesses of Dionysus, the notorious Maenads, were said to work themselves up to a bacchic frenzy, which Robert Graves claimed was induced by the *Amanita muscaria* toadstool, the hallucinogenic red fungus with white spots.[24] Dionysus, bull-horned with his bull's foot, was, at least to the Greeks, a vinous figure because he presided over that period of the year when the dying solar bull was sacrificed to sow its seed.

The practice of human sacrifice in the ancient world, and whether or not it took place, is disputed, although it appears here and there in myth. If Greek physicians declined to undertake dissection and autopsies, for whatever reason, they may have considered it abhorrent to defile the human body, an attitude shared by religious leaders. In his study *Human Sacrifice in Ancient Greece*,[25] Dennis D. Hughes is sceptical of sacrifice in the majority of examples, and concludes that the case in not proven. Evidence from archaeology, he says, has not been forthcoming – unless, of course, we have failed to recognise it.

We cannot fail to recognise it in ancient Mexico, however. That the Maya threw the bodies of ornately attired young girls and children into the limestone cenotes, or natural wells, at the sacred site of Chichen Itza is not disputed. In Yucatan, the cenotes were the only regular source of water, being in effect cisterns, and depended on the Chacs, the four rain gods who were thought to live at the bottom of the cenotes, for replenishment. While drowning, the victims were supposed to plead with the Chacs to send rain.

Human sacrifice certainly occurred regularly in India until recent times, before the British authorities in the mid-nineteenth century managed to find ways of preventing it. Frazer, quoting from the observations of General John Campbell in Dravidian Khondistan, tells of the sacrifice of young men (*purusha-medha*) as a means to encourage the harvest. The victim was hacked to pieces, (as Osiris was hacked to pieces), and the bloody morsels of flesh distributed to villages throughout the region, where they were ceremonially buried in the fields.[26] Significantly, the sacrifices were to a goddess, and in some examples the victim was held fast in a cleft or split made in the branch of a tree.

The Tswana tribes in Africa are reluctant to admit to human sacrifice as a part of their rainmaking rites, and its existence is doubtful. Informants say that it may have occurred 'in the old days' when a small boy was chosen and killed 'in great secrecy . . . when the boy was alone'. Today, they merely sacrifice a sheep.[27]

To sum up, then, the sun in antiquity was imagined as a red bull, or other suitably virile animal, whose decline in the autumn sponsored the fertilising rains, and also provided nourishment from the springs of water that burst from the earth. The death of the bull was thus equated with life, and so the sacrifice that became a feature of all religions ensured future survival and prosperity. If the rains failed to arrive, and drought threatened, more drastic measures than the killing of a black bull or ram had to be taken, of which human sacrifice may have been a feature.

The death of the celestial bull to encourage rain and fertility of the earth is in fact part of the formula upon which all religions and mythologies are based. It reached its ultimate and almost mystical height in Rome, in the symbols of the worship of Mithras.

CHAPTER 15

Scorpion, Snake and Dog

Did the Roman troops who worshipped Mithras ('also a soldier' as Kipling described him) understand the extraordinary symbolism that surrounded this slight, almost feminine figure? We cannot know, for Mithraism was a mystery religion, its devotees sworn to secrecy. What little we do know about it – once a close competitor to Christianity – can only be learned from its extravagant monuments, which Roman followers had spread across Europe, from England to Africa, from Iberia to the Black Sea.

'Had it not been for the birth of Constantine in AD 272, we might all be Mithraists at the present moment,' wrote the archaeologist F. Legge in 1912.[1] The Christians took no chances, and the competition was made to suffer, as Mithraic shrines were raided and defaced by axe and hammer. Sufficient evidence has remained, though, to offer perhaps the richest opportunity for study and speculation in the whole field of comparative religion. In an endeavour to undertsand what lay behind the design and execution of Mithraic temples, frescoes, mosaics and statues, scholars gather internationally to meet at symposiums, to exchange views, deliver lectures and publish papers.

The centrepiece of the religion of Mithras that excites such interest, and to which a worshipper's eyes were drawn in Mithraic temples, was the scene either carved in relief in stone or rendered as a mural or mosaic, and known to scholars as the 'tauroctony', in which Mithras sacrifices a bull.

The hero, wearing his Phrygian cap, tunic and trousers and a billowing cape, straddles a quiescent bull and pulls back its head with his left hand. His right hand grasps a dagger, which he plunges into the bull's shoulder. The bull's tail – or in some examples the wound itself – sprouts three ears of corn. A dog and a snake leap to drink from the wound. A scorpion grasps the bull's testicles. Sometimes a crab or a lion are present, and a cup to catch the semen.

This is compelling imagery, the more so since we do not know what it means, and of course every detail does have a meaning. A raven perches behind Mithras, usually on his cloak, which often carries seven stars, a number sacred to Mithras. At either side of the scene are the torchbearers, the twins known as Cautes and Cautopates. These have their own symbolic attributes. Cautes on the right holds his torch pointing up; Cautopates on the left is pointing down.

The tauroctony from the altar-piece in the Mithraic temple at Heddernheim in Germany is three-sided and turns on iron pivots. Here the bull-slaying is framed by several cameos and a zodiac, including scenes of Mithras performing various functions. On this as on many other versions there are references to the number seven, by the inclusion of seven trees and seven fiery altars. On the reverse, the sequel to the tauroctony and its eventual outcome, the bull lies dead, Mithras having dragged it back into the cave from whence it came. The sun-god Sol hands Mithras a big bunch of grapes.

The forceful symbolism was no doubt designed to impress neophytes with its blend of mystery, celestial references to astronomy and astrology (which in the ancient world were one and the same) and its scale of grades or degrees through which the initiate must pass to achieve full acceptance as a graduate. There were seven grades, each one may have demanded some physical effort or endurance and suffering.

We do not know how these various elements came to be crystallised into such a complex of iconographic oddities called Mithraism. Mithras himself probably evolved in Persia from a borrowed Indian god Mitra, whose close companion, and perhaps twin, was the early Vedic deity Varuna. In Persia Mitra became Mithra, and in Rome Mithras. His name comes from the Persian word *mihr*, 'sun', while *mihras* means 'lion'.

One scholar, James Moulton, suggested that Mithras may have derived from an Assyrian word *metru*, meaning 'rain', perhaps related to an Indo-European word *mih*, 'piss' and 'be wet'.[2] The original Indian word *mitra* seems to have meant 'contract', the contract is between Mithras and Sol, the sun god, and their task is to slay the bull.

Actually, his antecedents will not tell us much, except that the religion and its arcane symbolism was probably developed in Asia Minor and Phrygia. It was here that the lion-bull combat also realised its full expression, to migrate throughout the ancient world. It features some twenty or thirty times in the relief carvings in Persepolis, and is almost certainly the inspiration behind the Mithraic bull-slaying scene, the tauroctony. The motifs that regularly appear with Mithras and the bull – the scorpion, snake and dog – had long been established in Syria and Mesopotamia.

FIG. 39 The tauroctony, Mithras slaying the bull.

On stones carved in the second millennium we find the sun, moon, star of Ishtar (Venus), goat-fish (Capricorn), bull, scorpion, snake, bird and dog, and a lion-headed man holding a dagger – symbols later adopted and employed by the Mithraists.

The first modern authority to study and evaluate Mithraism was the nineteenth-century Belgian scholar Franz Cumont,[3] whose interpretations centred on the conflict between good and evil – the bull is good, and the source of life; the snake and scorpion are evil. The concept is based on Zoroastrian Dualism where, in the Persian creation legends, the powers of good, led by Ahura Mazda, is set against the powers of evil, led by Ahriman. The followers of Zoroastra were fire-worshippers, which suggests a strong solar cult leading to the emergence of Mithra.

Although Cumont's contribution held sway for close on a hundred years, his theories have been overtaken by scholars today who point to the strong astronomical and astrological features that embellish the icons. The general opinion now (with variations and reservations) is that the tauroctony is a star chart covering a specific area of the night sky during a period of the year when certain constellations can be identified. Controversy persists over which constellations are represented and why. Thus we have Taurus for the bull, Hydra for the snake, Canis Major (and possibly Minor, too) for the dog, Scorpius for the scorpion, Crater for the cup, Corvus for the raven, Gemini for the torchbearers. Since religion itself had evolved from man's close relationship with the natural world, especially in the skies, the behaviour of heavenly bodies was incorporated in religious symbolism, by the temple priests, or by a nation's rulers.

The night skies – and the monthly performance of the moon – had led the Sumerians to establish a calendar, but it was the Assyrians who first realised the value of primitive astronomy as a means of interpreting the force of destiny; astrology then gave considerable power to the elbow of the priestly caste, who of course developed it. In *A History of Astronomy*, Antonie Panne-koek explains that omens played a very influential part in the development of religion. 'The faith in omens existed in primitive man as a natural consequence of his belief that he was surrounded by invisible spiritual powers which influenced his life and work. It was vital for him to win their favour and aid, to appease or avert their hostility and to discover their intentions. Exorcism, offerings, incantations, charms and magic connected with his work occupied his daily life. Most of these spirits had their abode in the heavens. Thus in early times the conception of a close connection between the stars and man's destiny had already risen in the minds of the Mesopotamian priests.'[4]

Astrology needed to develop a system of reference, and used as a basis those animal symbols that already identified some of the constellations – the scorpion, the bull, the dog and the serpent – which led to the invention of the zodiac and its completion in Babylonia in the fourth century BC. Constant observation of the brilliant, clear night sky (dust- and sandstorms permitting) in Mesopotamia led to the recognition of constellations and their seasonal places in the heavens, their rising and setting marking some natural occurrence or, more important, the agricultural seasons.

It would be noticed, for example, that a certain constellation always rose before dawn around the time of the summer solstice, and although it could not be seen during the day, observers would fix its approximate position. If the sun's path, the ecliptic, was seen to pass through this position, and dwell for some period in this 'house', then that constellation was assigned to the zodiac, and given a name – in this example, Leo.

Astronomy as an exact science could only develop slowly, and discoveries took a long time to gain general acceptance and recognition. The earth was flat until the Greek scientists Thales and Aristotle proposed the novel idea that it was spherical. While the solstices had been observed since man first deliberated on the annual passage of the sun, we do not know who fixed the equinoctial points, where the ecliptic (the imaginary arc that traces the sun's apparent path through the sky relative to the stars) crosses the celestial equator, but the equinoxes were seen to occur in spring, in Aries, and in the autumn, in Libra.

The constellations marked the seasons, those on the ecliptic were the zodiacal 'houses' through which the sun passed during the course of the year, and the Mithraists acknowledged the importance of the zodiac in their monuments. The strange lion-headed man in the coils of a giant serpent is often marked, on the statues, with the signs of Aries, Libra, Cancer and Capricorn, being the equinoxes and solstices respectively, because the leonine figure represented the seasonal influences in the journey of the sun; in one icon we see him spitting a stream of water (which some have mistakenly identified as wind) on to a fiery altar.

FIG. 40 Babylonian zodiac, *circa* 2000 BC.

In identifying the stars, and placing them in their right context, one needs to account for the phenomenon known as precession, where because of a natural wobble in the earth's axis, stars and constellations rise later as the centuries progress. Thus in 3000 BC the constellation Leo rose in early July, but by the time of Christ the group rose in August. The stars in the tauroctony are those with traditional associations such as Hydra and the dog (Canis Major) with the searing heat of summer, and so they leap to drink from the wound, because the dagger of Mithras has struck water, and this is why in some versions of the scene, the wound sprouts vegetation, and why some terracotta models of bulls' heads feature human breasts – the breasts of the goddess of spring waters.

The killing of the bull, like the lion-bull combat icon, was given dramatic intensity by way of its celestial references, a formula recognised throughout the ancient world, and which in Mithraism reached the final stage of its development. (It still exists today, in the arcane form of the Tarot deck of cards, the symbols of which were all taken from Mithraism — the Fool is the bull, the Juggler is Mithras, and other Mithraic references can be found in the pack.)

Its meaning, the sacrifice of the great solar bull in order to bring forth new life, was within the compass of divine influence, as it had been since the Assyrian Adad stood on the back of a bull waving his axe and thunderbolt (respectively sun and rain) with the sun, moon and stars.

Although it might seem that Mithraism made a spontaneous appearance in the Roman world, it was in fact the end-product of a long gestation that began perhaps with the early foundations of Babylonian astronomy. A religion of such complex and compound symbolism could not have arrived on the Roman scene ready-made, as it were, and Mithraism was certainly syncretic, borrowing elements from Anatolian, Babylonian and Persian cults. Those mystery religions that sought to establish an intensive spiritual rapport with the divine usually achieved their goals through the often severe process of initiation so that the soul might be purified and prepared for the afterlife.

Mithraism cannot be studied in isolation, for it is part of a great complex of ancient religions and cults of the Near East, featuring such as Men, Attis, Adonis, Sabazius, Dionysus — each of whom symbolise in their own way those features of severity, asceticism, deprivation, self-denial, mutilation, exclusivity, savagery, common to mystery religions, features that are both their strength and their weakness.

Self-mutilation seems to be a feature of solar cults, as evident in practices of the Aztecs and the Maya, where *nezoliztli*, 'to prick oneself', meant piercing the ears and tongue with cactus thorns, and was part and parcel of their savage and bloody rites of sacrifice. Bloodletting, and the triumph of willpower over pain, would then be a feature of profound subservience to the gods in order to influence the course of nature — rain especially — and the future security of the self and that of the community.

The Romans were attracted to oriental religions, and we find that the cults of Cybele, Isis, Mithras, Dionysus and Sabazius, and the less-familiar Jupiter Dolichenus flourished together in Rome where practically every day saw the celebration of some feast or another. Theirs was a pragmatic approach: religions that had survived, and were rich in symbolism, were therefore successful, especially if they had spread beyond their boundaries of origin to attract new converts. They worked, and so were pressed into the service of the Roman Empire.

Some of these religions were introduced by foreign mercenaries in the Roman army; Syrian troops were probably responsible for the cult of the Hittite deity Jupiter Dolichenus (the cult eventually spread as far west as Wales) who wore military costume, a Phrygian cap, and seems to have combined Greek, Roman and Anatolian features.

FIG. 41 The Syrian storm god, Jupiter Dolichenus.

The source of all these bull-centred cults may be traced back to the Sumerian god An, 'the great bull of heaven'; to the Elamite god Enlil 'whose horns shine like the brilliance of the sun'; and to Assyria where people worshipped the bull-horned sun-god Adad. Enlil was also 'Lord of the Winds' who may have inspired the billowing cloak of Dolichenus, and later of Mithras. They may be traced back further still, to the bull cults of prehistoric Asia Minor, so clearly represented at Çatal Hüyük. Mithraism was a compilation of all of these pagan cult elements, reaching a peak of extravagance in Imperial Rome by combining mysticism with currently fashionable astrology, and the exclusivity of a secret society.

Most successful religions employed recondite imagery, never using one symbol when a dozen would do, a practice that remains with the Roman Church today. The richer and more enigmatic the symbols that surrounded the deity, the more powerful was the call to devotion – or so it was hoped. Of course, the strength of mystery religions lies in this secrecy and exclusivity, attracting followers particularly in those societies with strong hierarchical structures and strict social divisions such as the military. In essence, however, religious life in the ancient world flourished in relation to agrarian life, especially so in regions of uncertain climatic temperament where drought and disease were prevalent.

Even the Mithraic grades of initiation and achievement (progressive orders of rank rather like that of the military) carried motifs influenced largely by fire, water and agriculture – the sun and the moon, cups and lamps, sickles and a scythe, the bull's shoulder, a 'fire shovel', thunderbolt and sistrum. The sistrum, its design perhaps based on the shape of a scorpion, was a rattle possibly used in rain-making ceremonies; it was also a female symbol peculiar to the worship of Isis, symbolising both the fertility of women and of the earth.

One of the grades, nymphos, means 'Bride', and the initiate, although male, becomes the 'bride' of the god. The German scholar Georg Creuzer claimed that Persian Mithra was fused with the Anahita, goddess of spring waters and rivers, and this bisexual identity may be why Mithras is regarded by some as effeminate – he sometimes wears the dress of the androgynous Attis, who castrated himself in the service of the goddess Cybele.

It is unlikely that a bull-sacrifice, especially one of such prominence, would have taken place without the influence of a goddess, the most likely one being the Persian 'holy water spring, Ardvi Sura Anahita', the goddess from which all waters on earth flow. Clothed in thirty beaver skins, Anahita 'purifies the seed of men, and the womb of females'.[6]

Identified with Ishtar and Cybele, a goddess of love and war, the worship of Anahita spread with that of Mithra. Her sacred animal was a bull, her emblem a torch, as it was of Mithras. It is more than likely that the two deities were at some time combined, Anahita losing her identity in that of the god, who became notably effeminate. Herodotus mentions this, deciding that Mithra was in some way assimilated to the goddess Mylitta, or that they were one and the same.

These hints of effeminacy through emasculation make Mithras seem an unlikely candidate to inspire devotion among the soldiery, yet the act of self-sacrifice by castration demanded considerable courage. One has only to see the iron clamps on display in the British Museum, employed by the gallu priests of the goddess for tearing off the testicles, to appreciate this. Perhaps such self-denial and fortitude commended itself to the army where ritual suicide was a feature of the Saturnalia in December, when a soldier, chosen by lot, cut his throat and expired in his own blood on the altar of Saturn. The Phrygian hat worn by Mithras, sometimes Perseus, Attis, Men, Sabazius and others, probably denotes their allegiance to goddesses of springs such as Cybele, Anahita and Artemis, whose priests were eunuchs.

Regardless of whether or not a goddess played a role in encouraging water, it is clear that water was an essential part of Mithraic liturgy, perhaps in the form of baptism, and provision for a water supply existed in every Mithraeum. The sanctuaries contained water basins (some in groups of seven) with conduit and drain pipes, with basins set in the floors, and in niches in walls.[7]

In the famous Mithraeum at Ostia there is a 'ritual' basin and a mosaic of a crater adjacent to a mosaic of a burning altar. Another in Rome had a well in which were found an amphora and boar's tusks. Baptism symbolised the sun's winter passage through water, the head representing the sun, touched with water. Some forms of baptism required total immersion of the body, which grew to symbolise purification.

Sanctuaries were often sited above or near springs or streams, the Mithraeum in London being in the valley of the Wallbrook. Figures of Mithraic significance, such as lion statues, or statues of the reclining god Oceanus, had conduit pipes set in the mouth, from which water flowed. The prominent leonine elements in Mithraism are featured in statues of lions with holes in the mouth as provision for a water spout, and a lion statue with an upturned urn between its front paws, from which water flows. Conduits, drains and basins were hewn from solid rock, as were the cave-like interiors of the temples themselves.

Mithras, a torch in one hand, a sword or dagger in the other, was born on the banks of a river from a rock around which a serpent was coiled. In a version of the rock birth, he turns to look to the left, and towards a big bunch of grapes, which he holds. In one of the scenes of the bull-slaying, the god Sol presents Mithras with a gift of grapes, and on a number of coins we find a grape-cluster in the shape of a bull's head.

The significance of the grapes points to autumn, more specifically to the month of September when Romans gathered the grape harvest, signalled by the rising of the star Vindemiatrix in the constellation Virgo. It points to the time that the sacrifice of the celestial bull took place and, of course, the arrival of the rains that gave life and vigour to Anahita's springs of the earth. The creation of springs is symbolised by having Mithras stab the bull in the shoulder, and it features again in the icons where Mithras seems to be anointing Sol with the bull's shoulder, and again as one of the initiation grade symbols.[8]

The most recent proposal, by Roger Beck,[9] for the meaning of the bull-sacrifice, the tauroctony, suggests that the constellations represented by the snake, the dog, the scorpion, the raven, the bull itself, the twins and other symbolic features, delineate a map of the route through which the soul travels. Judging from the commentaries of contemporary philosphers, such as Macrobius, and the second-century Neoplatonist Porphyry, the essence of Mithraism seems to have centred on the celestial journey of the soul, involving its ascent and descent – like the sun – climbing the seven-stepped ladder which features as one of the many Mithraic symbols.

The notion of a ladder to heaven, a 'Jacob's ladder', a 'soul-ladder' of seven steps, can be compared to the Sumerian ziggurat pyramid of seven steps, the seven steps in every Mithraeum that led to the altar, and the seven gates through which Ishtar passed. There is not much evidence in Mithraic iconography to symbolise this soul journey in any recognisable way, since the psyche or soul has few acceptable analogies – the Greeks settled for bees or butterflies or snakes to represent this essentially abstract idea, although there are a few examples of winged figures climbing soul ladders, but the way through the stars starts, apparently, through a gate located in the constellation Cancer, at the summer solstice, and leaves through the gate at the winter solstice in Capricorn.

Since these are the 'gates' through which the sun enters and leaves, ascends and descends, the soul's journey would appear to be identified with the passage of the sun. One is led to conclude that at its most fundamental level the Mithraic religion was principally solar. This may have been the source of all religions, which drew their inspiration not from within, but from without.

Furthermore it must be said that any commentaries on Mithraism from contemporary writers such as Celsus and Porphyry[10] are largely biased, and were possibly influenced by Platonic notions of the soul and the stars, which are divine. The idea of celestial immortality and the journey of the soul was central to the mysteries of Attis and Isis, and the cult of Sabazius, with which Mithraism had much in common. The cult shared with Mithraism the same wealth of symbols such as the Phrygian costume, the Twins, snakes, a bull, the raven, a cup or vase, the bull's shoulder, wheat ears, pine cones, thunderbolt, and so on, and all ultimately to do with the success and the identification of the god, fused with the goddess, as rainmaker, promising good fortune.

Is the scene of the tauroctony an allegory of the agricultural year, or does it have a more esoteric meaning? Can it be shown to represent a chart of the constellations along the route of the soul? Recent attempts to find constellations that might symbolise the features in the tauroctony,[11] such as Taurus for the bull and Scorpius for the scorpion, have questioned why some, such as Scorpius, are on the ecliptic, and qualify as one of the twelve zodiacal constellations, while others such as Hydra are not included. The torchbearers are Gemini, the Twins, but where is Cancer? The crab is in fact included on some versions of the tauroctony, but if zodiacal constellations are part of a supposed star chart, where are Virgo, Leo, Libra, Aries, and so on?

Virgo, by general agreement, is represented by the bull's tail, which sprouts wheat ears, and can thus be identified by the first magnitude star of the constellation, Spica, called 'the wheat ear'. Except that the same triple motif is found on the tails of ceramic stags of the fifth millennium, and on horses with triple tails on coins of the first century AD. It was a convention, because 'the fructifying power of oxen is supposed to reside especially in its tail'.[12]

One feature that strikes the viewer of the scene is the invariable and exaggerated posture adopted by both Mithras and the bull. The purpose of this, I suggest, is to imitate the shape of the constellation Leo, and it is why the god pulls back the bull's head, to conform to the well-defined shape of this group of stars. Leo, rising at the summer solstice, represented the sun as did Mithras himself. Mithras is the solar lion who kills the bull. The bull also

represented the sun, and is but a version of Mithras himself, as
Porphyry suggested.

FIG. 42 The importance of astronomy in ancient religions led to the development of Mithraic symbols. The tauroctony and the constellation Leo.

Mithras is therefore the bull's 'twin', who slaughters the bull as
one twin traditionally killed the other in the rite of succession –
for the 'feminine' twin is always the one to perform the slaughter.
It is exactly comparable to the deaths of Talos, of Osiris, of Balder,
of Attis, and all those victims emasculated in the interests of the
goddess. The scorpion grasping the bull's testicles is in fact
performing the act of castration. The bull is the dying sun, and
following its death is dragged back to its cave. Here it will
undergo its metamorphosis, to generate life in its female role, as
the buried carcass was thought to generate bees. The cave is an
important feature of this symbolism, emphasised by the cave-like
interiors of Mithraic temples, many of them hewn from solid
rock.

The Mithraic solar bull is represented by the constellation Taurus, which followed the rising of the Pleiades in late April or early May when, said Virgil, 'the gleaming bull with golden horns ushers in the year'. Gemini rose a week or two later, and their setting occurred around the same time as that of Taurus, which explains the positions of the torchbearers. The star groups featured are there because of the seasonal influence each was thought to possess. Corvus, the raven, had long been associated in myth and folklore with drought, because the star group rises during the parched summer months. This is why it perches close to Mithras as he strikes water with his dagger, and the bird is invariably included in the tauroctony. With the death of the bull the fruits of autumn can be gathered, and the ground prepared for sowing.

On separate limestone carvings, the torchbearers show their specific interests. Cautes stands beneath a bust of the sun-god Sol, with a pine cone, cock, ears of corn, a dog, lion and double axe. He also has a tree newly in leaf, juxtaposed with a bucranium, or bull's head. Cautopates stands with lowered torch in the company of a scorpion, a bust of Luna or a crescent moon, a fruit-bearing tree, a snake, fish, reeds, and an upturned pitcher from which water flows. His foot rests on a bull's head.

The twins – like Mithras and the Bull – represent the two courses of the waxing and waning sun, and the influences of fire and water through the seasons, with Cautes at the start of the agricultural year with the solar symbols of the pine-cone and the cock and the double axe. Cautopates stands for the autumn and winter, with the fruit-bearing tree, and such water symbols as the fish, reeds, snake, and the flowing amphora. Here perhaps we see the influence of the Vedic Mitra, god of rain and storms, and of the wide pastures.

Most examples of the tauroctony include Luna, sometimes on a chariot drawn by horses, sometimes by bulls, and going downhill. The cresent moon represents the descent of the year into winter when the moon stands higher than the sun. Where the sun symbolises fire, the moon symbolises water. Roger Beck suggested recently that the tauroctony, in addition to being a route map for souls, describes a lunar eclipse, or the fading of lunar light by the proximity of the sun. The identity of the bull as lunar had been suggested by Porphyry, but apart from a resemblance between a bull's horns and the lunar crescent, and the creature's death as winter approaches, the symbolic bull is rarely identified with the moon.

In the ancient world the bull was the fertile power of the sun, and the only connection with the moon comes from the similarity of the crescent to the bull's horns. This is perhaps why Cancer, the crab, is associated with the moon, because its claws were thought to resemble the lunar crescent – in astrology Cancer is the house of the moon, even though it is the constellation which marks the summer solstice.

Beck sees Cancer as an important feature since it is the house of the lunar bull. This zodiacal constellation rarely appears, however, in the company of other signs. I have pointed out that Mithras and the bull together adopt the pose and shape of Leo, yet there is no comparable weight given to Cancer, a faint group of stars whose only claim to the zodiac is because the ecliptic passes through it at the solstice, when the sun begins to move backwards, like a crab. The sign of Cancer is in fact to be found in the figure of Mithras who, like Perseus, and like Nike, looks backwards during the act of sacrifice.

The scene of the tauroctony occurs in the months of autumn, and the most satisfactory seasonal clue is provided by the figure of Sol presenting Mithras with a bunch of grapes. We can quite accurately identify the date of the tauroctony to Roman viewers, in the first centuries AD. On 30th October, just before sunrise at 5 a.m., about 100 AD, they would have seen Leo, Hydra, Crater and Corvus, Gemini, Canis Major and Virgo, all together in the first flush of dawn. Taurus and Orion were slipping away, and soon Libra and Scorpius would appear. The new wine would have been fermenting from the grape harvest, and the cattle would lift their heads, like the Mithraic bull, to smell the oncoming rains.

Recent attempts by several scholars to seek in the symbolism of the Mithraic religion esoteric, celestial and stellar meanings would seem to ignore the powerful evidence of solar influences, and moreover the long historical precedence of nature worship. Mithraism may have been founded in southern Anatolia, in the city of Tarsus in Cilicia, the birthplace of St Paul, a centre for mystery religions of the East. Here, it was able to draw upon many sources for its iconography Babylonian, Neo-Hittite, Phrygian, Assyrian, Achaemenian Persian, and Greek.

The Argive Greeks who had settled in Cilicia introduced the figures of Perseus (or developed Perseus from Mithra as the philologist Creuzer had suggested), Heracles (grafted onto the local deity Sandan) and Triptolemus the grain-sower. Cilicia was said to be the richest district in Anatolia, 'an alluvial plain more than a hundred miles in length, where soil and water and climate combine to make the growing of all things possible ... one hundred and fifty thousand labourers come down from the surrounding mountains each year for the harvesting'.

Those monuments to Mithraism that remain preserve no clear indications of the struggle between light over darkness, the triumph of good over evil, the cosmic conflict between Ormazd and his twin Ahriman, central to Persian mythology and Zoroastrianism. This spiritual battle did not inspire the slaughter of the bull, for while Mithras is undeniably light and the sun, the bull does not represent darkness and malign forces. The rather alarming lion-headed figure with wings, in the coils of a great python (the Devil in the Tarot pack) undoubtedly represents the

FIG. 43 Ningishzida, Babylonian god of underground waters (*left*) and the Mithraic lion-headed man. Some 1500 years separates the two.

two elements of fire and water. It is likely that he is a version of Mithras himself. As such, the figure represents the seasons, since he holds a thunderbolt, and in some examples is blowing water from his jaws. Mithras, as a development of Adad, is a cosmo-logical super-hero.

The seven stages or grades of initiation are each represented by symbols that have more to do with the earth and sky rather than the soul, but it is nevertheless likely that aspects of redemption, spiritual group-bonding through initiation and purification rites, and other emotional aspects, played their part. A form of baptism is likely, particularly in view of the importance of water in the shrines, and a sacramental, Eucharistic meal was certainly celebrated, of which there is plentiful evidence. After all, any religion worthy of the name – and the liturgy – is nothing without some form of ceremony.

For many thousands of years men had founded their cults, religions and mythologies on the attempts to establish control, or at the very least influence, on the forces of the natural world. The prehistoric bull cult of Çatal Hüyük and the historic though arcane bull cult of Mithras developed from the same needs, and under the same sky. It also gave, of course, a powerful sense of security and purpose through worship, ritual and sacrifice, and a power structure shared between the ruler and the priesthood. This was partly the reason why Mithraism became so influential in the Roman legions.

The prime achievement of Mithras, and his true *raison d'être*, was the guaranteed provision of fertilising waters, and therefore the renewal of life. Although there are plenty of celestial references, the tauroctony was never a 'star chart', but a cosmological setting of the forces of nature at a vital season of the year. Mithras is the god of plenty, the god victorious over drought and famine, and for good measure over disease. He is capable of performing miracles, striking water from a rock. By sacrificing the bull, he appears to create life from death, and he presides over the eventual resurrection of the sun, thus he is 'Sol Invictus'. To his followers he promises life in the hereafter, and by baptism in his purifying waters he guarantees their salvation – this is why Mithraism was such a close competitor to Christianity.

He shakes hands with Sol, having fulfilled his 'contract' to both the sun and his followers. If his cosmic powers contained an inherent Zarathustrian vowed intent to conquer the forces of evil, then the military were happy to have Mithras on their side, while the grades of initiation with all their severities tested the metal of the legions. Mithras, also a soldier, kept them true to their vows.

CHAPTER 16

Fear of the Future

The sun in remote antiquity was perhaps not revered for itself so much as for its influences on daily life, and the life of the year. Men and women of the Stone Age did not fall on their knees to adulate and praise a fiery disc in the sky but elected to worship and to attempt to influence the sun's creative powers. They could not of course have identified the sun as a planet, as an incandescent sphere of raging gases and elements, nor did they attempt to represent it in their art. There are no pictures of the sun as a ball of fire – such representations did not occur until much later in Mesopotamia and Egypt. The sun's daily and annual journey across the sky was unfailingly regular, and so determined the seasons. Because its actual nature was unknown, and a mystery, men resorted to interpret its forces by way of the abstract, by way of symbol and simulation. Nature herself provided a ready-made system of solar imagery in the activities of wild animals, and the seasonal behaviour of trees and springs and rivers. The eastwards orientation of places of worship and tombs has persisted in many religions where veneration of the forces of nature is evident. A well-known symbol from Egypt and Assyria (devised by the Egyptians, borrowed by the Assyrians) was a combination of a sun globe, with the wings of a vulture – regarded throughout the ancient world as a storm bird – and two uraeus snakes, representing the combination of sun and rain. It was positioned above temple doorways, and it hovered over the sacred Assyrian tree.

The Assyrians, in identifying solar power with their national god, Assur, placed his image in the disc shooting an arrow, and in so doing strengthened greatly his role in the eyes of the people (and by the way the influence of the priesthood), because the solar arrow that pierces the ground creates a spring. It usefully combined the martial with the fertile and productive attributes of the deity. Acknowledging the value of this idea, the Persians substituted their own god, Ahura Mazda, in the winged disc. It is exactly the same imagery as that displayed by Mithras, god of the legions.

FIG. 44 Symbols of sun and rain – Egyptian winged disc and the Assyrian god Assur. The disc is the sun, the wings are those of a vulture, while the snakes are sacred uraeus serpents of royalty.

The arrow that strikes from afar is the arrow of Apollo, the arrow of Mithras, of Robin Hood, and of Sagittarius (a constellation of the winter skies), arrows that strike water. Perhaps the so-called arrows or spears engraved in the Palaeolithic caves had the same meaning.

The progress of these mythologies from primitive beginnings to complex, inspirational and artistic conclusions was long and slow, and we cannot even guess where and when it all began, but the remarkable process by which symbols, and especially number symbols, evolved led to a structure of considerable strength and elegance, and was directly responsible for the development of art and literature. Indeed, mythology and religion, and their by-product, folklore, were the outcome of the boundless creativity of human imagination, stimulated by the instinct for survival, and fear of the future, and these depended directly on the elements, on the sun and the rain.

In my view, the origin of mythology was simple and fundamental, and with it mankind was able to fulfill other needs, those of a spiritual and mystical nature which continued to employ the original solar symbolism, because it was an endless wellspring for themes of infinite variety.

That mythology and ancient religion centred on the recognition of sun and water as the first and foremost essentials of life, long before and into the time that spirituality gained a foothold, has been proposed in various forms for centuries, and generally discredited. Scepticism is not supported, however, by the evidence we have to hand, though it is true that some myths are difficult or impossible to penetrate, and seem to contain no reference to fire or water, and have no obvious connection with elemental nature. Yet for the most part, the myths and religions of the ancient world were mundane, and they served a valuable function. Thus the limping of Hephaestus was not an affliction, but a divine yet practical asset.

Symbolism responded directly to vital needs. Heinz Werner, in *Symbol Formation*, put the point well when he wrote that, 'close and precise knowledge of the hard facts of life is for primitive people with a narrow subsistence margin a necessary condition for survival'.[1]

Since the Neolithic period, all the gods of the ancient world displayed their close connection with the products of the earth, even as late as 400 AD with Mithraism. The purpose was to show their influence with the fertilising, nourishing and quickening elements through their attributes – Nemesis with apples, Ishtar and Aphrodite with pomegranates, Athena with olives, Artemis with honey, while corn was an obvious favourite, appearing with Zeus, Jupiter, Dionysus, Sandan, Adad, Isis and Osiris, Mithras, Demeter and Persephone, and Triptolemus. Several deities further displayed cornucopias and bunches of grapes. The fruits of the earth were used to petition gods in times of drought and famine, and so the Hittite god Telepinu, for example, was exhorted to send rain following gifts of grain, figs, wine and oil, all most probably buried in pits in the ground.[2]

The fringe benefits offered by the divine powers included success in war through the agency of Athena, Ares or Mars, Apollo and the Dioscuri, the latter being particularly solicitous in helping the Spartans. Zeus and Apollo were noted for oracular advice and healing. Christianity managed to disassociate itself from the pagan influences of animism and nature worship, although it continued to observe its solar origins through baptism, the Eucharist, and seasonal festivals.

One of the most notable and perhaps extraordinary aspects of the growth of myth and religion was the emphasis placed upon animals, and to a lesser degree on plants. I have suggested earlier that cave artists of the Palaeolithic used the horse and the bison to symbolise the fertile qualities of sun and water because their characteristics of swiftness, strength and virility were admired, but mainly because animals powerfully represented the otherwise abstract influences of the elements.

Since symbolism is a form of disguise, the system by which symbols are developed has made sure that many are very difficult to understand. The symbolism of numbers, for example, motifs such as the swastika and triskeles, the trident, double axes, bull's heads, rams with three legs, limping goldsmiths and priests with dirty feet, and divine twins. And yet a simple action can sum up the entire process, the action where Poseidon, one of a divine triad, Lord of the horse, of springs, rivers and the sea, bangs his trident on the ground to create a spring, for here is the sun touching down in the winter to promise and deliver rain and spring water, Poseidon's horse ridden by the sun galloped across the land, striking with its hooves, and bringing fertility, as Pegasus created the Hippocrene spring on Mount Helicon.

In England, this symbolism of the sun's journey to earth was to be marked for thousands of years by the horses cut into the chalk of the downs, especially the Uffington Horse with its strongly stylised figure, leaping across the hills, just where the chalk aquifers meet impermeable gault clay and greensand, and the water emerges as springs along the 'Spring Villages' of the Vale of the White Horse. Such figures cut into the turf, revealing a stark white outline, and traditionally 'scoured' each year by villagers proud of their ancient heritage, have been imitated, with variations, elsewhere. Perhaps the most startling variation is the ithyphallic Cerne Giant above the village of Cerne Abbas in Dorset. The giant is clearly visible on a hillside, close by a spring called St Augustine's Well.

Since it cannot be traced in local records and archives prior to the eighteenth century, researchers are unable to authenticate the figure as either Romano–Celtic or prehistoric. Those who favour the Romano–Celtic provenance claim that the Giant is a representation of Hercules with his club. What is interesting is that the Giant closely resembles the outline of Orion, the constellation that rules the sky in winter, during the months of rain, and which in ancient times was associated with storms.

The constellation almost certainly inspired the designs of several martial figures, including Jupiter Dolichenus and Apollo, and was identified with Tammuz and Osiris. Orion had a dog, the adjacent star group Canis Major, which contains the dog-star Sirius, and

aerial photography has revealed the faint outlines of what appears
to be a dog, once cut in the chalk, on the north side of the Giant.

Until the date of the Cerne Giant can be satisfactorily
authenticated, it is impossible to know if the figure is a hoax, cut
in the chalk by eighteenth-century antiquarians, or whether it is
truly ancient. If this figure, of no mean size, is a hoax, it would
surely have demanded considerable planning and marking out,
and cut by a team of workers with spades and trowels. How could
such an event go unnoticed and unrecorded in a well-populated
Dorset village, a vast phallic figure that magically appeared
overnight?

The very fact that the figure is located so close to a holy well, a
figure resembling Hercules who freed the springs of Lerna from
the Hydra, suggests an ancient history. The Cerne Giant may
have lain for centuries, hidden beneath the turf like the accom-
panying dog, and preserved in folklore until revealed by amateur

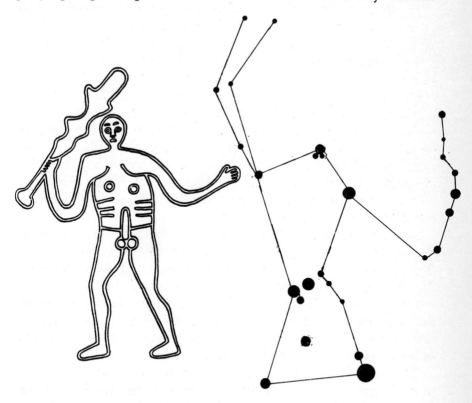

FIG. 45 The Cerne Giant and the constellation Orion.

excavation. The Giant's phallic attributes persuaded those that guided the morals of the village to play down their rather sensational discovery.

It is my firm contention that the principal function of all gods and goddesses was to represent the sun and to create water. As the sun and rain strike the earth, so Apollo and Artemis with their bows achieve the same end when they 'strike from afar', as Athena strikes with her spear, Nemesis with her branch, Ares and Chrysaor with their swords, Adad and Jupiter Dolichenus and Odin with their axes, Perseus with his sickle, Hercules with his club, Indra with his hammer, Zeus with his thunderbolt, Loki with his mistletoe shaft.

There are indeed several words in Sanskrit for 'to strike', all related to words meaning 'horse', 'gold' and 'yellow', 'to shine', and 'thunderbolt'. The 'strikers' seek water, and they set in motion the chariot of the sun to carry them on the journey that will terminate at the end of the year. Indeed, this is how and why they were first established, and their attributes symbolise this function. They were all, like Tammuz, 'faithful sons, and daughters, of the fresh waters of life'.[3]

One recurring theme along the routes of prehistory has been that of burial, heads in particular. Decapitation was an intrinsic part of solar rites. It featured in the medieval legends of Europe, especially among the Celts. In Arthurian romance, the victor of a combat or tournament decapitated the loser. There is a distant parallel here with the curious ball games played among the Aztecs and the Maya of Central America, where decapitation had a long history.

The game was played with a rubber ball between two teams, each of seven men including a captain (not unlike the team of Morris dancers), in a ball-court located at a sacred site. Fixtures may have been planned following a successful battle between warring tribes, for it has been suggested that one team was made up of prisoners of war, and the outcome was heavily loaded in favour of the victors. The captain of the losing team was beheaded, to join the skulls of previous victims displayed in rows on a *tzompantli*, or 'skull platform'.[4]

That this was a water-inducing rite may be inferred from a relief at Chichen Itza where a victorious player holds aloft the loser's head while snakes fan out from the headless body. In

Central America the rainy season began
with torrential rains in June, the time of
the winter solstice in the southern hemisphere. Perhaps the losing team can be
taken to represent the sun in decline at
the winter solstice. This does not fit in
with the facts, however. The author
Frederick Raphael, who has made a study
and has written about the Maya at Chichen Itza, said that the captain of the
winning team was also beheaded . . .

The head was sacred regardless of
whether it was human or animal. The
head of a horse or bull seems to have
exercised as much influence as that of a
human skull. In the shrines of Çatal
Hüyük in Anatolia, both the bucrania and
the skulls of the occupants were part of a
remarkable and complex symbolism.
James Mellaart, who excavated the tell,
recorded in detail this now-famous site which can claim, with
Jericho, to be one of the oldest cities in the world, dating from
about 6200 BC. A tell or hüyük is a settlement mound formed by
the repeated building of mud-brick houses on top of, and
replacing, those that had collapsed.[5]

FIG. 46 Stela from
Veracruz showing a
headless ball player. From
Coe, *Mexico* (1988).

The site is on the alluvial Konya plain, where the rainfall is
lowest in Turkey, the country then teemed with aurochs, pig and
red deer. Excavations showed remains of domestic sheep and goat,
while the crops were emmer and einkorn wheats, bread wheat
(*Triticum aestivum*) six-row barley (for bread and beer) and pea,
watered by irrigation from the river. There were almonds, acorns,
pistachio, apple, and hackberry (*Celtis australis*) for wine-making.
All in all, life appears to have been well-supported, with
childbirth, pneumonia and fevers the main causes of death.

Throughout the entire settlement clay models of bulls' heads
were found protruding from shrine walls, some with wavy horns
imitating water. The clay figure of a goddess was found giving
birth, like Pasiphae, to a bull. 'Decorating the east wall of a shrine
were two rows of women's breasts modelled in clay over the
lower jaws of wild boar. On the corresponding wall of another

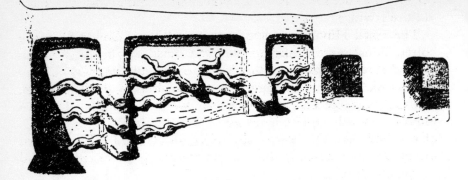

FIG. 47 Bulls' heads modelled in clay. From a shrine in Çatal Hüyük, Anatolia
The wavy horns are probably in imitation of water.

shrine a pair of breasts each contained the head of a Griffon
vulture the beak of which protruded from open red-painted
nipples.'[6]

Other walls displayed reliefs of leopards in a heraldic pose, and
carefully painted with leopard spots. Certainly the most dramatic
examples of shrine decoration were those of wheeling vultures,
painted in red ochre, some with human legs, apparently attacking
headless human figures. Beneath the murals a basket contained
a human skull. The bones of the dead were wrapped in cloth,
and buried beneath the sleeping areas in dwellings. This suggests
that the dead were excarnated, stripped of flesh, before the bones
were gathered. It is likely, given the association of vultures, and
their preference for carrion, that the birds carried out this
mortuary task. The heads of the dead were probably removed
before the bodies were exposed, the heads being regarded as
sacred, and performed the function of encouraging rain. Excarnation was probably a widespread practice throughout the ancient
world, and due to the need for a supply of selected bones. Quite
recently in England, a Neolithic excarnation platform was
discovered, high on Longstone Rake in the Peak National Park in
Derbyshire, and it may have supplied burial chambers in local
sites.

The red-painted birds were representations of, or in the service
of, the goddess, and this is why some have human legs. They are
red because they were painted with red ochre, the stuff of life, and

because they are solar, as the Assyrian and Egyptian solar disc has a vulture's wings.[7]

The Çatal Hüyük goddess was not a 'Death Goddess'[8] in the conventional sense, bringing about the death of men, but in the sense that she brings about the demise of the sun. She was perhaps of the nature of Mut, the Egyptian 'Great Mother', the 'lady of the sky', and was represented as a vulture and also as a lioness (at Çatal Hüyük leopards replaced the lions, but they remain the hunters of the bull, like the lion in the lion-bull combat). Mut was not merely vulture-headed, she was emphatically mammiferous and ithyphallic too.[9]

Mut was compared to the vulture goddess Nekhebet 'The Mother', identified by the Greeks with the birth goddess Eileithyia, the suckler and nourisher of children. That the vulture was a rainbird is evident from the Babylonian Imdugud, the thunder-cloud personified, the cloud imagined as an enormous vulture

FIG. 48 Vulture mural in a shrine in Çatal Hüyük.

floating in the sky, the name was composed of *imi*, 'rain' and *dugud*, 'cloud'.[10] The red vultures with human legs are rainbirds. The clay breasts in the shrines contain vulture skulls because the goddess supplies the vital water of life. The juxtapositioning of bulls' heads and breasts further suggests water.

The little headless human figures are solar, because their heads have been buried, as the sun is 'buried' in winter, encouraging the flight of the vultures – the storm clouds – to deliver rain. This is the meaning implicit in one of the shrine murals, depicting wheeling vultures and headless figures, mentioned above. I suggest that the headless remains of the dead were left in the open as carrion for the vultures, encouraging the beneficial influence of these venerated birds of the goddess. This was not human sacrifice, for society regarded the deceased as donors towards the common good of the living.

The persistent claim that in Anatolia and the Near East a Great Goddess, such as Cybele and Anahita, was the predominant divine figure is certainly due to the severe restriction of water in general. Marija Gimbutas mentions the desiccation of the climate in the Balkans during the sixth millennium BC shown by palaeobotanical research, indicated also by the water-inspired decorations on many artefacts.[11]

This Great Goddess then, who has captured the imagination of many writers, was an aspect of the sun that descended in winter and arose in spring, and paradoxically was responsible for its demise. The nemesis of the celestial, solar bull was brought about at Çatal Hüyük by the goddess and her leopards, and we see a bull hunt in one of the shrine murals where the bull and a boar are pursued by hunters in leopard skins. The relationship between goddess and bull, the fertiliser of the goddess, was profound and the androgynous identity of the two almost complete. Her offspring is the bull, or the bull-headed minotaur, or the young god, which she later kills, as the female spider devours the male. The bull as the catalyst of rain was a stylised image developed by the potters of Samarran and Halaf ware, 5000 BC, where raindrops fall from the bull's horns. The idea of water, as a tangible element, can be conveyed by wavy lines, descending patterns of lines, and raindrops, but it was more effective to show the natural forces that regulated the seasons, forces that were abstract and needed to be expressed through female human and male animal symbols.

This was realised through stylised and beautifully conceived designs which included scorpions (making the bull and scorpion two of the oldest symbols), rivers of water upon which ducks float, and antelopes from which rivers of water flow. In South Africa, among the Bushmen, the eland – an antelope – is the most highly prized animal, featuring in the rock-art of the region, although it does not constitute a part of the hunter's diet. In this, the art and the animals depicted bear close comparison to the cave paintings of the Palaeolithic. The killing of an eland is thought by the Kgatla tribe in Botswana to herald plenty of rain,[12] a survival of beliefs that go back to the bull hunts of Çatal Hüyük.

Stylisation in art is a lengthy process, whereby a conventional image, such as a bull's head, becomes progressively abstract and abbreviated, while retaining the essential features. It is a means of emphasising matters of importance and cultural significance. Water symbolism became more and more stylised throughout the ancient world, a process that started in the Palaeolithic (perhaps well before, if we knew how to interpret it). The religious iconography of the Anatolian settlements, especially Çatal Hüyük with its bulls and goddesses, vultures and human bones, is decidedly elemental.

Remarkably, we still respond to a primal urge to acknowledge solar rites, although they are now regarded as superstition, when we drop coins into ornamental ponds and wells, and it is directly parallel to rituals mentioned earlier, where animals were cast into lakes, rivers and the sea, and children were thrown into the cenotes of Mayan Chichen Itza.

The probability of human sacrifice may be evident from the preserved remains dug from peat bogs. The recently discovered Lindow Man, and the Danish Tollund Man, both show signs of having been ritually killed. The act is entirely solar, the corpse, the coin, object or animal symbolising the sun, and the sun's fertile influences, the 'water sun' that goes through water at the winter.[13]

'The survival of holy wells, "wishing" wells and well-dressing ceremonies in sophisticated modern societies attests to their importance even in countries with an abundant rainfall.'[14] Sometimes we throw in several coins ('Three Coins in a Fountain') and confirm the act by making a wish. The idea that the donor benefits in some way, by 'sympathetic magic' perhaps accounts for the extraordinary wealth of offerings. The Mayan cenotes yielded shells, stalagmites, pots, mirrors, the bones of jaguars, dogs, deer, turkeys, parrots and owls.[15]

An exhibition of open-air swimming pools was held at Waterloo station in London, and within forty-eight hours one pool had accumulated 217 coins, five finger rings and a beer mug.[16] A spring in Denmark yielded 540 silver and 5394 copper coins covering a period from the fourteenth century to the present.[17] In Britain, Celtic societies deposited prestigious metal-ware objects in watery contexts such as lakes and bogs. From the seventh century BC through to the late Iron Age, bronze and iron artefacts were the votive deposits in water. Even swords have been thrown in rivers, and particularly in east-flowing rivers.

One explanation of these acts is that the votive objects were sacred, and needed to be removed from this world and placed beyond human recovery and re-use, either by throwing them in rivers or burying them in pits.[18] This supposes a somewhat metaphysical objective, whereas votive acts were usually inspired by more utilitarian needs, and more likely motivated by self-interest or the interests of the tribe.

Sacred objects placed beyond human recovery are unlikely to include those designed as the focus of worship: excavations of the well at Carrawburgh, beside the Roman fort at Brocolitia in Northumberland, produced twenty-four undamaged altars, a human skull, and 13,000 coins.[19] The potential haul from the circular pool in the Roman remains at Bath is hard to assess since visitors continue to deposit coins of all values and all nationalities. Modern shopping arcades in town centres with ornamental ponds and fountains are strewn with coins dropped in by passing shoppers. Visitors to Cerne Abbas throw coins in St Augustine's Well, guarded by the Cerne Giant mentioned above.

The habit must stem from a powerful and atavistic impulse. When Stonehenge was in the care of the Department of the Environment, the authorities erected a scale model of the monument by the side of a path leading to the circle. The model regularly received deposits of votive coins. A mile to the south-east of Avebury, and at the end of a stone avenue, lies a site known as The Sanctuary, once containing concentric rings of stones and wooden posts, possibly supporting a roof, and of an earlier date than the Avebury circle. Rings of concrete posts now mark the position of the original structure, and when I visited the site recently, I saw that the central post bore an assortment of votive objects, including two 5p pieces, a penny and a dime, along with a conch shell, a bouquet of wheat and wildflowers, some feathers and pieces of flint.

The shards of flint observe a tradition so old as to be timeless, and were one of the most frequent deposits in what are called 'ritual pits', which the Greeks knew as *bothroi*, and were recognised throughout the ancient world. The contents of the pits might seem to be a random deposit of communal rubbish, except that they included objects that we now know to be highly symbolic of fire and water.

Shafts in the sanctuaries of Belgic Britons were found to contain horse skulls, jawbones and teeth, the complete skeleton of a horse, a carefully placed circle of horse teeth; also boars' tusks, dogs' skulls, charcoal, burnt flints and stones in several layers. Comparable to the deposits in the Mayan cenotes, a site at Ewell in Surrey had ten shafts that yielded a decapitated dog, the bones of a cock and the skulls of ravens, the assorted bones of bulls, boars and hares, a bronze figurine of a river god, and a scattering of unopened oysters.[20]

A significant addition was horse and bull hides, and the forelegs of horses because, of course, it was in the hooves that the dynamic power of water-raising was located. The ox skull-and-hoof combination was apparent much earlier at Arpachiyah in Iraq where, about 4000 BC, pendants and paintings of bulls' heads and hooves were laid down.[21]

In Britain, the pits are often located near henges and barrow graves, varying in depth from a few inches to forty feet, and more often than not dug to form a circle. The Maumbury Rings outside Dorchester in Dorset is a henge monument containing forty-five shafts cut into the chalk at depths of up to 36 feet. Most contained the burnt and unburnt skull and antler fragments of red deer, pig bones, flints, antler tools, charcoal, pottery, chalk objects and fragments of unburnt human skull, although this is apparently exceptional, for most human remains found on Neolithic sites were cremated.[22]

At Dorchester in Oxfordshire, three concentric ditches and a circle of fourteen pits were uncovered. The ditches held ox, sheep, pig and dog bones, the pits contained the cremated remains of at least 128 individuals from childhood to middle age, each burnt in a large pyre of wood. Animal and human bones were mixed; ox bones predominted, and of these mainly the shoulder and leg bones.[23] A ring of seven pits at Cairnpapple in Scotland each contained a small deposit of cremated bone, as did the Aubrey holes forming the first stage of Stonehenge.

There is a decided connection between these mixed deposits and the mortuary customs of prehistoric societies, except that these customs do not seem to have much to do with reverence for the dead. If anything, the human remains were classed as votive deposits along with pottery sherds and animal bones. Pottery sherds are common, and pots were deliberately smashed before burial because a broken pot symbolised the spilling of water, and by the same token, rainfall. A great quantity of sherds, weighing in total 24 pounds, were found during excavation of a Neolithic barrow on Whiteleaf Hill, Buckinghamshire.[24] It is likely that all burials in the ancient world were votive and interred in order to encourage favourable conditions, hence the inclusion of boars' jaws, stalagmites and stalactites, or other symbolic objects.

From a period around 4700 BC some 40,000 tombs were created along the Atlantic seaboard from Spain to Scandinavia. Most were of stone, or of timber covered with soil. All were monumental in size – and there all similarity ends. Designs varied, as did the contents. Some tombs contained but one person, others several. Some bones were burnt, others were not. Disarticulated bones, gathered together and perhaps collected from different individuals, were more of a common find than that of an entire skeleton. Some bodies appear to have been defleshed or had decomposed ages before being interred – and here are links with the mortuary customs of Çatal Hüyük.

Many bones were broken and swept into a pile, and were mixed with cattle bones, charcoal, flints and pottery sherds. Sexes varied, as did age groups. There appeared to be no common factors, no uniformity. 'The people who built and used these great structures seem to have taken a positive delight in making exceptions to every rule by which we try to discern their behaviour.'[25] Some tombs showed evidence of huge fires, deliberately lit and stoked like a kiln, after the bones had been interred – a mass cremation that may well have had a solar significance, like the midsummer fires lit to celebrate the sun's turning point, although it is impossible to know at what season the fires were begun. My own view is that the fires simulated the sun's descent into the earth, and were probably lit in the autumn, possibly around November. Here was the origin of the bonfires set alight at peak solar times of the year – the midsummer solstice, and later in the year as the sun's strength weakened. The word bonfire comes from bone fire, and seems formerly to have meant a funeral pile, a pyre.[26]

Burials in round barrows, or chambered long barrows, where the corpse was interred, sometimes clothed, and accompanied by grave goods, clearly belong to the category of conventional funeral practices, and show some reverence for the departed. Perhaps families chose either to bury their dead, or to dedicate their bones as votive deposits for the common benefit of the community.

Where only part of the body was interred, and shared its resting place with cattle bones and lumps of burnt flint, we may assume that the bones were in the nature of an offering, and so were votive. They possess a similar significance to that of sacrifice, like the buried heads of the Danaides, the heads in Çatal Hüyük and in Jericho, buried under the floors of dwellings, in the same way and with the same intentions that Neanderthalers buried the skulls of cave bears under the cave floor.

This is why we find the emphasis on skulls and long bones. It may seem to us a macabre thing to do, to bury family skulls under the floor at home (often in the sleeping area) as they did in the ancient Near East. The purpose, however, was not devotional, but entirely practical, for it was hoped that the powerful influence of the solar head, and the long bones that strike water, would bring nourishment and fortune to the family.

Excavations at Jericho revealed 30 skeletons, many of which had been decapitated, and the bones later collected and burnt in the centre of a tomb, with the crania disposed around in a circle.[27] At the Fussell's Lodge burial chamber in Britain, the skulls were separated from the stacks of long bones, which were then burnt. Bones and artefacts may have been stored, to be used later when a votive deposit was needed, perhaps to plead for rain on behalf of the entire community, hastening the return of the earth's springs and confirming the dynamic relationship between the elements of fire and water.

CHAPTER 17

Holy Fire

Here and there in this book I have mentioned the belief that the sun spent the winter in a cave. Deep in the winding passages of the earth was the solar forge that created life and introduced the smith-gods Hephaestus, Vulcan, Agni, Tvashtri and Wayland to the pagan pantheons. The lame smiths could take the form of bulls, or like Agni travelled on a bull, because the sun, in penetrating the earth, was the herald of the fertilising rains.

Mithras enticed the solar bull from its cave, sacrificed it, and dragged it back again. The Mithraeum shrines were in imitation of caves, usually in rock-cut grottoes. The Minotaur lived in a cave, for this is what the labyrinth represented – the cave of the sun, with its seven windings or passages, indicating the period of the sun's winter residence.

The sun performed magical tasks in the earth as the womb performs the magic of creation, and so the cave or labyrinth, like the womb with its seven cells, was the source of all life, and the birthplace of the gods. In the ancient world, caves were the province of the birth goddess. Zeus was born in a cave on Mount Dikte on the island of Crete (though there are other claims to this honour – Mount Ida, Mount Juktas, or Mount Lykaion in Arcadia), perhaps the same one into which he was cast (when robbed of his sinews) by Typhon. According to the early Christian writers Justin Martyr and Origen, Jesus was born in a cave, and lived with his mother in a grotto. Ian Wilson, in *Jesus the Evidence*, adds some support to this view: 'For centuries Christians have imagined Jesus's birth to have been in the stable of an inn, surrounded by farm animals, but this conception does not derive from the gospels. The Greek text of Luke speaks of a *katalemna*, a temporary shelter, or even a cave; and it was over a cave that the Emperor Constantine built Bethlehem's Church of the Nativity.'[1]

Krishna was born in a dungeon in which his mother Devaki had been imprisoned, like Danae, the mother of Perseus. Apollo was born 'where no rays of sunlight could penetrate' under Delos. The original sanctuary at Delos, later to become the temple of Apollo, was a cave, consecrated by the Phoenicians and taken over by the Greeks.[2] Sacred caves existed throughout ancient Greece, according to the second-century travel writer Pausanius, and were as common as temples. Apollo, Hercules, Hermes, Cybele (a goddess of stones and caverns), horse-headed Demeter and Poseidon were alike worshipped in them. Black Demeter, Hecate and Cinderella, and the Japanese Amaterasu — all female versions of the winter sun — lived for a time in caves. Mohammed retired to a cave in the Mountain of Light, and the great cave at Gibeon is said sometimes to emit a supernatural glow, as if the sun were contained within.[3] The Phoenician god Melkarth woke from his winter sleep in his sacred cave on the 25th December.[4]

All the sacred sites in Palestine are shown as grottoes ('grotto' from the Latin *crypta*, and the Greek *krupte* meaning 'vault'). The vaults of churches are really the ancient caves of the sun. While acknowledging that the earliest temples were in rock-hewn grottoes, the *Encyclopaedia Biblica* dismisses the association between caves and sacred Christian sites as the 'arbitrary invention of legendmongers'. Yet at Bethlehem the Manger is in a cavern, long used as a Mithraeum where the resurrection of Tammuz was celebrated. The Holy House at Nazareth is a grotto, and on Carmel is the cave of Elijah. The holy fire which breaks forth each Easter from the Sepulchre in Jerusalem is connected with caves and grottoes, the abode of the sun. The body of the crucified Jesus was taken to a sepulchre hewn out of rock.

The most celebrated cave in the Bible lands is said to be under the Haram mosque at Hebron, the cave of Machpelah, reputedly in three parts and containing the sepulchres of the three patriarchs Abraham, Isaac and Jacob, and their wives Sarah, Rebecca and Leah.[5] I say 'reputedly' because access is not permitted, and seems not to have been since the twelfth century when it was visited by the Rabbi Benjamin of Tudela. This cave also contains the head of Esau, the 'red and hairy' twin of Jacob. The sun's hair is one of its best-known attributes, and so the head of Esau, like that of John the Baptist, beheaded in a crypt in the church of the Baptist at Sebustieh, were powerful representatives of solar influence.[6] John Robertson, in *Pagan Christs*, mentions the cave as being the earliest form of temple. 'It is easy to understand how to half-civilised man caves would have a hundred mysterious significances, as places for dwelling or meeting made by the Deity himself; and fire or sun worshippers would have the special motives supplied by finding in caves the remains of fires of earlier men, and by the not unnatural theory that the sun himself went into some cave when he went below the horizon at night.'[7]

It seems, then, that men in primitive times imagined the sun as entering the earth at sunset, and spending long periods of time underground in winter. The idea that a mountain on the horizon of the world is the abode of the sun is ancient, and on Mesopotamian seals we see the sun god Shamash arise at dawn from the mountains, probably the Zagros range.

Although cave cults were undoubtedly important, we cannot jump to the conclusion that anything deposited in a cave shows evidence of cult practices unless some form of ritual seems to have been observed; in Gamble's caves, Kenya, tightly flexed and red-ochred burials were found, dating from around 13,000 BC. Evidence of cave-bear skulls and bones, 'Venus' figurines, and the Great Ofnet example we saw earlier, where ochred skulls were interred in a packed group, plausibly reflect cave cults. Cave worship was powerfully represented in Central America where altars, shrines and stairways occur in sacred caves. They were used for the worship of rain and earth deities, and as depositories for human remains and of clay figurines, which were found in great quantity. The Maya historian, Sir Eric Thompson, writing in 1972, said that pilgrimages to caves still continue in areas where European influences have not penetrated in strength. In ancient Peru the Wari culture, which predated the Incas by some 500 years, had sacred caves in the mountains where they interred human skulls. In Crete, the floors of caves were littered with the remains of sacrificed animals, while the Greeks were particularly devoted to cave cults, where the Corcyrian cave on Parnassus was sacred to Apollo and Dionysus. In the Diktaean cave, one of the several claimed birthplaces of Zeus, stalactite columns bore evidence of votive offerings embedded in crevices.

Stalactites and stalagmites are, of course, formed by the action of water percolating through limestone, depositing sediments of calcite and gypsum. In Israel, in the Mount Sedom area, salt caves were formed from the mineral halite or rock salt and perhaps inspired the legend of Lot's wife.

Stalagmites were venerated as the aniconic embodiment of the birth goddess Eileithyia in Cretan caves, and several scholars have pointed to this as a source of cone and pillar worship. Pillars were erected in shrines, sanctuaries, and even in the palaces in Minoan Crete. The archaeologist Marija Gimbutas,[8] who has excavated in Crete, refers to the worship of stalagmites in caves from the Neolithic period, and their probable relation to pillars. In France, the Tuc d'Audoubert cave is noted for its magnificent stalactite hall. At Les Trois Frères a narrow gallery leads to an extensive cave and to a chamber of stalagmites and there's a large, painted stalagmite gallery at Pêche-Merle.

In Çatal Hüyük, Mellaart found stalagmites obtained from the Taurus mountains, some fifty miles south, as part of the inventory of shrines where they accompanied figurines. The veneration of these water-formed pillars of limestone perhaps began in the Palaeolithic, and limestone formations occur throughout the Middle and Near East, and in Europe.

Claud Conder, surveyor with the Palestine Exploration Fund, described chalk, sandstone, and dolomitic limestone with flint bands, formations abounding in springs. The Jordan rises as a full-grown river issuing from a cave at Banias. The sacred Adonis river pours from a cave surrounded by a theatre of vine-clad crags at Af'ka. The river Nahr Sebta, thought to issue intermittently every seven days, rises as the 'bubbling spring', the Ain el Fuwar, in a cave, the site of a legend of a princess imprisoned, like Danae, by her father. The Ain Hesban spring flows from a cave, as do the springs of Moses under Pisgah.[9] When Apollo flayed the centaur Marsyas he hung his skin in a cave through which a river flowed.[10] As with many myths, you need to read between the lines to grasp the true meaning. Marsyas challenged Apollo to a flute-playing competition. Marsyas was the loser, and was killed and flayed by Apollo − the scene was a popular one in classical art. We then learn that the equine Marsyas's flute once belonged to Athena. Apollo was therefore Athena's agent, the 'lion' that kills the solar horse in the cave of winter.

Caverns of stalagmites and stalactites seem to have made a profound impression on those groups of people that lived in or near areas with springs and limestone formations, but then the cave complex as a whole possessed a powerful, numinous atmosphere because it was supposed that here was the source of life. The creation legends of the Flood featured caves and mountain tops as places of refuge, where life was preserved and renewed.

Caves, and in particular those on the slopes of mountains, were dedicated to birth deities and were revered as the birthplace of gods. In Kashmir, Hindu devotees gather in great numbers during September for the annual pilgrimage, the *Amarnath yatra*, to visit the lingam of Shiva, a pillar in a cave near Panchtarni in the Himalayas.

Shrines were often located at a high place where the sun was seen to enter the earth and where precipitation occurred, where the rain soaked into the rock and burst out as springs on the lower slopes, a natural phenomenon underlying those myths where a storm god spilled his semen on a rock, and led to the idea of rocks as the abode of, or forms of, the goddess. In Vedic myth Parvati, the wife of Siva, was called 'The Mountaineer' and takes her name from the word *parvata*, 'a rock', from the Sanskrit root *PA*, 'to drink'. Siva is 'lord of the hills' and dwells on Mount Kailasa. He is regarded as the source of five sacred rivers flowing from the Himalayas.

In Mesopotamia, Ninhursag was 'The Lady of the Mountains'; the Anatolian Cybele was worshipped as a black stone; Athena was goddess of the rocky citadel, the Acropolis of Athens. This explains why Hephaestus ejaculated his semen on Athena's thigh, for he was the limping sun of winter, spilling rain like semen, and she was the goddess of the rocks; Athena's nursling was Erechtheus, part male child, part female serpent. The progeny of these rock births, of the 'rock that begat thee', were often androgynous, perhaps because the rock absorbed the seminal donation of the sky god, and in time delivered the spring waters of the goddess.

Mithras was born from a rock around which a water-snake was coiled, and Sir Arthur Evans correctly perceived that 'The real origin of the connection of Mithras with rocks and mountains should be sought in cloudland'.[11] The rock-birth of Mithras may explain the sanctity attached to all rocks. From the caves and rocks of the earth rose the sun, and we may suppose that the earth goddess represented by rocks, and trees and springs, annually gave birth to the sun (as the goddess gave birth to the bull, her son, her lover, and eventually her sacrificial victim) as the sun rose from the high peaks of the mountains. We may suppose that every goddess of springs is also identified with rocks, and we know that Zeus as a rain-god impregnated Hera on a mountain peak, probably Mount Cithaeron, and certainly in a cave, since Hera was predominantly a birth goddess and closely identified with the birth goddess Eileithyia. In the hymn to the Delian Apollo, the poet sings: 'Thou hast delight in all rocks, in the steep crags of tall mountains, in rivers hurrying seaward, in shingles sloping to the tide, and harbours of the sea.' It is almost unavoidable to compare the cave to the womb, a place of increase, of fecundity, where rainwaters rushed through limestone channels to nourish the earth warmed by the sun's generative heat.

This would have been the matrix, the model, for every shrine and temple, grotto and crypt, catacomb and chapel, and came from the observation of the structure of the womb and the cave. Take note, though, that this was the symbolised, seven-cell womb of the sun, a structure with which the human womb was later, and wrongly, accredited.

Many but not all caves were formed by a narrow passageway leading to a cavern or gallery. The Franco-Cantabrian limestone caves, such as La Pasiega, Montespan, Les Combarelles, and Font-de-Gaume, have passages, grottoes, labyrinths and chambers. In his book *From Cave to Cathedral*,[12] E. O. James records the evolution of places of worship in cult and religion but seems to avoid seeing a direct development from the vaulted caves to the similarly vaulted cathedrals. The so-called 'passage graves' of the Neolithic, where a long entrance tunnel leads to a domed chamber, may be compared to the design of a church where the nave leads to the transept above which a dome is often located.

Temples were hewn out of rock in imitation of the cave, and temple design regularly conformed to a standard entrance where a pair of upright pillars supported a lintel. The more primitive types, and the passage graves and long barrows had rough-hewn monoliths supporting a large slab or capstone forming a trilithon, taken to the ultimate of Neolithic grandeur in the massive trilithons of Stonehenge. I suggest that this was the form leading to the construction of dolmens or chamber tombs and 'coves', and that their purpose was to stand as a symbolic cave, a structure of influential potency. Sir Norman Lockyer, in 1906, mentions the similarity between the cave and the dolmen, and that the successors of the natural cave are representations of a cave built of stone, especially in the French *allées couvertes* 'a stepping-stone, as it were, between the natural cave and the dolmen.'[13] The *allée couverte* is a passage-grave or *tholos*, where a long stone gallery opens into a circular chamber or *cella*. In ancient Greece the inner chamber of temples, the *adytum*, was originally a cave, and was often wholly or partly subterranean. It was also known as the *megaron*, which Robertson Smith says can hardly be true Greek, and mean 'hall', but is rather to be identified with a Phoenician word *me'arah*, meaning 'a cave'.[14]

FIG. 49 Dolmen in Palestine (left) and a tholos or domed passage grave at Arpachaya, Mesopotamia.

It would be wrong to claim that the people who built these monuments saw them as emitting a form of radiation, like a spacecraft, but it seems likely that a certain magical influence was believed to be channelled through them. They were a means of establishing an interrelationship between man and the heavens. Building a dolmen was an act of dedication, and votive opportunity, in much the same way as a sacrifice was a petition for good fortune.

For one thing, they were usually on elevated sites, the 'high place' closer to the sun, and where the rain was first most likely to fall, and for another they were always strategically related to water. Dolmens were discovered in abundance in the Near East by the Palestine Exploration Fund, formed in 1865 as a pioneer archaeological society, employing officers of the Royal Engineers, including Claud Conder and the future Lord Kitchener. Conder surveyed some four hundred dolmens, standing stones and cromlechs, or stone circles, on the mountains of Moab. The dolmens were always built on the slopes of hills, usually with a central feature such as a circle, but with no particular orientation.

Many bore cupmarks with intersecting channels, very like those found in Western Europe. Conder supposed that they were cut to receive libations, perhaps of blood. I would suggest they were symbols of the labyrinth, and of caves as the abode of the sun, as were the stone circles.

At 'Ain Jideid this centre is found in the great stone circle of Hidanieh, just above the spring, while on the south the hill top is occupied by a great cairn and the slopes thickly strewn with cromlechs. *In every case the monuments are located in the immediate vicinity of a spring. In districts where no springs occur, no cromlechs are found, although suitable material could often have been obtained* [my italics].[15]

Several of these circles had dolmen gate entrances, that is, trilithons of a design similar to those of Stonehenge. The stone monuments of El Mareighat stand on a knoll located above the springs of Zerka, while on the cliff above the Jideid spring stands 'an enormous stone circle' on the south side of Mount Nemo. Where the Jordan flows from its cave are dolmens and menhirs and the remains of stone circles.[16]

The comparison between the dolmens of Palestine and those of the West of England is striking. Spinster's Rock in Devon, said to be a chamber tomb, stands on an elevated site and close to a lake. Trevethy Quoit in Cornwall is on high ground, some 500 metres from two streams and springs. At the promontory of Land's End in Cornwall, in a relatively small area of basalts, granites and dolerites, are hut circles, wells, springs and streams, outcrops of rock, and several well-known monuments dating from the Bronze Age, including the Boscawen-un circle, the Long Stones, the Lanyon Quoits, the Men-an-tol holed Stone, the Men Scryfa inscribed stone, and the Nine Maidens stone circle.

The Men-an-tol is an upright stone with a hole in the centre, like a ring doughnut, through which sick children were passed (three or nine times, against the sun) in the hope of a cure. 'Superstitions connected with "passing through" are common all over the world. In Madras children are passed under the sills of doorways, and many sacred holes and clefts are crawled through in India.'[17] Here is the passing of the sun through the door of winter, and through the water that effects the cure.

Water is the principal element here, and stone erected by groups that recognised an ancient system of belief, the source of this lithic heritage, which began in the caves of the Palaeolithic and persisted into historical times. It is safe to say that wherever there was water in the ancient world one might have expected to find a sanctuary, and vice versa. Plato described sanctuaries known for springs that eventually dried up.[18]

The reverence for water, linked to the passage of the sun through the year, was exceeded only by – and engendered by – the fear of drought, which was central to the entire system of belief, and the idea persisted even where water supplies were reliable. Indeed, where water supplies are abundant, as in Britain and Ireland with their long dark winters, the wealth of stone monuments seems to celebrate this reliability.

Here lies the single source of all myths and related symbols. From this source there arose the idea that the influence of the sun and water could be appealed to through oracles, through ritual – especially sacrifice – and that water and stone had powers of healing.

Over the centuries man attempted to establish a workable relationship with nature through a variety of methods, in order to stimulate the sun's powers. Paintings of animals that seemed to symbolise the subterranean activity of the sun decorated remote caves. The deposit of votive objects in rivers, lakes, bogs, and wells had a similar purpose, as did the burial of figurines, and of cremated bone in pits.

All these diverse activities, and in many places quite complex systems of belief and devotion, had simple solar origins which were first formed in the minds of men perhaps millions of years ago. Wherever they originated, they spread far and wide, each society developing its own individual means of expressing this belief through the creation of symbols and myths, and of gods and goddesses who would act on their behalf.

Groups which spread westwards across Europe during the Neolithic Age – the Celts, the Beaker folk – whoever they were, constructed buildings of earth and stone, which archaeologists call 'passage graves' and 'chamber tombs', and the mortuary houses known as long barrows, round barrows and cairns, like the Clava cairns of Inverness. These chambers, often placed at the end of a long passage or tunnel, with cists leading off from the side, were an imitation of the caves of the sun, and the bones deposited therein – human and animal – were solar offerings.

FIG. 50 A reconstruction drawing of Fussell's Lodge ossuary, where bones
were cremated. From Ashbee, 1970

This was sympathetic magic, superstition if you like, and arose
originally from the idea of the sun entering and warming and
fertilising the earth, in order to reawaken nature. Fierce fires or
holocausts were deliberately created in the ossuaries and mortuary
houses (the 'bonefires' mentioned above), sweeping through the
chambers and leaving a mass of cremated and partly burned bone.

As we saw with the buried skulls of Çatal Hüyük, the simplest
ritual in maintaining a magical rapport with the sun and the earth
was to dig a hole in the ground and to inter the appropriate votive
object – the jawbone of a boar, perhaps, or a scattering of shells or
cremated bone or pieces of burnt flint or chalk. The purpose of
this was to simulate the entry of the sun into the earth, as we
throw coins into wells.

Almost anything, it seems, would do – even the digging of the
hole might be sufficient unto itself. In Britain, the Neolithic site at
Maumbury features a ring of deep pits. Although fewer than half
of the 45 shafts have been excavated, three were found to contain
nothing but chalk rubble, the remainder having an assortment of
bones, flints and pieces of pottery.[19] Excavators of a long barrow at
Thickthorn Down found no trace of a burial, other than the leg
bones of oxen, although there were secondary (possibly Beaker
folk) burials on top of the mound.[20]

We now know that buried skulls, both human and animal, were especially powerful talismans in solar religions and cults. Stuart Piggott noted the deposits of horse and ox skulls, with the forefeet only, but also the evidence of buried horse and cattle hides.[21] Here would seem to be a reason for the importance attached to hides and skins – the flayed skin of Marsyas, the Golden Fleece of the Argonauts, and the flayed skin of the Aztec rain-god Tlaloc. The rituals receive some support from myth, where three gods (perhaps Zeus, Hades and Poseidon), after a bout of drinking, urinate on the hide of a bull and bury it.

The progeny of this bizarre token is the giant Orion, born of the earth, and the Greek pun on pissing with rain – *ouron*, and *oureros*, 'to make water'. Orion, the great constellation of winter, is associated with rain and storms, which the buried hides encourage.

Rain is the element expelled from the orifices of gods and goddesses in the myths of ancient Mexico, where rain was *kaxal ha*, 'to defecate'. An icon from the Madrid Codex of the Mayas shows water pouring from the anus of a rain-god, and from the breasts, armpits and between the legs of a goddess – probably Ix Cheel – wearing a serpent headdress.[22]

The most highly developed form of the relationship with the earth and the elements was the construction of great monuments. In Egypt the pyramids of Gizeh contain passageways, galleries and chambers like caves in a mountain, and the monuments are directly related to the river Nile. Even though, as has recently been proposed, the pyramids are closely allied to celestial bodies, in particular the star Sirius and the constellation Orion, they have their origins in solar and water symbolism.

The helical rising of Sirius, or Sothis, the dog-star, marked the inundation of the Nile and the start of the agricultural year. In early times Sirius was represented as a woman, in reality a form of Isis, and later identified with the cow Hathor, because of course they were goddesses of water. This is probably why in Egyptian myth the sky is feminine and the earth masculine, representing the vegetation-sprouting body of Osiris, consort of Isis. It is also why Osiris is identified with Orion, since the constellation Orion or Sah, the 'fleet-footed' and the 'father of the gods', rises with Sirius.

The waters of the goddess rejuvenated the body of Osiris, and so every deceased Egyptian king and indeed every dead person, was believed to become an Osiris. Knowing this makes it easier to grasp the idea that the dead have powers of fructification, like the solar bull sacrificed in its cave, or the cult of the buried skull, and were employed as votive offerings. It was not essential that the whole body be represented, a part of the skeleton would suffice. This is why digging a ring of small pits, and interring cremated human bone was the foundation of Stonehenge, which finally brings us, as it were, the full circle.

CHAPTER 18

Full Circle

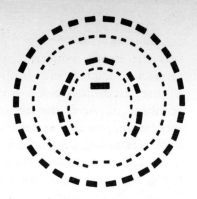

Everything in the world of myth and folklore, of ancient cult and ritual, can perhaps be traced back to that brief moment in time when Neanderthal hunters made a symbolic gesture of thrusting the leg bones of a bear into the eye sockets of its whitened skull. This sacred combination may have become, during the course of some 50,000 years, the foundation of a modern symbol – the skull and crossbones of death. In prehistory, especially in the cold climate of the Pleistocene, it was a death to be encouraged, to be celebrated and revered, for while the leg bones might magically summon up springs of water, the skull was invested with the fertile powers of the sun, interred in a cave where it might encourage and regenerate life.

With this in mind, it is easy to appreciate the significance of the discovery made by the archaeologist Emile Bächler of cave-bear cults at Wildkirchli and Drachenloch in the Swiss Alps. The bear skull with the long bones thrust through its eye sockets is the earliest example that has come down to us of primitive solar worship and symbolism as it was observed by Neanderthalers perhaps 60,000 years ago, and even so it must have undergone the process of gradual development over previous millennia. The importance of this find and its wider implications should not be underestimated, for it points to the considerable cultural development and intelligence reached by so-called 'primitive' man. Here was the combined symbol of sun and water, the elements that created life in the earth. The leg and foot bones were venerated, even as late as the Bronze Age, and a belief is retained in parts of the world today that bears obtain nourishment by sucking water from their paws during their long winter of dormancy. The theme of nourishment tells us why birth-goddesses such as Artemis were associated with bears, and adopted the theriomorphic form of bears.

The place chosen by Neanderthalers for this simple ceremony

was the bear's winter refuge, the cave, the abode which the Greeks associated with birth-goddesses. Much later, in the minds of the mythologists of ancient Greece, fire and water would combine to work the annual miracle of regeneration when the sun's entry to the underworld would be guided by the phallic herald Hermes, bearing his caduceus of serpents.

And so, wherever there was a source of water in a landscape of stone, flint and chalk, from Portugal to Palestine, from Ireland to Poland, from where crystal brooks cascaded down the hills through the harsh and arid maquis scrub, here men and women made a solemn investment. They built monuments that best imitated the womb of nature, and performed rituals of sacrifice that convincingly imitated the activity of the fertilising elements. They built the coves and the dolmens and stone chambers in which skulls and long bones could be interred, or cremated ashes sprinkled, or water ceremonially spilled, and pottery sherds strewn. They erected circles and enclosures of monolithic stones, a male and a female, to represent the combined powers of generation.

In southern England, they erected their monuments of increase on the chalk, for the chalk downs of Wessex are the major aquifer in this country. Like a huge sponge, the formations can hold water for months after a rainfall, and the level below ground, the water table, may fluctuate in places from between three feet at its highest down to 35 feet in the dry season.

Botanists digging in the fossilised remains on prehistoric sites worked by man have found evidence suggesting a drier climate in the early Neolithic, although it is unlikely to have resembled the seasonal drought conditions frequently experienced in Mediterranean regions.[1] The dependable supply of the chalk and the character of the land, with a good though flinty topsoil, easy to cultivate with primitive tools, accounts for the early agricultural settlements in the area, where crops of emmer and einkorn wheats flourished.

Those wonderful, sweeping and almost treeless downs that make up Salisbury Plain are a part of the Cretaceous formations extending across southern England, meeting another band of chalk stretching down to meet it from Yorkshire, through Lincolnshire and East Anglia. The strata forms three layers – upper, middle and lower chalk, each possessing a different character. Peter Reynolds, who pioneered the Butser Hill experimental prehistoric farm, told me that the upper chalk retained water to nourish the topsoil, while the middle chalk was less easy to farm, and is grudging.[2] Best in some respects is the lower chalk in the valleys, for here it meets a seam of impermeable clay; the water cannot percolate through, so it runs off through fissures to form springs on the lower slopes.

One of the notable features of chalk country are the bourns, or winterbournes, clear and shallow streams – some of them mere brooks – that dry up in the spring and summer months when the water level has fallen below the level of the valley. In those places where an ancient watercourse has cut deeply through the broad folds of the hills, the riverbed is low enough to breach the water table even at its low summer level.

Where these gentle issues of water occur you get a perennial stream, gradually maturing as a dependable river bordered with reeds, rich in water plants and fish. Such are the rivers Kennet and Avon in Wiltshire. Where a group of springs, issues and tributaries collect and form a more or less continuous supply, you have the headwaters of a perennial river, the domain of the goddess, and it is here that prehistoric builders often placed their stone circles, dolmens and barrows and henges. There is no fundamental difference between the monuments built at the headwaters of the river Kennet – Silbury Hill, The Sanctuary, the West Kennet long barrow, the circle of Avebury – and the great sanctuary of Dan at the source of the river Jordan.

In early prehistoric times, before forest clearance began, the Kennet river may have had to force its way through profuse undergrowth, broadening to form marshes and watermeadows. The building and damming activities of beavers helped in this, and we know that beavers were a part of the scene in the once-virgin lands of Britain.

Although forest clearance had long been in progress in Neolithic Britain, there remained large areas of untamed woodland to inhibit the free flow of surface ground water.[3] Rather than running off down slopes to the valleys, water would soak in through the fissures in the sedimentary rock. It is possible that even the intermittent chalk streams had a longer season in spate. In parts of the country, poor drainage turned the land into a fen; much of prehistoric Oxfordshire and Somerset was fen country.

The barrow builders chose to erect their earth and stone chambers, with their deposits of ancestral bones, mainly on chalk downland; of the 250 long barrows in the country, over half are on the Wiltshire chalk.[4] They are also grouped around the headwaters and tributaries of the rivers Wylie and Kennet, those on the Chilterns around the river Lea, and on Kent chalk around the river Stour. The Lincolnshire barrows keep to the chalk, and close to water.

Another fairly consistent factor is the position of monuments on ridges and high ground, something they share with many stone circles. As many as eight in ten orientated east-west, with the chamber facing east. The best-known and one of the largest British long barrows, at West Kennet, dated about 3700 BC, is on an elevated site, and its length of 328 feet seems disproportionate to the small chamber at its eastern end.

The exaggerated length of these barrows perhaps represents the hill or even the symbolic mountain range, penetrated by the cave-chamber of the sun, in the same way that round barrows, heaped over their token burials, are diminutive hills. The excavators of West Kennet found the skeletal remains of some forty-five individuals, probably seasonally interred over a period of 1500 years.[5]

Old bones may have been removed as new ones were added. In respect of the long-established osteal rites, preference was for long bones and skulls, one that seems to have been universally observed throughout prehistory, the long bones swept into heaps, the skulls placed in rows. There were also bones of beavers from the nearby river Kennet. The round barrows too follow a general pattern, being sited as they are on aquifers and well-drained land-masses,

FIG. 51 Long barrow cist containing long bones and skulls at Millin Bay.
Drawn from Ashbee (1970).

on chalk, limestone and rocky moors close to rivers. Barrow
building is covered by a period roughly 4000–1200 BC (long
barrow construction began around 4000 BC, and continued until
the Bronze Age, 2000 BC, when the style gradually changed to the
round barrow form), and the societies that built these monuments
– there are over 40,000 of them – occupied an area that covered
most of western Europe.[6]

It cannot be a coincidence that the majority of large passage
graves and chambered barrows are found along the Atlantic
seaboard, where the westerlies bring monthly rainfall. Indeed, the
Atlantic is mainly responsible for the most consistent (some would
say persistent) and the most reliable wet-weather patterns across
the entire landmass. The early farming communities, arriving from
the drier east, bringing livestock and handfuls of primitive grain,
found a favourable climate and created an environment of wheat
and water upon which, eventually, great civilisations would be
built. Here, in river valleys of tumbling streams littered with
building material, in forests teeming with game, on the chalk,
limestone and basalt formations favourable to the blessings of
springs and wells, the settlers were inspired to express their
atavistic veneration of fire and water.

These people, with perhaps an ancestral folk memory of
drought and disease preserved in myth and legend, acknowledged
their fortune, insured their future, and repaid their debt with the
construction of lithic edifices such as Avebury and Stonehenge.
There would also have been, in a community wealthy enough and
powerful enough to have built these huge earthworks, no small
amount of social and personal prestige, civic interest and self-
aggrandisement to be gained from such endeavours.

There may have been, however, a further reason for the spread
of stone monuments – the dolmens, circles, passage graves and
stone rows, along the Atlantic seaboard. This was the widespread
belief in Western Europe that the sun plunged into the sea in its
descent to the underworld. In his book *Clear Waters Rising*, travel
writer Nicholas Crane mentions this belief, which attracted pagan
pilgrims to Cape Finisterre in Spain.[7] A labyrinth design, found
cut into a rock in Galicia, may have been engraved by one such
pilgrim, perhaps a traveller from the east. Crane further mentions a
legend of a sunken city, in the sea off this western coast. Is the
'sunken city' in fact the sun? Could such legends have led to the
idea of Atlantis, really a solar myth? Does the sun's winter decline

account for the concentration of monuments on western promontories, in Brittany, Cornwall and the west of Ireland? Taking this idea a stage further, could the symbolic importance of the west have been the reason for the proliferation of stone circles in Britain and Ireland?

For thousands of years the human imagination had linked stones with water and life because stone – especially limestone and the bands of flint mined from the chalk – absorbed the waters from the sky and returned it as springs and rivers. It was widely believed that rocks were living things, and contained within them the spirit of the goddess – Parvati, Athena, Cybele, Demeter. The excavation of a megalithic passage grave or *allée couverte* at Tressé in the Forêt du Mesnil, France, revealed two pairs of human breasts carved in relief on the end stone.[8] Close inspection showed that one pair seemed to represent the breasts of a young girl, the other those of an older woman, comparable perhaps to the breasts of Persephone and Demeter.

When, as societies progressed and orthodox religions took over pagan cults, and the shrines, tombs and barrows were gradually replaced by churches, these latter buildings respected the eastwards orientation of the barrow builders, the nave and vault taking place of the chamber tomb, itself an imitation of the mountain cave of the sun, but the churchyard retained the reverence for stones, and bones buried in the earth.

Within its walled enclosure, the church continued to retain a devotional and solemn atmosphere, but now of life on earth and the life hereafter, symbolised by heroic self-sacrifice and divine resurrection. Once, long ago, this symbolism referred to the death and resurrection of the sun. This nucleus of life was always solemnised by enclosure, whether it be a cave, a constructed stone chamber, stone circle, dolmen, or simply a ring of pits dug in earth or hewn out of rock. Such was the original plan of Stonehenge.[9]

Stonehenge in its earliest form was a circular ditch and bank, inside which there were fifty-six shallow pits, many containing cremated human bone, called the 'Aubrey Holes', after their discoverer, the seventeenth-century antiquary John Aubrey. The site was marked out in a large circle perhaps because this was the sphere of the sun and the sphere of influence – at 97 metres across it was large by the standards of other circles in Britain, but nowhere near the circumference of Avebury.

The ditch and bank, with an entrance at the north-east, were dug out with picks made from the antlers of red deer. The Aubrey Holes were each cut to a depth of about three feet and were equally spaced. Shortly after the holes were dug, they were filled up again, partly with burnt chalk. This first stage was a modest achievement really when you compare the digging of the holes to the work that must have gone into the ring of pits at Maumbury – 45 shafts at an average of 34 feet deep.

The setting out of the Stonehenge ground plan took place, according to the latest findings, around 2600 BC, and the stage of building known to archaeologists as 'Stonehenge I' began about the time that work started on Silbury Hill. The Aubrey Holes, with the Heel Stone and its partner, and possibly the avenue down to the river Avon, seems to have sufficed as a ceremonial site for the next 700 years. This means that the A-holes were for a long time a feature in themselves, and the now-famous stones added to emphasise the cultural and religious importance later attached to the site.

Is there any significance, then, in the number of holes? Fifty-six is divisible by seven, and the presence of four stones in pairs, known as the 'Station Stones', later erected on the circle (some of the existing holes were cut into by the stone's bases) shows that each pair were placed seven holes apart, the two pairs sited twenty-one holes apart. They were also placed exactly either side of the monument's north-east/south-west axis. If they were markers, what did they signify?

Fifty-six does not appear to be a significant number, while twenty-eight, if in reference to the number of days between new moons, falls just short of the synodic month. Neither fit in to the number of days – approximately 182 – between the solstices. Tempting though it is to try and find a numerical equation, the idea that the circle of holes might have been planned to represent a cycle is best forgotten. Even if the builders were skilled astronomers there were easier ways to pinpoint the solstices.

The obsession to discover meaningful alignments dies hard. Maybe Mesolithic, and later Neolithic man, did set up stones to form a backsight, aligned to distant features, such as a cairn or hilltop (like sighting along the barrel of a gun) to mark the rising and setting of the sun and moon at divisions of the year. I do not think, however, that this is what happened at Stonehenge, nor at Avebury. It is claimed that the site upon which Stonehenge stands was deliberately chosen, because here and only here do significant lunar and solar alignments meet at right angles; the four Station Stones were thus arranged in a rectangle to mark the most southerly rising of the moon, and its most northerly setting. These alignments coincided with those of the midwinter sunset, and the midsummer sunrise. Yet the important midwinter sunrise is not marked by any stone, and I doubt that the builders of Stonehenge placed much importance on the setting of the moon.

According to astronomer Richard H. Phillips[10] the calculations are in fact inaccurate. Stonehenge stands on latitude 51.19 where the lunar and solar alignment is 90. 67. If a true right angle was important to the builders' requirements, they should have erected Stonehenge further north. Since the angle is dependent on latitude only, and not longitude, the chalk downs of the Chilterns would have been the ideal spot, through which passed an ancient track (the Icknield Way), and where are found the heads of two perennial rivers (the Thame and the Lea). Sarsen stones can still be found nearby at Aston Rowant. Here, the aforementioned lunar and solar alignments meet at exactly 90.00 at latitude 51.45, passing through Tring. An even better choice would have been on the Dunstable Downs, where there were a half-dozen long barrows.

In any case, why go to such trouble when alignments to all the risings and settings of the sun and moon throughout the year could have been determined by posts, or stones set on the perimeter of a circle, and viewed from a backsight, or backsights, in the centre? No stone circle exists in which such a simple arrangement was made. The astronomer Sir Fred Hoyle has suggested that the Aubrey Holes could have been used to predict eclipses, by moving counters around in a certain way, but at least five of the holes may have been later buried by mounds on which two of the Station Stones were erected. Gerald Hawkins also proposed the idea of eclipse prediction, using the Aubrey Holes, but as John Wood made clear in his book *Sun, Moon and Standing Stones*, 'Perhaps the *coup de grâce* for this proposal is that there are other and simpler methods of eclipse prediction not requiring this high degree of intellectual sophistication.'[11]

The vexing question as to whether or not there are celestial alignments at Stonehenge has no satisfactory answer. As Aubrey Burl and others have pointed out, you can find an alignment on practically anything.[12] It is possible that the axis deliberately faces towards the summer solstice, and we know that the original entrance saw a change in orientation, and was widened more to the north-east – the direction of the solstice sunrise.

Yet a position to indicate the more important winter solstice, as I have said, does not appear to have been marked – at least not by any recognisable features. The 900-plus other stone circles of Britain do not share significant alignments, either with features in the surrounding landscape or with celestial bodies, in spite of the efforts of the Scottish surveyor Alexander Thom and other astro-archaeological enthusiasts to find them.[13] The large stones at Stonehenge, and the gigantic monoliths at Avebury, are hardly ideal for observing accurate astronomical phenomena.

The only recognisable uniformity in the prehistoric monuments of Britain is their very diversity, except that most stone circles are indeed circular, save for a few egg-shaped examples.[14] Stonehenge has never performed a measuring function – it was not a Neolithic computer, nor a type of celestial timekeeper designed to aid priests or farmers planting crops, or even women determining their menstrual periods. These things were achieved by simple observation – the farmer more likely depended on the rising and setting of the Pleiades, and in the Mediterranean region the movements of migratory cranes, to tell him when to sow and reap. In classical times, the rising of the stars in Virgo signalled the start of the grape harvest.

The stages in the building of Stonehenge were working towards a design which seems to have undergone changes in detail but not in its basic formula. First, the builders dug a circular ditch and bank with a banked entrance path, and then the circle of holes which chanced to arrive at fifty-six, although an even number was probably desirable. The holes were then ready to receive votive deposits of bone, and artefacts, and it is likely that these were interred seasonally, perhaps in the autumn, in much the same fashion as the cave artists made their seasonal drawings.

It is in reference to the cave that I believe Stonehenge and all circles owe their origins. As I suggested in the previous chapter, the concept of the cave lay behind the design of the Cretan labyrinth, and the passage graves, gallery graves and chamber tombs, originating perhaps in early Mesopotamia with the domed tholoi. There is a resemblance between Stonehenge with its final seven circles and the seven paths of the labyrinth, but the ground plan was based upon the European passage grave, and this is perhaps why the Station Stones are found on either side of the axis in place of the side chambers or cists, which they may symbolically represent. Compare this with the plan of the Neolithic structure, with its trilithon entrance stones, at Alcalar in Portugal (Fig. 54), and New Grange in Ireland (Fig. 52).

The kerbstones around New Grange, and certain of the long barrows and cairns, suggest the design of stone circles, within which animals sacrifices were seasonally performed. In his fine study *The Stone Circles of the British Isles*, the archaeologist Aubrey Burl, draws attention to a link with these monuments: 'The possibility of passage-graves being a source for the development of stone circles is interesting. These mounds with an orthostatic passage leading to a sepulchral chamber are widespread in the British Isles, especially in Ireland and Scotland. The Boyne cruciform-chambered tombs, of which New Grange, Meath, is the best-known, are concentrated in five great cemeteries ... across central Ireland.'[15]

It is of particular significance that New Grange was designed to include a unique 'light box' of stone which conveyed a ray from the rising sun down the passageway of the tomb, exactly at the point of the winter solstice. Burl, referring to R.E. Hicks (1975) mentions that the etymology of New Grange may possibly derive from *An Uamh Greine*, the 'Cave of the Sun', from *grian*, 'the sun'.

It it relevant, therefore, that the four small satellite passage-graves around New Grange also face towards the south-east, the ruined chamber of one containing a stone basin with a rayed circle chiselled on it like a sun-pattern facing down the passage towards the midwinter sunrise, further evidence of the association of the sun and death in the mind of prehistoric man ... Many of the earliest monuments of Britain had plans in some way related to the movements of the sun ... The same astronomical aspect is found in megalithic tombs whose entrances customarily were built between north-east and south east ... It is not improbable that some of the first stone circles, sites of ceremony and religion, continued the beliefs inferred from earlier monuments ...[16]

There seems to me good evidence that the monuments, the chamber tombs, the passage graves, the long barrows, were not sepulchral, and it was in order to encourage life, and the turning point at the sun's winter journey, its period of terrestrial residence, and its passage through water, that they were constructed, and the votive bones interred. Why, though, were not all passage graves and long barrows equipped with a similar 'light box' to admit the rays of the winter sun?

I can only guess that the most widely accepted, potent and efficacious presence of solar power was afforded, not by the sun's rays, but primarily by the votive interments, the skulls and bones, burnt flint and chalk, and pottery sherds and the deliberate use of fire, because these rites were a positive and human act of propitiation and investment. In other words, by interring a bone, or despositing a votive object, such as a chalk phallus or figurine, the celebrant was enacting the role of the sun. This may explain why the entrances to the chambers were often sealed off by a large portal stone. The deposits possessed intrinsic generative power comparable to the seed in the womb and which, unlike the brief shaft of light from the sun, was made permanent.

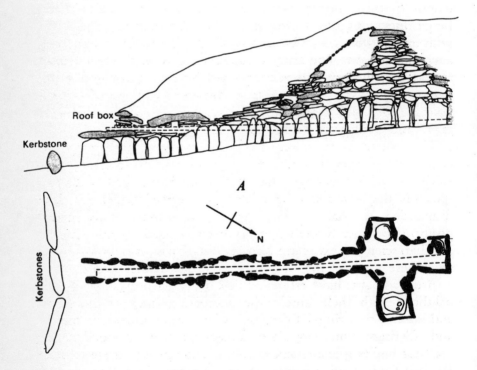

FIG. 52 Diagram of New Grange. Dotted lines indicate the path of the sun's rays at the winter solstice.

Another method of inducing representative solar power was by fire, the 'bonefires'. Excavators of several sites found evidence of fire within the chambers, of conflagrations so intense that many of the interred bones were literally cremated. The fires were deliberate and may be explained as simulations of the sun's entry and its residence in the earth,[17] of the 'magic' brought about by the action of solar fire in these artificial caves of the Eileithyiae, the goddesses of childbirth, the forges of Hephaestus, and the labyrinth of Ariadne.

I am faced with a dilemma here. If the burials and cremations were not sepulchral, how can the grave goods be explained?[18] Throughout the long years of prehistory, from the time of the Neanderthalers, single and multiple burials were sometimes adorned with necklaces, seashells, bone pins, and accompanied by weapons and pottery, all suggesting reverence for the departed.

The sepulchral and the votive must have been integrated in some way. It is possible that, after some acceptable and appropriate length of time, bones of the ancestral dead, in particular the long bones and skulls, were disinterred – disarticulated, and mixed with animal bones – to be used votively, as part of an extremely ancient tradition. The truly sepulchral burial, with the deceased attired in jewellery and accompanied by rich grave goods (the practice in Egypt, and the later round barrow burials of the Bronze Age) may mark the transition towards the conventional grave and tomb that we recognise today.

The entrances to circles, like the passages of the chamber tombs, were often marked by portal stones, and there is good evidence at Stonehenge that the Heel Stone had a partner (possibly the now recumbent 'Slaughter Stone') which was later dismantled, or that the Heel Stone was moved to its present position. Because Stonehenge has been ravaged by time and by less than scientific excavations in the distant past, it is impossible to say where some of the now missing stones actually stood.

Archaeologists have estimated that the inner horseshoe, the big trilithons with their lintels, the alternating rings of bluestones and sarsens, two rings of dug and refilled holes known as the 'Y' and 'Z' rings, which appear to form a spiral, were added during the later building phases known as Stonehenge II and Stonehenge III. What is important is that the total number of rings forming the ground-plan of Stonehenge (including the ring of A-holes), is seven, a structural constant shared with the Cretan labyrinth and its seven rings. The design was widely recognised in the ancient world, and has been found scratched on rocks throughout Celtic areas of Western Europe as far west as Ireland.

Part of the aura of mystery and the mystique of Stonehenge has evolved from the idea that the huge stones were dragged over rough country from distant sources to their resting places, the sarsens at Stonehenge having been brought from the Marlborough Downs, twelve miles to the north.

Sarsens cover a wide area of southern England from the eastern end of the Chilterns to the western edge of Salisbury Plain, a distance of over a hundred miles. The majority were residual boulders buried beneath the surface of the land. It is more than likely that the stones of Stonehenge were local, and brought to the surface during the Neolithic land clearance in preparation for sowing. The geologist Dr G. A. Kellaway told me that sarsen has the property of being relatively malleable while remaining under the soil, hardening only by prolonged exposure. The newly dug stones were thus easily dressed by the circle builders, allowing them to shape the sarsens without perhaps too much effort.[19]

A well-known theory about the bluestones is that they were dragged from the Prescelly hills on the Pembrokeshire coast, a distance of about 180 miles, fording the Severn at Tewkesbury or Gloucester. This would have entailed a considerable effort of manpower and transport since the stones each weighed about two tons and would have had to be lashed on rafts for the proposed river routes (down rivers themselves strewn with boulders and almost impossible to navigate). The source of these stones of ophitic dolerite was first identified in 1923 by the geologist H. H. Thomas, who also proposed the most likely route taken by the Stonehenge builders.[20]

There is plenty of evidence of ophitic dolerite around Prescelly, scattered across the hills. The outcrops are not hard to locate. There are, however, sources of igneous rock nearer to Stonehenge than Prescelly – Dartmoor being one. A more plausible but rather more prosaic (and therefore less appealing) reason for the appearance of the bluestones on Salisbury Plain was put forward a century ago by geologists Judd and Gowland, and recently by Dr Kellaway, who maintains that they were carried by meltwaters from the first Ice Age some two and a half million years ago and possibly by solifluction (the movement of soil softened by meltwater) over frozen subsoil or tundra.[21]

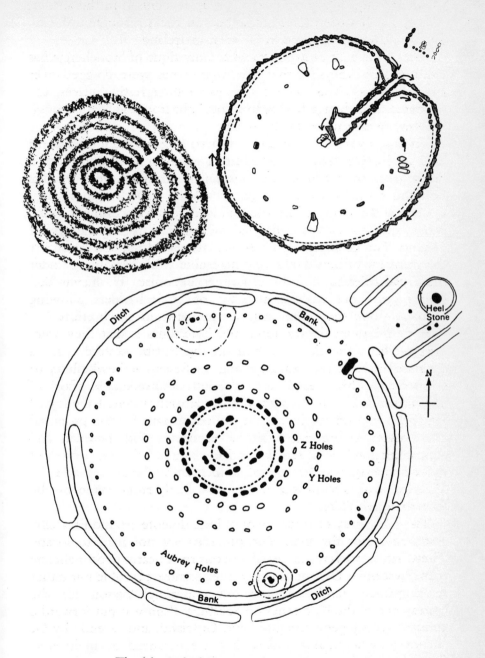

FIG. 53 The labyrinth design may have influenced the spiral form
of this passage grave in Wales (above), and the plan of the rings
at Stonehenge.

The transport of the bluestones is part of the modern folklore of Stonehenge and serves to compound the aura of megalithic magic that gives the monument its air of mystery. The fact that a stray bluestone has been found in the structure of a barrow eleven miles west of Stonehenge, some way from the supposed route from Prescelly, has done little to temper the enthusiasm of many believers in the long haul from Wales.

Clearing areas of stone for the purposes of agriculture, in addition to clearing forests, was a feature of Neolithic life in many parts of Britain. The construction of monuments was perhaps a recognised act of faith and an insurance against crop failure and drought, during the clearances.

Perhaps this is why there is evidence of 'woodhenge' circles where trees have been felled, to be replaced by the more permanent ones of stone. It is possible that Stonehenge was once a wooden structure, and there is clear evidence of post holes around the entrance, and in the south-eastern quadrant of the circle.[22] Perhaps we should take with a pinch of salt such romantic visions of massive boulders being dragged a hundred and fifty miles across wild country to their point of destiny on Salisbury Plain, just as we should dismiss the mystic lines of alignment, but we might accept the possibility of the seven rings at Stonehenge as having the same symbolism as that of the Cretan labyrinth. By the very same token that Theseus slew the Minotaur in the labyrinth, we may imagine that oxen were sacrificed in the henges, such as at Arbor Lo on a limestone plateau. The rituals probably took place in the autumn, before the ploughing and sowing, and the decline of the sun towards the winter solstice, which the sacrifice simulated.

All stone circles, from the modest ring of Nine Stones at Winterbourne Abbas in Dorset to the huge earthwork at Avebury, were places designed to celebrate and encourage increase and prosperity, and to reduce the nagging fears of drought and disease. They represented the sun's fertile influence in the earth, and its gift of water, and it is why huge circles such as that of Marden and Avebury, both in Wiltshire, are located at the headwaters of chalk rivers.

The ancient monuments, the barrows, the dolmens, the chamber tombs, the wood and the stone circles, while being separate entities in terms of design, all fall into the same category. If we want to understand the meaning and purpose of the stone circles of Stonehenge and Avebury, we have to regard them not as places devoted to primitive astronomy, nor as monuments in deference to the dead but as centres of activity which contained and generated the germ of life, released by sacrifice and solemnised by ritual.[23]

The stone circle was simply a stage in the development of an idea, a concept, which began in the caves, progressed to the rock-cut grottoes and shrines, and thence to the dolmens, passage graves, long barrows and circles. You can see this in the similarity of designs. All were forms of enclosure, and all deliberate enclosures were favourable to, and encouraged, the wonder of creation, as does the human womb, and by way of analogy the womb of the earth.

The fact that the enclosures were now open to the skies, instead of being subterranean, had a practical purpose in that they were more closely related to the sun and rain, and could be sited in places where agriculture might benefit and water be encouraged to flow.

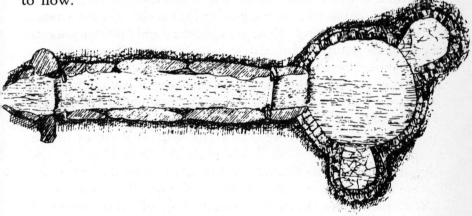

FIG. 54 Passage grave at Alcalar in the Algarve, Portugal.

On the domed granite plateau of Dartmoor in Devon there are over sixty stone rows, either single, double or treble rows of low boulders, and 80 per cent culminating in a small circular cairn. The rows are part of a complex of cairns and circles and dolmens, and their presence at the headwaters of many rivers and streams attest to their origins. They were also located in areas of abundant stone, for stones and rocks had an almost numinous quality, and were thought to absorb rain and generate life. They can be favourably compared with the impressive stone rows at Carnac in

Brittany, and were perhaps built by the same tribes migrating northwards from the Breton peninsula. A recent theory suggests that even Stonehenge may have been designed and constructed by settlers from Brittany.

It is significant that the majority of circles have even numbers of stones, because they symbolise the androgynous nature of the sun. The stones were indeed selected, or dressed with mauls, to represent male and female pairs. This may be why the Heel Stone and two of the Station Stones at Stonehenge are supported on ditched mounds, being the male counterparts of their opposite female stones.

Observers have pointed out the identity of male and female stones in the Avebury avenue, and have suggested that the twin circles, each surrounding a Cove and Obelisk at Avebury, has the same significance. A feature of the early phase of Stonehenge was an avenue, perhaps marked by stones like the avenue at Avebury. The uniformity of this design was noted by Burl: 'Where an avenue of stones is associated with a stone circle it almost invariably leads from a source of water, indicating the importance of water in the ceremonies that took place in the rings.'[24]

Avebury is close to the Winterbourne stream, and the Kennet river, and by five local springs in the chalk stratum on which Avebury is built. It is marked by Silbury Hill. Yet we need to be careful about attributing the direction of the avenues towards water. The avenue of stones at Avebury leads to and from the Sanctuary, a complex small circle on a hill. The Stonehenge avenue heads north-east before deflecting down to the river Avon, where there may once have been a ford. The main avenue at Callanish, on the Isle of Lewis, leads away from water, although the monument is close by the sea.

An English folktale which I read as a child tells of a youth who lived near a stone circle. A local legend said that once every hundred years at midnight the stones would leap from the holes in which they stood and rush down to the nearby river to drink. Each vacated hole revealed a treasure of gold, and if the lad was quick, and grabbed some before the stones returned, the gold was his for the keeping.

At the appointed hour he watched as the stones lifted themselves from their positions and rumbled down to the river. The boy jumped into a hole and began to fill a bag with gold. All too soon he heard the great stones thundering back, and climbing desperately up the rope he had used to lower himself down, escaped just in time before the stones settled back into their places for the next hundred years.

The tale has variations where stones go to drink, bathe in the water, or dance, some turning around three times. Preserved in folklore is the evidence from phrase and fable that may be more persuasive than the physical evidence remaining. Here is the sun, suggested by the golden treasure and the number three, plunging into water at the winter solstice. The Roman historian Diodorus Siculus reported (second hand) the existence of an island, possibly Britain, with a sacred enclosure (possibly Stonehenge) dedicated to Apollo.

The solar identity of Stonehenge, like that of Apollo and the healer Achilles, is further emphasised by the reputed healing properties of its stones. 'For in these stones is a mystery, and a healing virtue against many ailments,' observed Geoffrey of Monmouth in the twelfth century, 'for not a stone is there that is wanting in virtue of leechcraft.' In the eighteenth century the legend still persisted. In 1707 the Reverend J. Broome reported that 'if the stones are rubbed, or scraped, and water thrown upon the scrapings, they will (say some) heal any green wound, or old sore'.[25] Just as Achilles scraped the rust from his spear to cure Telephus.

References to healing are of considerable importance in the understanding of ancient beliefs. Oracular prophecies, divination, sacrifice, votive offerings, the fixing of rags to sacred trees, bathing in sacred rivers and other superstitious practices, perhaps including devotional rites in stone circles, were and still are employed as remedies against injury and disease. The function of healing is symbolised by the descent of Hermes – the 'psychopomp' or conductor of souls – into the underworld, bearing the caduceus, the wand entwined with serpents, adopted as the symbol of the medical profession. Hermes is the sun's messenger, the herald, and his descent heralds the approach of winter, and brings to an end the hot period and its associated diseases. In the ancient world, summer was disease time, winter brought the healing waters. The caduceus is probably, in its original form, the branch of the goddess's tree, the 'Golden Bough', while the snakes symbolised the arriving rains.

That part of the Avebury complex known as the Sanctuary, on an elevated site by a trackway, predated Avebury by 500 years. It was contemporary with Stonehenge I, and like Stonehenge was constructed in stages, six rings of oak posts juxtaposed with rings of stone in even pairs. The discovery of a human skeleton during excavation, plus a large quantity of human bone, has been interpreted as a sacrifice or dedication burial. Its site by the headwaters of the Kennet shows that the Sanctuary might fulfil the requirements of a solar shrine, although I must admit that there should be seven, rather than just six post rings. It is linked to the later Avebury by the avenue of paired stones, and I would suggest that the great circle of Avebury is actually a development, and grander concept, of the Sanctuary.

The nearby Silbury Hill was also built in stages, for it was estimated to have taken 18 million man-hours to complete, given a force of 700 people over a period of about 10 years. The hill, 130 feet high, was constructed of six layers, or steps, on a natural terrace, making seven layers in total, although this is probably not deliberate number symbolism.

Silbury is surrounded by a ditch (now almost totally filled by accumulated silt), quarried to allow a flow of water from a brook issuing from nearby Beckhampton to surround the hill. The original depth of the ditch is an estimated 16 to 20 feet deep, and since the water table is at times only 3 feet below the surface, the water could have formed a moat all year round.

A recent explanation by Michael Dames[26] of the purpose of Silbury is that the hill is a man-made, landscaped representation of the great Mother Goddess herself. This is no more fanciful than the idea that Stonehenge represented a menstrual timetable, and we know that springs were always the special province of the goddess. Silbury must have had a powerful, symbolic meaning to be worthy of such effort, and the same is true of the great stone circles.

Many will have died without seeing the results of their sweat and toil, unless the meaning and purpose was implicit in every stage. The builders who lay the foundation stones of a cathedral have no need to see its completion, content in the knowledge that they are building the house of God. Those who dug the fifty-six Aubrey Holes may never have imagined the completed splendour of the massive trilithons that were the unique style of the later Stonehenge. The holes were sufficient unto themselves, and their creators.

The effort and man-hours needed to build the monuments

must have been staggering. The ditch around the Avebury circle had been cut to a depth of 30 feet, displacing some 200,000 tons of chalk, hacked out with antler picks,[27] and its purpose was unlikely to have been defensive; the depth of the ditch around Stonehenge was a mere six feet by comparison, and most stone circles do not have ditches at all. Neolithic communities built sites known to archaeologists as causewayed enclosures. They were surrounded by a ditch, often with a series of banks of earth and entered by one or more causeways bridging the ditch. Their purpose is uncertain but many were strategically placed on hill tops, so were perhaps defensive. This typical design may have been followed in the construction of ceremonial sites, the ditch being an architectural convention. The most famous, and the largest, is Windmill Hill, just over a mile from the Avebury circle. In the bottom of the perimeter ditches, archaeologists found human bones, and noted the frequency of skulls and long bones, which we can now claim to be an essential ingredient of prehistoric cult and symbol.

Although Avebury is built by the Winterbourne stream, the streams were then, as they are today, intermittent bourns, the water emerging from fissures in the chalk, flowing in the winter and spring, dry in the summer and autumn. The Avebury circle stands on a spur of the Middle Chalk formation, in the river valley, where water yields are higher than elsewhere in the area. In fact, the Winterbourne and Kennet rivers are fed by the only five springs for some considerable distance, in the chalk formations.

It was also the reason, I suggest, for the construction of Silbury. The hill was built to revere and to celebrate and to mark a permanent water supply. Although the Winterbourne stream was dry from early spring until the rains of late autumn, the low-lying depression at Silbury breached the water table. When archaeologists dug shafts through the Silbury ditch in 1886 the water level was only 8 feet below the natural surface, while probing suggested that the original ditch had been dug to between 16 and 20 feet.[28]

Today it has become silted up, but without the silt the moat around Silbury would be permanently filled with water, unless abstraction lowered the level. Here was the seemingly magical, permanent spring that supplied the builders of the Avebury circle with water, and since springs were presided over by goddesses, Michael Dames's proposition that Silbury was the goddess herself is not far wide of the mark. The legendary King Sil will certainly

FIG. 55 Silbury Hill, from a drawing made in 1723 by William Stukely.

have distant associations with the goddess Sul of Bath who, by the way, was a goddess of vengeance, according to the archaeologist Dr Miranda Green.[29]

Silbury was a monument built by a people who had probably inherited a sun and water mythology that originated with the birth of mankind. If this theory is to be accepted, then it follows that other monuments may have been inspired by the same ancient beliefs. Another large mound, though smaller than Silbury, can be seen in the grounds of Marlborough School, where water-meadows would once have formed. Situated like Silbury in the valley bottom, it may mark a spring, or the point where the Kennet becomes perennial. These were not the only votive hills in the area. The antiquary Sir Richard Colt Hoare excavated in 1809 'an enormous tumulus', having a deep and wide ditch around it 'which in winter is full of water'.[30] This was Hatfield Barrow at Marden in the Vale of Pewsey, and it stood originally some 30 feet high (Silbury is 130 feet), within a huge causewayed enclosure, in the bank of which excavators found stags' horns and the skeleton of a man, possibly a foundation sacrifice. Colt Hoare sank a shaft from the summit to the floor of Hatfield Barrow and found a quantity of charred wood, the bones of red deer, as well as two small parcels of burned human bones. He concluded though that the hill was not sepulchral, but perhaps a High Altar, or Druid *locus consecratus*. Colt Hoare returned ten years later and 'had the unexpected mortification to find that the great barrow had been completely levelled to the ground, and no signs remained of its previous existence'. Marden is midway between Avebury and Stonehenge, and was near an old trackway, but of considerable importance is the stream running through the enclosure. This is the river Avon, and its perennial headwaters are but a few miles away to the north-west.

Avebury, with its surrounding ditch 30 feet deep, will have contained water for much of the year, since even today the water table at its lowest (from records between 1915 and 1935) is about 35 feet below the natural surface. This is perhaps why the ditch was quarried with so much effort. The circles are closely allied to nearby springs and conveniently built wherever there was a suitable supply of stone. We cannot reconstruct the ceremonies that took place in the circles, but it is likely that water was brought into them, and that sacrifices occurred at certain seasons of the year, most probably in the autumn. The circles will have been built in respect of the continued reliance on the elements of nature that encouraged the fertility of the soil and the health and future of mankind.

In conclusion, then, this book has been about water and the sun, their importance to the prehistoric and early historic communities, and how water was thought to be a gift of the sun (a gift that could just as easily be withheld). The declining sun in its male role delivered the rain that fertilised the womb of the earth. In its female role it descended into the subterranean regions, and through the seven months of winter warmed the barren earth, eventually to create the waters of life to bring forth the springs and rivers, and nature's green bounty. The need for a reliable supply of seasonal rain became of even greater importance with the introduction of agriculture.

Mankind has always responded to and felt the need to participate in this dynamic formula because of his total dependence on it, and in so doing created religion. He created, too, the extraordinary myths and symbols that expressed the formula, achieving this through synthesis, by taking the abstract and making it concrete, equating human and animal characteristics (which are in many respects identical) with the forces of nature.

Rocks, stones and wood, with which he had worked for a million years, possessed their own creative powers because they were in a sense extensions of himself, and he worked them into his own likeness. Rocks and trees were especially female because they were products of the earth; the fruits of the tree and the waters from the rocks nourished man through his formative years. The veneration of rocks and trees by issues of water was an early stage of religion.

The caves were female, too. This is why Zeus, among others, was born in a cave, why caves were the province of the birth goddess, why Ariadne was able to guide Theseus out of the labyrinth, and why, in the painted caves of the Palaeolithic, engravings of female figues adorned the entrances. It is why the phallic stag-man, the 'Sorcerer', and the phallic bison, prance on the cavern walls, and why Hephaestus, the limping sun of winter, having dutifully spilled his semen on the rocks above, was guided by the phallic Hermes to work the forge of the underworld.

The cave was the nucleus of life which could with effect be simulated, encouraged, imitated, reproduced. By carrying out some form of appropriate activity — burying a skull, lighting a fire, sacrificing an animal or a human being, making a drawing, men and women contributed to the process of nature, to the evolution of life. In this way mankind developed ritual. Again, by the process of synthesis and simplification, digging a pit and depositing therein a votive offering, a favourable effect might be achieved.

At the beginning of this book I mentioned a myth in which two brothers slew a third (the third or winter sun), wrapped his head in a red cloak, and buried it under mount Olympus. In this ritual is contained the essence of all prehistoric mythology. Objects daubed with ochre symbolised the Sun. Figurines, phalli, skulls, pieces of flint or bone buried in the earth, represented the votive internment of the sun's magical powers to induce nature to release her gifts.

This delicate balance of life and death led in time to the development of dolmens and standing stones, portals through which the sun in his and her majesty might be encouraged to pass, and their erection by a spring would encourage water to flow. Building a passage grave to imitate the cave of the sun, introducing the potently influential skulls and bones, and siting it in an elevated position near a river, might ensure the fertility of the land, and the advancement of crops. Its stones would be life-enhancing, and death-cheating, and have the beneficial properties of healing.

Enclosures of almost any kind were the microcosmic centres

where the forces of nature could be induced to work in man's favour. This, then, was the purpose of the stone circles of Stonehenge and Avebury, and the wood structures of Woodhenge and The Sanctuary, the long barrow and the round barrow. They were, and so remain, the caves of the sun, and Stonehenge in particular is what legend and tradition have always held it to be, a temple of the sun, a Stone Age church, and place of worship and a source of life. The position of these enduring monuments on the heights of Salisbury Plain and the Marlborough Downs, where stone was once abundant, were essential to the communities whose hoes and ploughs first tilled the virgin chalklands of southern England.

Acknowledgements

Many people have helped me in the research for this book, always with enthusiasm and kindness. I would like to thank the staff of the following libraries for their valuable assistance and patience: the University of Bristol, the School of Oriental and African Studies, the Wellcome Institute for the History of Medicine, the Folklore Society, the London Library, the British Library, and the libraries of Bath and Bristol. There are people with whom I have corresponded but have never actually met, and who gave freely of their advice. They include Professor R. J. Atkinson, Dr J. E. Wood, Richard Phillips, Dr B. D. Yallop of Greenwich Royal Observatory, Ken Sheldon of the Federation of Astronomical Societies, Professor B. M. Hibbard at the University of Wales College of Medicine, and Phil Bristow who sent me some star charts. I received invaluable help from Tina Brown and Trevor Maggs of Condor PR on computer technology. Equally helpful advice was generously given by the geologist Dr Geoffrey Kellaway, by Dr Peter Reynolds at Butser Ancient Farm, Professor Ian Fenwick at the Department of Geology, University of Reading, Professor A. T. Hatto at Queen Mary College, London, and by Vin Robinson of Wessex Water, Reading. The initial idea for this book was accepted with enthusiasm by Tom Maschler of Jonathan Cape, and guided through its many stages of difficulty by my editor at Cape, Tony Colwell, and by my agent, Anne Dewe. I would also like to thank Dr Joe Berke, Suzy Bitner, Nicholas Crane, Dick Evans, and Eve Goldsmith. I hope that I have traced sources of pictures still under copyright, and I am grateful to Professor James Mellaart for permission to reproduce drawings from his book *Çatal Hüyük*, to the Accademia Nazionale dei Lincei, to Revista Veleia, Hunting Aerofilms, *Nature* (Macmillan), the Ordnance Survey, University of California Press, J. M. Dent, the George Ortiz Collection, the Institute of Classical Studies, and Thames and Hudson. Finally, the most sincere expressions of gratitude remain woefully inadequate when I come to thank my wife, Fiona, for her support, helpful suggestions and critical comments, without which this book would never have been completed.

Notes and References

Abbreviations

AJA	*American Journal of Archaeology*
BAR	*British Archaeological Reports*
EB	*Encyclopaedia Biblica*
FLS	*Folklore Society, London*
JHA	*Journal for the History of Astronomy*
JNES	*Journal of Near Eastern Studies*
OCD	*Oxford Classical Dictionary*
PEF	*Palestine Exploration Fund*
PSBA	*Proceedings of the Society of Biblical Archaeology*
PPS	*Proceedings of the Prehistoric Society*
RAI	*Royal Anthropological Institute*
SBA	*Society of Biblical Archaeology*

Notes

Chapter 1   *Skulls and Stones*

1 Kirk 1974, 1983 edition pp. 41–4.
2 Frazer, various works.
3 Graves 1961. Paperback edition 1975, p. 11.
4 Frazer 1898. ed. 1931, p. 8.
5 Bremmer 1987.
6 Dowden 1992, p. 169.
7 Hawkins 1970.
8 Lockyer 1906.
9 Allegro 1973.
10 Drews 1911.
11 Graves 1955. See also Graves, *The White Goddess*, 1961. 1975 edition p. 45.
12 Gilbert & Cotterell, 1995.
13 Bauval & Gilbert, 1994.
14 Ucko 1962–3, p. 43.
15 Roe 1970. 1974 edition p. 104.
16 Mellaart 1967.
17 Kenyon 1957.

18 Ashbee 1970, p. 63.
19 Burl 1976, pp. 146–84.
20 Ibid.
21 Ashbee 1970, p. 88.
22 Conder 1878, p. 48.
23 Bonnefoy & Doniger 1991, Vol. 1, p. 61.
24 Walters 1928, p. 177.
25 Green 1995, pp. 194–5.
26 Thompson 1972, p. 179.
27 Dames 1976.
28 Burl 1976, p. 315.
29 Conder 1882–3, p. 79.
30 Hoskin 1996, p. 282.

Chapter 2   *Sex and Symbol*

1 Dulaure 1805, p. 158.
2 Hannay 1922.
3 Anon. *Crux Ansata*, 1892, no. 1 (one of a 'Phallic Series' published in the 1890s).
4 Inman 1869, p. 11, plate IV. figures 2, 61, 136.
5 Allegro 1973, p. 70.
6 Gubernatis 1872, Vol. 1, p. 249. See also Gimbutas 1974, p. 107.
7 Séjourné 1962, p. 40.
8 Slater 1968, pp. 94–100.
9 Conder 1884, p. 341.
10 Roheim 1930.
11 Roheim 1972, p. 169.
12 Redgrove & Shuttle, 1978, p. 189–90, 203.
13 Reed 1965.
14 Chippindale 1983, p. 242.
15 Hatto 1953, p. 151.
16 Ucko 1962–3, p. 48.
17 Gimbutas 1989. p. xx. More accurately a 'gylany', from *gy*, 'woman', and *andros*, 'man', where men and women had equal status. Gimbutas says society changed from gylanic to androcratic.
18 Ucko 1962–3, p. 39.
19 Goldbert 1977, p. 30.
20 Farnell 1921, p. 175.
21 Howe *AJA* 1954, Vol. 58, p. 3 and p. 212.

Chapter 3   *The Lion's Head*

1 Grinsell 1976, p. 119.
2 Coles & Higgs 1969. 1975 edition p. 219.
3 Mellaart 1967.
4 Jacobsen 1976, p. 106.
5 Lindsay 1965, p. 185.
6 Rose *OCD* 1968, pp. 881–2.

7 Conder 1886, p. 11.
8 Coles & Higgs 1969. 1975 edition pp. 286–7.
9 Burl 1981, p. 35
10 Sieveking 1979, p. 209.

Chapter 4   *The Breasts of Venus*

1 Bahn 1988.
2 Ucko & Rosenfeld 1967.
3 Coles & Higgs 1969. 1975 edition p. 248.
4 Bahn 1988, p. 152.
5 Ucko & Rosenfeld 1967, p. 182.
6 Bahn 1988, p. 138.
7 Clark & Piggott 1965. 1976 edition p. 69.
8 Mellaart 1967, pp. 83–84; figure 52, and plates 67, 68, IX.
9 Séjourné 1957, p. 52.
10 Bahn 1988, p. 140.
11 Bradley 1976, p. 25.
12 Bonnefoy & Doniger 1991, Vol. 1, p. 14.
13 Bahn 1988, pp. 169–70.
14 Ibid p. 173.
15 Bonnefoy & Doniger 1991, Vol. 1, p. 20.
16 Ucko & Rosenfeld 1967, p. 179.
17 Ibid. p. 49.
18 Bahn 1988, p. 95.
19 Ibid. p. 176.
20 Powell 1971.
21 *Compendious Vocabulary of Sanskrit*, 1885.
22 Marshak 1976, 1977 edition, p. 315.
23 Burl 1981, p. 31.
24 Jones 1951. 1971 edition pp. 277–8.
25 Cox, G. W., 1870, pp. 151–4.

Chapter 5   *Caves of the Sorcerer*

1 *Everyman's Dictionary of Non-Classical Mythology*, 1962, p. 49.
2 Dundes 1988, p. 1.
3 Ibid. p. 89.
4 *EB* 1903, column 290.
5 Dundes 1988, pp. 167–82.
6 Gelling & Davidson 1969.
7 *Larousse Encyclopaedia of Mythology*, 1959. 1964 edition p. 444.
8 Séjourné 1957, p. 77.
9 Rundle Clark 1959. 1978 edition p. 130.
10 Bahn 1988.
11 Ibid. p. 125.
12 Marshak 1972, p. 243.
13 Ibid. p. 171, figures 62a & 62b.
14 Van Buren 1933 and 1945, *passim*.

15 Marshak 1972, figure 129.
16 Barandiaran 1984, *passim.*
17 Bahn 1988, p. 177.
18 Green 1991.
19 Jones 1951. 1971 edition p. 299.
20 The Marlborough Bucket in Devizes Museum.
21 Drews 1910, p. 101 footnote.

Chapter 6   *Numbers Code*

1 Hopper 1938. 1978 edition p. 9.
2 Ibid. p. 78.
3 Ibid. p. 17.
4 Webster 1916, pp. 213–14.
5 Cook *Zeus* 1925, Vol. 2, p. 236 note 5.
6 Gilbert & Cotterell 1995, p. 270.
7 Usener 1903.
8 Dundes 1980.
9 Hopper 1938. 1978 edition p. 5.
10 Graves, R., 1955, Index: 'Hecate'.

Chapter 7   *Gods of Fire*

1 Gupta 1987, p. 35.
2 Müller 1897 Vol. 46.
3 Thienne, see Hinnells 1975, Vol. 1, pp. 21–39.
4 Plutarch, see Graves 1961. 1975 edition pp. 208 and 337.
5 Neugebauer 1951, p. 106.
6 *EB* 1903, column 4008.
7 Lloyd 1983. 1986 edition p. 27.
8 Speert 1973, pp. 110–11.
9 Redgrove & Shuttle 1978. p. 178.
10 Hopper 1938. 1978 edition pp. 207–8.
11 They are: Kali, Karala, Manojava, Sulolita, Sudhumravarna, Sphulingini, and Visvarupi. See Moor 1861.
12 Rose, see 'Leto', *OCD* 1968, p. 496.
13 Slater 1968, p. 144.
14 Lindsay 1965, p. 277.
15 Deep in one of the caves, the Palaeolithic cave artists modelled a bear in clay and covered it with a bear's pelt.
16 Cole, S. G., 1988, pp. 161–65; see in Haag, Marinatos *et al.*
17 Ibid.
16 The curious epithets of Apollo, Smintheus or 'Mouse Apollo', and Apollo Lykeios, 'Wolf Apollo', have been variously explained. Warren Dawson (*The Bridle of Pegasus* 1930) suggests that because mice were medicinal in ancient times, they were associated with the god of healing (Dawson was a medic). Others have suggested that Apollo was petitioned to rid grain stores of pests, and that mice damaged crops, and similarly that the wolves were a threat against which the Athenians waged constant war (Sallares, Frazer *et*

al.). I am more inclined to Conder's explanations (Conder 1884) that the wolf was a common emblem of dark winter (p. 51), and that the mouse was an emblem of the night. 'The Sminthian, or mouse-slaying sun-god treads upon it, and the wise god Indra rides on its back' (p. 89). The mouse too was perhaps an emblem of winter, like the winter sun, 'the Hiding One', as the mouse slips through holes in the ground.

Chapter 8   *The Nuptial Murders*

1 Conder 1883, p. 220.
2 Cook *Zeus* 1914, Vol. I, p. 438.
3 Kirk 1970, p. 183.
4 Withers & Vipond 1974, pp. 1 and 7.
5 Bier JNES 1976, No. 35, pp. 115–30.
6 Förstemann, see in Bowditch 1904, p. 422.
7 Pannekoek, 1961, p. 33.
8 Förstemann, see in Bowditch 1904, p. 437.
9 Ward, D., 1968, p. 89.
10 Farnell 1921, p. 175.
11 See Harris 1903 and 1906.
12 Cook *Zeus* 1914, Vol. I, p. 760.
13 Bonnefoy & Doniger, 1991, Vol. I, p. 70.
14 Harris 1906, p. 27.
15 Ward, D., 1968, p. 54.
16 See various works: Harris 1903 and 1906; Farnell 1921; Cook, *Zeus* 1914–40, 3 vols.
17 Farnell 1921, p. 184.
18 Boisacq 1916, also Chantraine 1983.
19 Graves 1955, Index: 'Polydeuces'.
20 See 'Der Ursprung der Mythologie' 1860, quoted in Cook *Zeus* 1914, Vol. I, p. 447.
21 Cox, G. W., 1870, Bk II, p. 22.
22 Stutely & Stutely 1977, 'Krishna'.
23 Conder 1884, p. 11.

Chapter 9   *Crippled Gods*

1 Delcourt 1982, p. 136.
2 Graves 1961. 1975 edition p. 331.
3 Nilsson 1925.
4 Caldwell 1989.
5 Friederich 1978, p. 65.
6 Stutely & Stutely 1977.
7 Darrah 1994, p. XIII.
8 Rundle Clark 1978, p. 104, and Graves 1975, p. 303.
9 Cramp (ed.) 1980.
10 Graves 1955, Index: 'Paris'.
11 Friederich 1978, p. 59.
12 Cook *Zeus* 1914, Vol. I, 719 ff.

13 Conder 1883, p. 294.
14 Cole, S. G., 1988, pp. 161–5
15 Gurney *Journal of Semitic Studies* 1962, No. 7. See also Jacobsen 1962, Vol. 1, p. 189 ff.
16 Homer *Odyssey*, pp. XIX, 460–90.
17 Miller & Taube 1993, p. 164.
18 Roheim 1934.
19 Taplin 1989, p. 103.
20 Euripides, see in Edmunds 1985, p. 49.
21 Bonnefoy & Doniger 1991, p. 499.
22 Frazer 1898, ed. 1931, p. 374.
23 Caldwell 1989.
24 Lindsay 1965, p. 84.
25 Symeonoglou 1985, p. 9.
26 Robert 1915.
27 Lang 1893, p. 87 ff.
28 Cook *Zeus* 1914, Vol. 1, pp. 459–61.

Chapter 10   *The Mask of Medusa*

1 Farnell 1896–1906, Bk IV.
2 Mackenzie 1913, p. 149.
3 Farnell 1896, Vol. IV, p. 6.
4 Wilson, L. M., *AJA* 1920, Series 2, No. 24, p. 233.
5 Blinkenberg *Revue Archéologique* 1924, Series 5, No. 19.
6 Graves 1955, Index: 'Danae'.
7 Boisacq, *Dictionnaire étymologique*, 1916.
8 Bent 1885, p. 64.
9 Jacobsen 1976, p. 128.
10 Barnes, in *The Times* 10 Oct 1992.
11 Wake 1888, p. 112.
12 Cook *Zeus* 1914, Vol. 1, p. 230.
13 Graves 1961. 1975 edition p. 210.
14 Frazer *Golden Bough* 1912, Vol. II, p. 32.
15 Mellaart 1975, p. 106.
16 Rose *OCD* 1968, 'Praxidikai'.
17 Gubernatis in Jones 1951, p. 276. Ernest Jones's *On the Nightmare* is a useful blend of etymology, folklore and mythology. The interpretations are less secure. Jones was Freud's biographer, and his comments weigh heavily in favour of a psychoanalytical approach.

Chapter 11   *The Evil Eye*

1 Dundes 1980, p. 107.
2 Mackenzie 1913, p. 6.
3 *Larousse Encyclopaedia of Mythology*, 1959, p. 195.
4 Bonnefoy & Doniger 1991, p. 161.
5 Ibid. p. 67.
6 Burkert 1979, p. 20.

7 Morris, *Animalwatching*, 1990
8 Mundkur 1983, *passim*.
9 Gimbutas 1974, p. 94.
10 *EB*, columns 3193 and 5366.
11 Ibid. column 61 note 3. Scholars are Professors of Semitic Languages Noldeke, Wellhausen and Jastrow.
12 Cheyne in *EB*, column 62.
13 Rieff 1959; and Jones in *Psychoanalysis* 4th edition, 1929, p. 145.
14 Freud, ed. Strachey, *Collected Works*, 1922, Vol. 18.
15 Mundkur 1983 p. 174.
16 Leibovitch 1953, *JNES* Vol. xii, and Sejourné 1962, p. 40. Coe 1980, revised edition.
17 Mundkur 1983, p. 67.
18 Deane 1833.
19 Coe 1992, p. 56.
20 Cook *Zeus* 1914, Vol. 1, p. 224.
21 Bonnefoy & Doniger 1991, p. 67.
22 Cook *Zeus* 1914, Vol. 1, p. 14; 1940 Vol. 3, plate lxii, and pp. 342–3. See also Frazer, *Golden Bough*, 1912 Vol. ii, p. 40.

Chapter 12   *Day of Blood*

1 Smith, W. Robertson, 1894, p. 171.
2 Mackenzie 1913, pp. 312–18.
3 Graves 1955, Index: 'Euryale', and 'Sthenno'.
4 Caldwell 1989, p. 10.
5 Dundes 1980, p. 246.
6 Burkert 1979, pp. 104, 120, 190.
7 Robertson 1910, second edition, p. 98, and EB, column 735.
8 Smith, W. Robertson, 1894, p. 174.
9 Kirk 1974. 1983 edition.
10 Versnel, in Bremmer 1987, pp. 121–52.
11 Frazer *Golden Bough* 1929, Vol. ii, p. 584.
12 Frazer *Golden Bough* 1907, Vol. 4, p. 291.
13 Graves 1961. 1975 edition, p. 210.
14 Cook *Zeus* 1914, Vol. 1, p. 157.
15 Walton 1968. *OCD*: 'Adonis'.
16 Rose 1968. *OCD*: 'Ancaeus'.
17 Homer *Odyssey*, xix, pp. 428–59.
18 Mackenzie 1910, p. 67.
19 Mackenzie 1913, p. 136.
20 Ibid., p. 26.
21 Lang 1893, p. 60.
22 Ellworthy 1900, pp. 63–6, figures 33–6. The weeping for Tammuz, observed by women, was probably a rain-inducing charm. The Canaanite god Moloch, to whom children were said to have been sacrificed by fire in order to alleviate a persistent drought or famine, may have been linked to the idea that children cry more readily (*EB*, column 3183). This was

certainly true in Mexico, where the Aztecs and Zapotecs sacrificed children to Tlaloc, the rain god. (Seler, in Bowditch, 1904, pp. 28 and 278.)

23 *EB*, column 4312, note 3.

24 Darrah 1994, p. 26.

25 Rundle Clark 1959. 1978 edition, p. 80.

26 Graves 1961. 1975 edition, p. 390.

27 Bettelheim 1955, p. 159.

28 Gimbutas 1974, p. 92, figure 52.

29 Mellaart 1967, pp. 83–4.

30 Stanner 1956, *Oceania Monograph*, No. 11, p. 96.

31 Ellenberger 1970, p. 546.

32 Baumann 1955.

33 Diószegi & Hoppál 1978, pp. 330–7.

34 Eliade 1964.

35 The Hungarian anthropologist Geza Roheim, who studied aboriginal cultures, said that the subincision wound is actually called a vagina in the aboriginal language. (Roheim 1934, p. 123.) Berndt & Berndt (1964, pp. 145–6), say that the wound is the womb of the Kunapipi, the Fertility Mother, while the penis itself is the male Rainbow Serpent (one example of a phallic serpent). The subincised penis therefore represents both male and female sexual organs.

36 Frazer *Golden Bough* 1890, Vol. 1, p. 368. This was the significance of the black mask. Blackness has always been a symbol of rain, and the sun in winter. The sacrifice of a black bull by the grave of a chieftan is still a rainmaking ceremony in times of drought among tribes in Botswana, and Frazer mentions the use of the blood of a black bull and a black goat in Africa and India as a rain charm, and a black goat sacrificed on top of a mountain.

37 Opie & Opie, *Oxford Dictionary of Nursery Rhymes*, 1951.

38 Lewis 1978, p. 98.

39 Lindsay 1965, p. 184.

40 Seler in Bowditch 1904, p. 268.

41 Bonnefoy & Doniger 1991, pp. 57 and 71.

42 Ibid. p. 175.

43 Mackenzie 1913, p. 323; see also Stutely & Stutely, 1977.

44 Robertson 1910, p. 147.

45 Frazer 1930, p. 168.

46 Parke & Wormell 1956, p. 190 note 6.

47 Parke 1967, and Homer *Iliad*, xvi, p. 220 ff.

48 Cox, M. R., 1893.

49 Various authors: see Rubenstein, B., and Marcus, D., in *American Imago*, Vol. 20, 1963.

50 Bettelheim 1975.

51 Glas 1946.

52 Freud, *Collected Papers*, 1913.

53 Bayley 1912. Reprinted edition 1974. There are many references to the Cinderella cycle in *The Lost Language of Symbolism*, and the author devotes

several chapters to the theme, taking tales from a variety of sources, such as the Song of Solomon.

54 *EB*, column 3741.

Chapter 13   *Goddesses of Death*

1 Parke & Wormell 1956, pp. 364–5.
2 Parke 1967, p. 151.
3 Hughes 1991, p. 77.
4 Marinatos 1988, p. 19, figure 15.
5 Mackenzie 1913, p. 149.
6 Sallares 1991, pp. 308–9.
7 Farnell 1896, Vol. 1, p. 265 ff.
8 Cook *Zeus* 1940, Vol. 3, p. 776.
9 Conder 1878, pp. 51, 83, 103. Perhaps this will explain the curious, prehistoric figurines with no features save for large staring eyes, or simply two holes in the head, the 'Eye Goddess' (see Crawford 1957), a figure whose later development must surely be Athene Glaukopis, 'the brilliant eyed', or 'grey-eyed' as Homer calls her. Perhaps she is also Athena, the 'owl-eyed'. In Homer, the fire of anger flames in the eyes, while Plato, Alcmaeon and Heraclitus believed that the eye was a source of fire.
10 Cole, S. G, in Haag, Marinatos *et al.* 1988, pp. 161–5.
11 Frazer *Golden Bough* 1907, Vol. 4, p. 164.
12 Friederich 1978, pp. 13–18.
13 Pack *OCD*: 'Tyche'.
14 Van Buren 1933, p. 120.
15 Frazer *Golden Bough* 1936 (the chapter 'Diana and Viribius'), Vol. 1, part 1, pp. 1–24.
16 Hopper 1978, p. 205.
17 Robertson 1910, p. 134.
18 Zuntz 1971, p. 140.
19 Cook *Zeus* 1925, Vol. 2, p. 410, note 0, and pp. 406–11. The symbolism that associates breasts with water has been acknowledged in the ancient world for thousands of years, a persistent theme that was noted by Norman Lewis in Italy where water-carriers dispense their water from earthenware *mmommere* shaped like a woman's breast, just as they appear on the murals of Pompeii – 'an excellent example of marketing ingenuity on the part of the ancients – and a cup of it costs three or four times the equivalent amount of wine.' Lewis 1978, p. 93.
20 Begg 1986, p. 144.
21 Smith, W. Robertson, 1894, p. 88.
22 Darrah 1994, *passim*.
23 Parke 1956, p. 365.
24 Cook *Zeus* 1914, Vol. 1, p. 490 ff. and p. 658.
25 Taplin 1989, p. 109.
26 Holt 1982. The solar hero Samson was weakened by a woman's hand, Delilah, goddess of springs. In the seventh month, Samson drives back his enemies with the jawbone of an ass, which later gives rise to a spring. The

excellent suggestion that the jawbone resembles a sickle comes from Reay Tannahill, *Food in History*, 1973, p. 62.

27 Jones 1910. 1971 edition, p. 268 *passim*.
28 Brand 1841, Vol. I, p. 285.

Chapter 14   *The Lion and the Unicorn*

1 Bunt *Antiquity*, 1930, p. 425 and p. 437.
2 Hartner, *JNES*, Vol. XXIV 1965, pp. 1–16.
3 Marinatos 1993.
4 Burkert, in Edmunds 1980.
5 Bonnefoy & Doniger 1991, Vol. I, p. 173.
6 Frazer *Golden Bough* 1907, Vol. 4, p. 136.
7 Cook *Zeus* 1914, Vol. I, p. 718.
8 Onians 1951.
9 Ibid p. 221.
10 Mondi, see in Edmunds 1980, p. 154.
11 Onians 1951, p. 175.
12 *Revue Celtique*, Vol. XL 1923, pp. 143–52.
13 Onians 1951, p. 183.
14 Ibid. p. 246.
15 Frazer *Golden Bough* 1936, Vol. I, pp. 250 and 291.
16 Schapera 1971. It is more likely that the animal is black to acknowledge the 'black' winter sun. In the myth of the Minotaur, the white bull sent by Poseidon at the request of Minos was the summer sun who will fertilise the earth-goddess Pasiphae.
17 Marinatos 1986, p. 36.
18 Dietrich 1974, p. 45.
19 Cook *Zeus*, Addenda Vol. 3, p. 110 note 1, p. 723 note 3.
20 Conder 1883.
21 Graves 1961. 1975 edition, p. 105.
22 Lindsay 1965, p. 57.
23 Quoted in Edmunds 1980, p. 41.
24 Graves 1961, p. 45.
25 Hughes 1991.
26 Mackenzie 1913, p. 89.
27 Schapera 1971, p. 104.

Chapter 15   *Scorpion, Snake and Dog*

1 Legge, *PSBA* 1912, p. 125.
2 Moulton 1911, p. 36 and p. 47.
3 Cumont 1896, 1899 and 1913.
4 Pannekoek 1961, p. 37.
5 Cook *Zeus* 1914, Vol. I, p. 394.
6 *Zend Avesta*.
7 Vermaseren 1956–60 *passim*.
8 The shoulder was a prominent symbol in ancient times, because the limb with the attached foot struck water – this is why the dog and snake leap to

drink from the wound. The Maenads in the retinue of Dionysus entreat him to appear to them with his 'bull's foot', for their vinous god with his wreath of grapes heralds the coming winter rains.

9 Beck in Hinnells, J. (ed.), 1990.

10 The philosopher Porphyry studied the religions of his times, but was primarily a chronicler, rather than an interpreter. As a Neoplatonist, he was certainly influenced by oriental mysticism and the concept of the World Soul, and the prevalent Platonic theories of the cosmos and the journey of the soul. His reports on Mithraism may well have been coloured by Neoplatonic ideas. He reported that initiates to the Mithraic mysteries were baptised with honey rather than water, because honey was hostile to fire. It is more likely that honey was used because it was thought to be a product of the sun, and more especially of Mithras himself. One of the Mithraic symbols was a lion with a bee in its mouth.

11 See Beck 1990; Ulansey 1989 and 1991 edition; Spiedel 1980.

12 Frazer *Golden Bough* 1912, Vol. 2, p. 43.

13 The double axe, a remarkable symbol derived ultimately from the butterfly and especially venerated in Crete, along with the bull. Several suggestions have been made about the insect's metamorphosis as being analogous to rebirth, to resurrection, although its main contribution to the symbolism of the double axe is because it appears in direct response to sunshine and flowers, as of course do bees.

14 Thienne, see Hinnells 1975.

15 Beck 1990.

16 Drews 1910, p. 184.

17 Childs 1917, p. 342.

Chapter 16   *Fear of the Future*

1 Werner 1963, p. 75.

2 Bier, *JNES*, Vol. xxxv, 1976, pp. 115–30.

3 Jacobsen, 'Tammuz', in *History of Religions*, Vol. 1, 1962, p. 189 ff.

4 Raphael in 'Stony Silence' in *Sunday Times*, 4/2/1996, and Thompson 1972, pp. 178–9.

5 Mellaart 1967. 1975 edition.

6 Ibid. p. 49.

7 Gimbutas 1974, pp. 195–200.

8 Mackenzie 1913, p. 75.

9 Ruthven 1976, p. 18.

10 Jacobsen, *JNES* No. 12, 1953, p.167, note 27.

11 Gimbutas 1974, p. 113.

12 Schapera 1971, p. 2 note 3.

13 The recent discoveries of bodies preserved by peat, and excavated from bogs in England and Denmark – respectively Lindow Man and Tollund Man – strongly support the notion of human sacrifice. Lindow Man had been bashed on the head, strangled, had his throat cut, and had been thrown in water as a possible votive act. Tollund Man had been strangled before his immersion.

14 Wendt 1963, trs. 1969, p. 97.

15 Thompson 1972, pp. 182–3.
16 *Antiquity*, Vol. XLVI., 1972, p. 233.
17 Clark, *Antiquity*, Vol. XVIII, 1944.
18 Wait 1985, p. 19.
19 Ross, *Studies in Ancient Europe*, in Coles & Simpson (eds.) 1968.
20 Ibid.
21 James 1965, p. 54.
22 Bradley 1976, *passim*.
23 Atkinson, Piggott & Sanders 1951.
24 Scott, *PPS* 11, 1936.
25 Hutton 1995.
26 Lockyer 1906, p. 204.
27 Ashbee 1970, pp. 54 and 63.

Chapter 17   *Holy Fire*

1 Wilson, I., 1984, p. 52.
2 Smith, W. Robertson, 1894, p. 200 note 1.
3 Conder 1883, pp. 296 and 302.
4 Robertson 1903, p. 308.
5 Conder 1882.
6 Conder 1878, p. 48.
7 Robertson 1903, p. 317.
8 Gimbutas 1974, p. 78.
9 For descriptions of sites, see Conder, 1878, 1883, *PEF Quarterly* 1882–3.
10 Lindsay 1965, p. 277.
11 Evans Sir A., 1885, p. 19.
12 James 1965.
13 Lockyer 1906, pp. 244 and 253, note 2.
14 Smith, W. Robertson, 1894, p. 200.
15 Conder, *PEF*, 1882, p. 77.
16 Ibid. p. 70, *passim*.
17 Conder 1883, p. 293.
18 Camp, see Tomlinson, R. in Haag, Marinatos *et al.* 1988, p. 172.
19 Bradley 1976.
20 Ashbee 1970, p. 58.
21 Piggott in *Antiquity*, 1961–62.
22 Thompson 1972, pp. 30, 31.

Chapter 18   *Full Circle*

1 Simmons and Tooley, 1981.
2 Pers. comm.
3 Several authors suggest a climatic change from drier to wetter conditions
from the late Neolithic through the Bronze Age. In Scotland, there is
evidence of a rise of water tables, with a more widespread formation of
blanket peat around 3000 BC. Bog conditions developed in Aberdeenshire
with rising water levels and increased humidity and water plants. North-

East Scotland and Aberdeenshire are noted for their concentration of stone circles and cairns.

4 Ashbee 1970.

5 Piggott 1962, p. 83.

6 Hutton 1991.

7 Crane 1996, pp. 1–2.

8 Collum 1935.

9 The standard authority on the development and construction of Stonehenge is R. J. C. Atkinson, *Stonehenge* 1965. See also Barnatt 1989, and Burl 1976.

10 Phillips 1996, paper and pers. comm.

11 Wood 1978, p. 17.

12 Burl 1976, p. 50.

13 Thom & Thom, in *JHA*, Vol. II, 1971; III, 1972; IV, 1973; V, 1974; VII, 1976.

14 Burl 1976, p. 33.

15 Ibid. p. 241.

16 Ibid. pp. 52–53.

17 It now occurs to me that the respect given to red ochre (Chapter 3), came from the belief that the appearance of ochre in the earth marked the passage of the sun during its subterranean journey.

18 Grave deposits of jewellery, ornaments and weapons were no doubt devotional, a personal gesture from the living to the dead. This aspect of mortuary practices must be viewed separately from the deposits of bones and skulls, and the flexed inhumations suggestive of sacrifice.

19 The geologist G. A. Kellaway, an adviser to the planning engineers of the M40 motorway, told me that during the construction of the motorway, gigantic sarsen stones were dug up and removed, stones far larger than those of either Stonehenge or Avebury. The word sarsen is supposed to have derived from 'Saracen', meaning 'foreign', a dubious derivation since the stones had always been local. It is interesting, though, that the word Saracen comes through Latin and Greek from the Arabic *sharq*, 'sunrise'.

20 Thomas, *Antiquaries Journal*, Vol. III 1923.

21 Kellaway, *Nature*, 1971.

22 In view of the symbolic character of the oak tree and its relation to thunder and rain, mentioned in Chapter 13, it is of interest that oak was used invariably in the construction of round barrows, and some henges. Woodhenge was made of oak, as was the Sanctuary.

23 This is not too far removed from the modern church. The association between church and pagan circle can be seen at Knowlton in Dorset, where a church stands inside the henge. See also Burl 1976, p. 12.

24 Ibid. p. 78.

25 Grinsell 1976, p. 15.

26 Dames 1976.

27 Malone 1990, p. 42. See also Malone 1989.

28 Dames 1976, pp. 56–7.

29 Green 1996.

30 Hoare 1821, Vol. II, pp. 5–7.

Bibliography

Allegro, John, *The Sacred Mushroom and the Cross*, 1973. London: Hodder & Stoughton.

Alviella, Goblet d', *La Migration des Symboles*, 1892. Paris. *The Migration of Symbols* (facsimile edition), 1979. Wellingborough: The Aquarian Press.

Ashbee, Paul, *The Earthern Long Barrow in Britain*, 1970. London: Dent.

Atkinson, Richard J., Cecily M. Piggott and Nancy K. Sanders, *Excavations at Dorchester, Oxon*, 1951. Oxford University Press.

Atkinson, Richard J., *Stonehenge*, 1956. London: Hamish Hamilton.

Austin, Norman, *Meaning and Being in Myth*, 1990. Pennsylvania University Press.

Bahn, Paul G., and Jean Vertut, *Images of the Ice Age*, 1988. Leicester: Windward.

——'Water Mythology', in *Proceedings of the Prehistoric Society* no. 44, 1978.

Barandiarán, Ignacio, 'Signos Asociados a Hocicos de Animales en el Arte Paleolitico', in *Revista Veleia* 1, 1984.

Barnatt, John, *Stone Circles of Britain*, (2 parts), 1989. Oxford: *British Archaeological Reports*.

Barrière, Cl., *Palaeolithic Cave Art in the Grotte de Gargas* (2 parts), 1976. Oxford: *British Archaeological Reports*.

Baumann, Hermann, *Das Doppelte Geschlecht*, 1955. Berlin: Dietrich Reimer.

Bauval, Robert, and Adrian Gilbert, *The Orion Mystery*, 1994. London: Heinemann.

Bayley, Harold, *The Lost Language of Symbolism*, 1912. London: Ernest Benn, 1951 and 1974.

Beck, Roger, 'In Place of the Lion. Mithras in the Tauroctony', in 'Studies in Mithraism', (ed. J. R. Hinnels), 1990. *Storia delle Religioni* 9. Rome: L'Erma di Bretschneider.

Begg, Ean, *The Cult of the Black Virgin*, 1985. London: Arkana (Penguin).

Bellamy, John, *Robin Hood, an historical enquiry*, 1985. London: Croom Helm.

Bent, James Theodore, *The Cyclades*, 1885. London: Longmans.

Berndt, Ronald and Catherine H. Berndt, *The World of the First Australians*, 1964. London: Angus & Robertson.

Bettelheim, Bruno, *Symbolic Wounds*, 1955. London: Thames & Hudson.

—— *The Uses of Enchantment*, 1975. London: Thames & Hudson, 1978, London: Peregrine Books.

Bier, L., 'A Second Hittite Relief at Ivriz'. *JNES* Vol. xxxv, 1976.

Blinkenberg, Christian S., 'Gorgone et Lionne', in *Revue Archéologique*, Ser. 5. No. 19, 1924.

Boisacq, Emile, *Dictionnaire étymologique de la langue grecque*, 1916. Heidelberg and Paris.

Bonnefoy, Yves, and Doniger, Wendy (eds), *Dictionnaire des mythologies et des religions des sociétés traditionnelles et du monde antique*, (2 vols.) 1991 Chicago: University of Chicago Press.

Bosanquet, Robert C., 'Laconia. Excavations at Sparta', in *Annual of the British School at Athens* No. XII, 1905–6,

Bowditch, C. P. (ed.), *Smithsonian Institution Bulletin* 28, 1904. Washington.

Bradley, Richard, *Maumbury Rings, Dorchester. The Excavations of 1908–1913*. 1976. Oxford: Society of Antiquaries, London.

Bremmer, Jan (ed.), *Interpretations of Greek Mythology*, 1987. London: Croom Helm.

Brown, Peter Lancaster, *Megaliths, Myths and Men*, 1976. Poole, Dorset: Blandford Press.

Bunt, Cyril G. E., 'The Lion and the Unicorn', in *Antiquity*, 1930.

Burkert, Walter, *Structure and History in Greek Mythology and Ritual*, 1979. Berkeley: University of California Press.

—— *Greek Religion*, 1989. Oxford: Basil Blackwell.

Burl, Aubrey, *Rites of the Gods*, 1981. London: Dent.

—— *Stone Circles of the British Isles*, 1976. London: Yale University Press.

Calasso, Roberto, *The Marriage of Cadmus and Harmonia*, 1994. London: Jonathan Cape.

Caldwell, Richard, *The Origin of the Gods, a psychoanalytic study of Greek theogonic myth*. 1989. New York: Oxford University Press.

Camp, J., in Tomlinson, R., 'Water supplies and ritual at the Heraion Perachora', *Early Greek Cult Practice, Proceedings of the 5th International Symposium, 1986* (ed. Haag & Marinatos), 1988. Stockholm.

Chantraine, Pierre, *Dictionnaire étymologique de la langue grecque*, 1983. Paris: Klincksieck.

Childs, W. J., *Across Asia Minor on Foot*, 1917. Edinburgh and London: Blackwood.

Chippindale, Christopher, *Stonehenge Complete*, 1980. Thames & Hudson.

Clark, Graham, 'Water in Antiquity', in *Antiquity* XVIII, 1944.

—— and Stuart Piggott, *Prehistoric Societies*, 1965. Harmondsworth: Penguin. Pelican edition 1976.

Clark, Robert Rundle, *Myth and Symbol in Ancient Egypt*, 1959 and 1978. London: Thames & Hudson.

Coe, Michael D., *The Maya*, 1966 and 1980 rev. ed. London: Thames & Hudson.

—— *Breaking the Maya Code*, 1992, London: Thames & Hudson.

Cole, Sonia, *The Neolithic Revolution*, 1970. London: British Museum Publications.

Cole, Susan G., 'The Uses of Water in Greek Sanctuaries', in *Early Greek Cult Practice, Proceedings of the 5th International Symposium, 1986* (ed. Haag & Marinatos), 1988. Stockholm.

Coles, John M., and Eric S. Higgs, *The Archaeology of Early Man*, 1969. London: Faber & Faber, and Peregrine paperback 1975.

Collum, Vera C. C., *The Tressé Iron-Age Megalithic Monument*, 1935. London: Oxford University Press.

A Compendious Vocabulary of Sanskrit, 1885. Published privately.

Conder, Claude R., *Bible Folklore*, 1884. London: Kegan Paul, Trench.

—— *Tent Work in Palestine 1878*, *PEF*.

—— *Syrian Stone Lord*, 1886, *PEF*.

—— *Heth & Moab*, *1883*, *PEF*.

—— *Palestine Exploration Fund Quarterly*, 1882–3.

Cook, Arthur B., *Zeus* (3 vols), 1914–1940. Cambridge, University Press.

Cornwall, Ian W., 'Soil science and archaeology from some British Bronze Age monuments', *PPS* 19, 1953–4.

Cox, Marian R., *Cinderella, Three Hundred and Forty-five Variants*, 1893. *FLS*.

Cox, Sir George W., *The Mythology of the Aryan Nations*, 1870. London: Kegan Paul, Trench.

Cramp, Stanley (ed.), *Birds of the Western Palearctic*, 1980. Oxford University Press.

Crane, Nicholas, *Clear Waters Rising*, 1996. London: Viking.

Crawford, Osbert G. S., *The Eye Goddess*, 1957. London: Phoenix House.

Creuzer, Georg F., *Symbolik und Mythologie der alten Volker*. Trs. J. D. Guigniaut, as *Religions de l'antiquité* (4 parts), 1825–5. Paris.

Cumont, Franz, *Textes et Monuments Figures Relatifs du Mystères de Mithra* (2 vols), 1896–99. Brussels.

—— *Les Mystères de Mithra*, 1913. Trs. T. J. McCormack as *The Mysteries of Mithra*, 1903. London: Kegan Paul, Trench.

Dames, Michael, *The Silbury Treasure*, 1976. London: Thames & Hudson.

Daniel, Glyn, *The Prehistoric Chamber Tombs of England and Wales*, 1950. Cambridge University Press.

Darrah, John, *Paganism in Arthurian Romance*, 1994. Woodbridge: Boydell.

Deane, John B., *The Worship of the Serpent*, 1830. London: Hatchard.

Delcourt, Marie, *Héphaistos ou la légende du Magicien*, 1982. Paris: Les Belles Lettres.

Dietrich, Bernard C., *The Origins of Greek Religion*, 1974. Berlin: De Gruyter.

Diószegi, V., and M. Hoppál (eds), *Shamanism in Siberia*, 1978. Budapest: Akademiai Kiado.

Dowden, Ken, *The Uses of Greek Mythology*, 1992. London: Routledge.

Drews, Arthur, *The Christ Myth*, 1910. London: Fisher Unwin.

Dulaure, Jacques, *Les Divinites Génératrices, ou du Culte du Phallus*, 1805. Paris.

Dundes, Alan (ed.), *The Flood Myth*, 1988. University of California Press.

—— *Interpreting Folklore*, 1980. Bloomington: Indiana University Press.

—— *The Cinderella Cycle, a folklore casebook*, 1982. New York: Garland.

Edgerton, Franklin, *A Buddhist Hybrid Sanskrit Grammar and Dictionary* (2 vols), 1953. New Haven and London: Yale University Press.

Edmunds, Lowell, (ed.), *Approaches to Greek Myth*, 1980. Baltimore: John Hopkins University Press.

—— *Oedipus: The Ancient Legend and Its Later Analogues*, 1985. Baltimore: John Hopkins University Press.

Eliade, Mircea, *Shamanism*, 1964. London: Routledge and Kegan Paul.

Ellenberger, Henri F., *The Discovery of the Unconscious*, 1970. London: Allen Lane.

Elworthy, Frederic T., *Horns of Honour*, 1900. London: John Murray.

—— *The Evil Eye*, 1895. London: John Murray.

Evans, Sir Arthur, *Archaeology*, 1885. London.

Evans, John G., *The Environment of Early Man in the British Isles*, 1975. Berkeley: University of California Press.

Everyman's Dictionary of Non-Classical Mythology (ed. Egerton Sykes), 1952. Revisions 1961 and 1962. London: Dent.

Farnell, Lewis R., *Greek Hero Cults*, 1921. Oxford: Clarendon Press.

—— *The Cults of the Greek States* (5 vols), 1896–1906. Oxford University Press.

Förstemann, Ernst, in Bowditch, C. P., 'Mexican and Central American Antiquities', *Smithsonian Institution Bulletin* 28, 1904. Washington, DC.

Frazer, Sir James G., Pausanius, *Studies in Greek Scenery, Legend and History*, 1898, ed. 1931. London: Macmillan.

—— *The Golden Bough: Myths of the Origin of Fire*, 1930. *Spirits of the Corn and of the Wild*, 1912. *The Magic Art*, Vols 1 and 2. 1929. *Adonis, Attis, Osiris*, Vol. 4, 1907. All London: Macmillan.

Freud, Sigmund, 'The Gorgon's Head', in *The Complete Psychological Works* (ed. J. Strachey), Vol. 18, 1922. 'The Theme of the Three Caskets', Vol 12 (1913). London: Hogarth Press, 1974.

Friederich, Paul W., *The Meaning of Aphrodite*, 1978. University of Chicago Press.

Gelling, Peter, and Hilda Davidson, *The Chariot of the Sun*, 1969. London: Dent.

Gilbert, Adrian, and Maurice Cotterell, *The Mayan Prophecies*, 1995. London: Element.

Gimbutas, Marija, *The Language of the Goddess*, 1989. London: Thames & Hudson.

—— *The Gods and Goddesses of Old Europe 7000–3500*, 1974. London: Thames & Hudson.

Glas, Norbert, *Cinderella, Meaning and Exact Rendering*, 1946. Stroud.

Gleadow, Rupert, *The Origin of the Zodiac*, 1968. London: Jonathan Cape.

Goldberg, Stephen, *The Inevitability of Patriarchy*, 1977. London: Maurice Temple Smith.

Goodison, Lucy, *Death, Women and the Sun*, 1989. London: *Institute of Classical Studies Bulletin*, supplement 53, University of London.

Grant, Michael, *The Myths of the Greeks and Romans*, 1962. London: Weidenfeld & Nicolson.

Graves, Robert, *The White Goddess*, 1961; paperback 1975. London: Faber & Faber.

—— *The Greek Myths*, 1955. Harmondsworth: Penguin.

Green, Miranda, *Sun Gods of Ancient Europe*, 1991. London: Batsford.

—— *Celtic Goddesses, Warriors, Virgins and Mothers*, 1995. London: British Museum Publications.

Grinsell, Leslie V., *The Folklore of Prehistoric Sites in Britain*, 1976. London and Newton Abbot: David & Charles.

Gubernatis, Angelo de, *Zoological Mythology* (2 vols), 1872. London.

Gupta, K., *Social Status of Hindu Women in Northern India, 1206–1707*, 1987. New Delhi: Inter-India Publications.

Gurney, Oliver R. 'Tammuz Reconsidered', in *Journal of Semitic Studies*, Vol. 7, No. 2, 1962.

Haag, Robin, Marinatos, Nordquist & Gullog (eds), *Early Greek Cult Practice, Proceedings of the 5th International Symposium, 1986* (at the Swedish Institute, Athens), 1988. Stockholm.

Hadingham, Evan, *Secrets of the Ice Age*, 1980. London: Heinemann.

Halm-Tisserant, M., 'Le Gorgonéion, emblème d'Athéna', in *Revue Archéologique*, 1986–7.

Hannay, James B., *Sex symbolism in religion*, 1922. Privately printed.

Harris, James Rendell, *The Cult of the Heavenly Twins*, 1906. Cambridge University Press.

—— *Boanerges*, 1913. Cambridge University Press.

—— *The Dioscuri in Christian Legends*, 1903. Cambridge University Press.

Harrison, Jane E., *Prolegomena to the Study of Greek Religion*, 1903. Cambridge University Press.

Hartner, Willy, 'Motif of the Lion-Bull Combat', in *JNES*, Vol. xxiv, 1965.

Hatto, Arthur T., 'Stonehenge and Midsummer', in *Man*, 1953.

Hawkins, Gerald S., *Stonehenge Decoded*, 1966. London: Souvenir Press.

Hinnells, J. R. (ed.), *Mithraic Studies*, 1975. Manchester University Press.

—— *Studies in Mithraism*, 1990. Rome: L'Erma di Bretschneider.

Holt, James C., *Robin Hood*, 1982. London: Thames & Hudson.

Hopper, Vincent F., *Medieval Number Symbolism*, 1969. New York: Columbia University Press.

Hoskin, M. A., 'Current Issues in Archaeoastronomy', *The Observatory* (ed. Clive Ruggles), Vol. 116, 1996. London.

Howe, Thalia P., 'The Origin and Function of the Gorgon Head', in *American Journal of Archaeology*, Vol. 58, No. 3, 1954.

Hughes, Dennis, *Human Sacrifice in Ancient Greece*, 1991. London: Routledge.

Hutton, Ronald, *The Pagan Religions of the Ancient British Isles*, 1991. Oxford: Blackwell.

Inman, Thomas, *Ancient Pagan and Modern Christian Symbolism*, 1869. Privately printed.

Jacobsen, Thorkild, *The Treasures of Darkness*, 1976. New Haven and London: Yale University Press.

—— 'Tammuz', in *History of Religions*, 1962, London: Weidenfeld and Nicholson.

James, Edwin O., *From Cave to Cathedral*, 1965. London: Thames & Hudson.

—— *Myth and Ritual in the Ancient Near East*, 1958. London: English University Press.

Janssens, Paul. A., *Palaeopathology*, 1970. London: John Baker.

Jones, Ernest, *On the Nightmare*, 1951. Paperback 1971. New York: Liveright.

Judd, John, W. 'Note on the Nature and Origin of the rock-fragments found in the excavations at Stonehenge', *Archaeologica* 58, 1902. See also Gowland, W. 'Recent Excavations at Stonehenge', ibid.

Jung, Carl. G., and Karoli Kerenyi, *Essays on a Science of Mythology* 1951. London: Routledge Kegan Paul.

Kellaway, Geoffrey, A., 'Glaciation and the Stones of Stonehenge', in *Nature* 233, 1971.

Kenyon, Kathleen. M., Digging up Jericho, 1957. London: Ernest Benn.

King, Leonard. W., *Legends of Babylon and Egypt, Schweich Lectures*, 1916. London: British Academy, 1918.

Kirk, Geoffrey, S., *Myth: its meaning and functions in ancient and other cultures*, 1970. Berkeley & Los Angeles: Cambridge University Press.

—— *The Nature of Greeks Myths*, 1974. Harmondsworth: Penguin.

Kraus, Theodor, *Hekate*. 1960. Heidelberg.

Kraay, Colin. M., and Max Hirmer, *Greek Coins*, 1966. London: Thames & Hudson.

Lang, Andrew, *Custom and Myth*, 1893. London: Longmans, Green.

Langdon, Stephen, H. *Tammuz and Ishtar*, 1914. Oxford: Clarendon Press.

—— *The Enuma Elish, Epic of Creation*, trans. 1923. Oxford: Clarendon Press.

Larousse Encyclopaedia of Mythology, 1959. London: Paul Hamlyn.

Legge, F., 'The Lion-headed God of the Mithraic mysteries', *PSBA* No. 34. 1912.

Leibovitch, J., 'Welfare in Ancient Egypt', *JNES*, 1953.

Lewis, Norman, *Naples '44*. 1978. London: Collins.

Lexicon Iconographicum Mythologiae Classicae (LIMC) 1986. Zurich and Munich: Artemis Verlag.

Liddell, H. G., & Robert Scott, *A Greek – English Lexicon*, 1966. Oxford: Clarendon Press.

Lindsay, Jack, *The Clashing Rocks*, 1965. London: Chapman & Hall.

—— *The Origins of Astrology*, 1971. London: Muller.

—— *Men and Gods on the Roman Nile*, 1968. Muller.

Lloyd, Geoffrey, E. R., *Science, Folklore and Ideology*, 1983, 2nd ed. 1986, Cambridge University Press.

Lockyer, Sir Joseph Norman, *Stonehenge and other British stone monuments astronomically considered*, 1906. London: Macmillan.

Mackenzie, Donald. A., *Indian Myth and Legend*, 1913, London: Gresham.

—— *Egyptian Myth and Legend*,1913. Gresham.

Malone, Caroline, *The English Heritage Book of Avebury*, 1989. London: Batsford.

—— *Prehistoric Monuments of Avebury*, 1990. English Heritage.

Marcus, D., in *American Imago*, Vol. 20, 1963.

Marinatos, Nanno, *Minoan Sacrificial Ritual*, 1986, Stockholm.

—— 'The Imagery of Sacrifice', in *Early Greek Cult Practice*, 1988 (see Haag).

—— *Minoan Religion*, 1993. Columbia: University of South Carolina.

Marshak, Alexander, 'The Meander as a System' (1976), in *Form in Indigenous Art*, (ed. P. J. Ucko), 1977.

—— *The Roots of Civilization*, 1972. London: Weidenfeld & Nicolson.

Mellaart, James, *Çatal Hüyük: a neolithic town in Anatolia*, 1967. London: Thames & Hudson.

—— *Neolithic of the Near East*, 1975.

Mercer, Samuel A., *The Religion of Ancient Egypt*, 1949. London: Luzac.

Miller, Mary E., and Karl Taube, *The Gods and Symbols of Ancient Mexico and the Maya*, 1993. London: Thames & Hudson.

Mondi, Robert, 'Greek and Near Eastern Mythology' in *Approaches to Greek Myth*, (see Edmunds), 1980. Baltimore: John Hopkins University Press.

Monier-Williams, Sir Monier, *A Sanskrit-English Dictionary*, new edition, 1899. Oxford: Clarendon Press.

Moor, Edward, *Hindu Pantheon*, 1861. London and Hertford.

Morris, Desmond, *Animalwatching*, 1990. London: Jonathan Cape.

Moulton, James H., *The Early Religious Poetry of Persia,* 1911. Cambridge University Press.

Müller, Max, *Sacred Books of the East*, 1897, Oxford: Clarendon Press.

Mundkur, Balaji, *The Cult of the Serpent*, 1983. Albany: New York University Press.

Neugebauer, Otto, *The Exact Sciences in Antiquity*, 1951. Copenhagen; and (1957). Providence, RI: Brown University Press.

Nilsson, Nils Martin, *A History of Greek Religion*, 1925. Oxford: Clarendon Press.

—— *Primitive Time Reckoning*, 1920. Lund (Sweden): Gleerup

—— 'Greek Art and the Medusa Myth', *AJA*, Series 2, 1920.

Onians, Richard B., *The Origins of European Thought*, 1951. Cambridge University Press.

Opie, Peter and Iona, *Oxford Dictionary of Nursery Rhymes*, 1951. Oxford University Press.

Pack, Roger A., 'Tyche' *OCD* 1968.

Pannekoek, Antonie, *A History of Astronomy*, 1961. London: Allen & Unwin.

Parke, Herbert W., *The Oracles of Zeus*, 1967. Oxford: Blackwell.

—— and Donald Wormell, *The Delphic Oracle*, 1956. Oxford: Blackwell.

Penglase, Charles, *Greek Myths and Mesopotamia*, 1994. London: Routledge.

Piggott, Stuart, *The West Kennet Long Barrow, Excavations 1955–6*, 1962. London: H.M.S.O.

Poulsen, Frederick. S, *Etruscan Tomb Paintings* (trs. Andersen), 1922. Oxford: Clarendon Press.

Powell, Thomas G. E., 'The Introduction of Horse-Riding to Temperate Europe', *PPS*, Vol. xxxvii, ii, 1971.

Ransome, Hilda M., *The Sacred Bee in Ancient Times and Folklore*, 1937. London: Allen & Unwin.

Raphael, Frederick, 'Stony Silence', *The Sunday Times*, 4/2/1996.

Redgrove, Peter, and Penelope Shuttle, *The Wise Wound*, 1978. London: Paladin.

Reed, Clyde F., *Stonehenge of Salisbury Plain, The Sex Machine*, 1965. Darlington, Maryland: privately printed.

Rieff, Phillip, *Freud, the Mind of the Moralist*, 1960. London: Gollancz.

Reynolds, Peter J., *Iron-Age Farm, the Butser Experiment*, 1979. London: British Museum Publications.

Robert, Carl, *Oidipus*, 1915. Berlin.

Robertson, John M., *Christianity and Mythology*, 2nd edition 1910. London: Watts.

—— *Pagan Christs. Studies in Comparative Hierology*, 1903. London: Watts.

Roe, Derek, *Prehistory*, 1970. London: Macmillan. 1974 edition, Book Club Associates.

Roheim, Geza, *Animism, Magic and the Divine King*, 1930. London.
—— *Australian Totemism*, 1925, London: Allen & Unwin.
—— *The Riddle of the Sphinx*, (trs. R. Money-Kyrle), 1934. London: Institute of Psychoanalysis.
—— *The Panic of the Gods and other essays* (ed. Werner Muensterberger), 1972. New York: Harper & Row (Harper Torchbook edition).
Rooth, Anna B., *The Cinderella Cycle*, 1951. Lund: Gleerup.
Rose, Herbert J., *A Handbook of Greek Mythology*, 1928 and 1953. London: Methuen.
—— 'Telephus' article in *OCD*, 1968.
Ross, Anne, 'Shafts, Pits and Wells − Sanctuaries of the Belgic Britons?', in *Studies in Ancient Europe* (ed. Coles & Simpson), 1968.
Ruthven, Kenneth K., *Myth*, 1976. London: Methuen.
Sakellarakis, Jannis, 'Votives from the Idaian Cave', in *Early Greek Cult Practice*, 1988 (see Haag, R.).
Sallares, Robert, *The Ecology of the Ancient Greek World*, 1991. London: Duckworth.
Schapera, Isaac, 'Rainmaking Rites of the Tswana Tribes', in *African Social Research Documents*, Vol. 3, 1971.
Scott, Sir Warwick L., 'Excavation of a Neolithic Barrow on Whiteleaf Hill, Bucks', *PPS* II, 1936, and in III, 1937.
Séjourné, Laurette, *El Universo de Quetzalcoatl*, 1962. Buenos Aires.
—— *Burning Water*, 1957. London: Thames & Hudson.
Seler, Eduard, 'Mexican and Central American Antiquities', in *Smithsonian Institution Bulletin* (ed. C. P. Bowditch), 28, 1904.
Sieveking, Anne, *The Cave Artists*, 1979. London: Thames & Hudson.
Simmons, Ian G., and M. J. Tooley, *The Environment in British Prehistory*, 1981. London: Duckworth.
Slater, Phillip E., *The Glory of Hera*, 1968. Boston: Beacon Press.
Smith, W. Robertson, *The Religion of the Semites*, 1894. London, A & C Black.
Smith, C., 'Nike Sacrificing a Bull', *Journal of Hellenic Studies*, Vol. VII, 1886.
Speert, Harold, *Iconographia Gyniatrica*, 1973. Philadelphia: S. A. Davis.
Speidel, Michael, *Mithras-Orion*, 1980. Leiden.
Spencer, Walter B., and Francis Gillen, *The Native Tribes of Central Australia*, 1899. London: Macmillan.
Stanner, William E. H., 'On Aboriginal Religion', *The Oceania Monographs*, No. 11, 1956. University of Sydney.
Stutely, Margaret E. L., and James Stutely, *Dictionary of Hinduism*, 1977. London: Routledge and Kegan Paul.
Symeonoglou, Sarantis, *The Topopgraphy of Thebes*, 1985. New Jersey Princeton University Press.
Tannahill, Reay, *Food in History*, 1973. London: Eyre Methuen.
Taplin, Oliver, *Greek Fire*, 1989. London: Jonathan Cape.
Thienne, Paul, 'The Concept of Mitra in Aryan Belief', in *Mithraic Studies*, Vol. I (ed. J. R. Hinnels), 1975.
Thom, Alexander and Archibald S. Thom, works on megalithic astronomy in *JHA* 2 (1971), 3 (1972), 4 (1973), 5 (1974), 6 (1975), 7 (1976).

Thomas, H. H., 'The Source of Stones of Stonehenge', in *Antiquaries Journal*, III, 1923.

Thompson, Sir John Eric S., *Maya History and Religion*, 1972. Oklahoma University Press.

Trueman, Arthur E., *Geology and Scenery in England and Wales*, 1938. London: Gollancz. Penguin edition 1971.

Ucko, Peter J. 'The Interpretation of Prehistoric Anthropomorphic Figurines', *Journal of the Royal Anthropological Institute*, Vols 92–3, 1962–3.

—— and Andree Rosenfeld, *Palaeolithic Cave Art*, 1967. London: Weidenfeld & Nicolson.

Ulansey, David, *The Origins of the Mithraic Mysteries*, 1991. Oxford University Press.

Usener, Hans, *Dreiheit*, 1903. Rheinisches Museum für Philologie, 58.

Van Buren, Elizabeth, *The Flowing Vase and the God with Streams*, 1933. Berlin: Hans Schoetz.

Versnel, H. S., 'The Case for Cronus', in *Interpretations of Greek Mythology* (ed. Jan Bremmer), 1987.

Wait, Gerald A., *Ritual and Religion in Iron-Age Britain* (2 parts), 1985. Oxford: *BAR*.

Wake, Charles Staniland, *Serpent Worship*, 1888. London: Redway.

Walters, Rupert C. Skyring, *The Ancient Wells, Springs and Holy Wells of Gloucestershire*, 1928. Bristol: St Stephen's Press.

Walton, Francis Redding, 'Adonis' in *OCD* 1968.

Ward, Anne. G. (ed.), *The Quest for Theseus*, 1970. London: Pall Mall Press.

Ward, Donald, 'The Divine Twins', *Folklore Studies*, No. 19, 1968. Berkeley: University of California Press

Webster, Hutton, *Rest Days*, 1916. New York: Macmillan.

Wendt, Herbert, *The Romance of Water*, 1963 Paris: Hachette. 1969,. London: Dent. 1969.

Werner, Heinz, and Bernard Caplan, *Symbol Formation* 1963. New York: Wiley.

Wilhelm II, Kaiser, *Studien zur Gorgo*, 1936. Berlin: de Gruyter.

Wilson, Ian, *Jesus: The Evidence*, 1984. London: Weidenfeld & Nicolson.

Wilson, L. M., in *AJA*, Series 2, No. 24, 1920.

Wilson, Thomas, *The Swastika*, 1896. Columbia: Smithsonian Institute.

Withers, Bruce, and Stanley Vipond, *Irrigation Design and Practice*, 1974. London: Batsford.

Wood, John E., *Sun, Moon and Standing Stones*, 1978. Oxford University Press.

Zuntz, Guenther, *Persephone*, 1971. Oxford: Clarendon Press.

Index